Bobby Dodd
on
Football

Robert L. "Bobby" Dodd

HEAD COACH *and* **ATHLETIC DIRECTOR**
GEORGIA INSTITUTE *of* **TECHNOLOGY**

Bobby Dodd

on

Football

Prentice-Hall, Inc.

ENGLEWOOD CLIFFS, N. J.

In memory of
William A. Alexander
The finest man
I have ever known

Preface

IN MAKING this contribution to books about the great game of football, we do so with the hope that every person who reads this book will find something that will prove interesting and profitable.

We have long believed that some of our greatest football teachers come from the "ranks"—from the group who were never "stars" in college, or, in some instances, never participated in athletics, but who have great qualities of leadership and other characteristics of great coaches. It is our hope, too, that some of our ideas will help them to get oriented in the coaching world. Naturally, we will be happy if those who have been coaching a long while find some of our suggestions beneficial.

In this book we have tried to "bring, bind, and blend together" the facts, fundamentals, and philosophy of football that have proved of value to us at Georgia Tech. We have had the benefit of suggestions made by all the coaches who are members of our staff at Georgia Tech, and, as a result, we have used many fine ideas that had their beginning in other colleges.

I asked my assistants, each of whom I consider an expert specialist in his field, to contribute a portion of the book.   Thus, I would give special thanks to coaches Ray Graves, Frank Broyles, Whitey Urban, Tonto Coleman, Lewis Woodruff, Bob Bossons, Sam Lyle, Bo Hagan, trainer Buck Andel, and publicity director Ned West.

We have tried to cover every maneuver in sufficient detail. We have included all the drills we use perfecting these techniques, and we hope these will be of special benefit to those new to the coaching game, and of interest to our more experienced coaching colleagues as well.

We gave much thought to the chapters on "Preparation and Game Organization," "Scouting," and "Training." We feel these are vital to successful coaching.   From personal experience we know that these aspects of the game are those in which the beginning coach frequently needs help in a special way. Regardless of his experience as an athlete, the beginning coach has usually had very little opportunity to become well acquainted with these aspects of the game.

It is our hope that the chapters "The Coach and Public Relations" and "Football Is a Game" will furnish suggestions that will make the road smoother and life happier for any coach. If any of our readers should get an idea or two from these experiences, we will feel that we are in a way paying on an obligation to the many who have given us the advantages of *their* experience.

Finally, we have made a few suggestions that we hope will help spectators enjoy the game more fully—for it is through their interest and support that football has truly become one of our great American heritages.

BOBBY DODD

Contents

vii

9   *Defensive Team Play (Cont.)*

overshift. Goal line defense vs. single wing. Defensing the split "T." 6-2-3 defense against the split "T." Defensing spread formations.

Punt mechanics. Protecting and covering the punt. The quick kick. Fielding and returning the punt. Blocking the punt. The place kick. The field goal. The kick off.

1

The Evolution of Football

J UST as man's comfort has progressed from the cave to the air conditioned home, the game of football has advanced from the roughest of beginnings to one of the most scientific and interesting of all athletic events.

Historians trace football, in its earliest form, back as far as 500 B. C. when it was played by the Spartans of Greece. The conquering Roman Legions picked up the sport and took it back to Rome where it became the military's pastime, much as polo was once the favorite sport of our armed forces.

Various types of the game football spread from this early start until by the 14th Century it was played in some form all over Europe. The sport became so popular in England, in fact, that it detracted from the practice of archery, mainstay of a warring nation, and caused Edward II to issue a proclamation:

1

"Forasmuch as there is a great noise in the city caused by hustling over large footballs, from which many evils arise, we command and forbid on behalf of the King under pain of imprisonment such game to be played in the future."

This was the first recorded de-emphasis program in football and it did not last very long.   Soon football was recognized as the national pastime in England.

Football was a mighty rugged sport in the 14th Century. One town would challenge another.   The "goals" would be municipal buildings, usually the town halls.   There might be miles of country between the two goals and everyone was elegible to compete.   Battles would rage for hours in some of these "games" before one side or the other would manage to kick the ball into the other's town and against the town hall goal.

The ball was always kicked in early football games and it was not until 1823 that, by chance, the principle of carrying the ball originated.

In the English public schools groups of boys would often play after classes with the game terminating at supper call, about five o'clock.   Such a group was playing the familiar kick game of football at Rugby School.   Student William Ellis, just before the five o'clock deadline, caught a punt that, under the prevailing rules, he should have kicked back or heeled for a free kick.   Instead, much to the surprise of everyone and the humiliation of his own captain who later apologized for his actions, Ellis tucked the ball under his arm and ran across the opponent's goal.

Ellis received only censure for his illegal run, but several of the Rugby football leaders became interested in the possibilities of a new type game in which running would be permitted. They revised the rules and thus invented "Rugby football" from which most of the principles of our present American game were derived.

Football, with very haphazard rules, was played on an intramural basis in several colleges in the United States throughout the 19th Century.   In the fall of 1869 William S. Gummere of Princeton challenged Rutgers, just twenty-five miles away, to a game between the two schools.   William S. Legget accepted for Rutgers and the first intercollegiate football game in history was played on November 6, 1869, with Rutgers winning six goals to four.   The two teams met again the following Saturday with Princeton emerging the victor 8–0.   These were "kicking-only" games, played under association football, or soccer, regulations.

Five years later McGill University of Montreal, Canada, introduced Rugby football to the intercollegiate picture.   The Canadians challenged Harvard to a game and it was agreed finally to have two contests, one under association rules, which Harvard was using, and one under Rugby rules, as the game was played by McGill.   On May 14, 1874, Harvard won the kicking-only game 3–0, and the Rugby contest the next day ended in a tie.   Harvard leaders liked the Rugby rules and decided to adopt them for their play.

Another important milestone in the evolution of football came on November 23, 1876, when the football leaders of Harvard, Yale, Princeton and Columbia met in Springfield, Massachusetts, and created the American Intercollegiate Football Association.   The Association then adopted the Rugby Union Code of football rules, with certain modifications, and scheduled a set of games for the year.   Football as it is played today is a direct descendant of the rules and regulations adopted at this meeting.

Through the efforts of Walter Camp, a Yale football leader,

the game became even more distinctly American in 1880. Following Camp's suggestions, the Association reduced the number of players on a side from 15 to 11, changed the size of the playing field from 140 by 70 yards to 110 by 53 yards, and abolished "sorum," the English method of putting the ball in play. Next followed the assigning of players with seven on the line, a quarterback, two halfbacks, and a fullback designated as they are today. Richard Hodge of Princeton introduced the principle of guarding a runner, or interference, and invented the first trap play. Signals, as such, were called for the first time in 1882—first as sentences, then as letters, and finally as numbers.

It might be interesting to note here that football was becoming so popular at this time that it was responsible for the naming of one of the world's best known schools. Until the year 1896 the official name of Princeton University had been College of New Jersey. Athletic teams of the school, since 1870, had worn on their shirts the name of the town where the college was located. This popularized the name to such an extent that in 1886 the school was officially renamed Princeton University.

There were many black days ahead for football, however. Great power and mass plays became so generally used that the public and educators alike became alarmed at the many deaths and crippling injuries resulting. There was little finesse to the game and it became dull and uninteresting as well as dangerous. Many college presidents either banned the sport entirely, or threatened to. Parents forbade their children to play.

This was the situation in 1905 when President Theodore Roosevelt, never one to evade what was becoming a national issue, stepped in and declared that if something wasn't done to improve the game—to cut down on the injuries and deaths —he would abolish it by executive edict.

The football leaders, now known as the Rules Committee of Football, met again in the winter of 1905–1906 with the fate of the game hanging in the balance. After a great deal of discussion, proposals and counter-proposals, they voted to rule out practically all mass formations. They prohibited hurdling and amended the rules to permit the forward pass. They increased the distance the offensive team must move the ball in three downs from five to ten yards and reduced game time to sixty minutes (divided into thirty-minute halves.)

Legalizing of the forward pass didn't make any immediate impression on the football teams of that day, although there are reports of one being thrown once in a while. None of the teams practiced pass plays as an offensive weapon and the first recorded pass in a game, by Moore to Van Tassel of Wesleyan in a losing game against Yale during the 1906 season, was pretty much of a desperation attempt. Later the same year Yale defeated Harvard 6–0 on a pass after the Eli had failed to score running and time was running out.

Most important changes in the next few years came about in 1910, when the game was divided into four fifteen-minute quarters, and in 1912 when the number of downs allowed the offensive team to advance the ball ten yards was raised from three to four.

Football regained some of its popularity, but it remained for two youths at a then obscure midwestern university to take the first real advantage of the medium that has made the game such a great spectator sport. The two imaginative boys were end Knute Rockne and quarterback Gus Dorais of Notre Dame University.

Army had an open date in its 1913 schedule and was looking around for a "breather" game with an easy opponent. Notre Dame, then practically unknown in the football world, was offered a thousand dollar guarantee (hardly enough to pay expenses from Indiana to West Point, where the game was to be played) to fill the opening.

Dorais and Rockne worked together at an Ohio resort town that summer. Hoping to be able to spring something new that might give them a slim chance to win over highly rated Army, Gus and Knute practiced the forward pass all summer in their leisure hours. They had this new offensive maneuver down to a fine science by the time they returned to school in the fall.

To make sure that Army couldn't concentrate on Rockne after the first pass or two was thrown, Pliska, another Notre Dame end, was privately tutored as a receiver prior to the game.

At last the day of the game arrived. Big Army punched out two quick touchdowns, as everyone had expected, and soon led 13–0. It was at this point that Dorais decided to unveil the forward pass. His tosses were the first the Army players had ever seen and they stood around helplessly while Dorais threw successfully time and again to Rockne. Then, when they concentrated on Rockne as Notre Dame had anticipated, Dorais calmly threw to Pliska and the game became a rout.

Notre Dame defeated Army 35–13 that afternoon and the forward pass went into the play book of every coach in the nation. Notre Dame's success encouraged the small colleges, proving that with the pass they could cope successfully against the brawn of the big school squads. Spectators loved the new inovation and flocked to see the more wide open games.

Another major step in making football a great spectator game was the numbering of players.

Washington and Jefferson College is credited with being the first team to put numbers on its players' jerseys, getting the idea from track teams and putting it in practice in the 1908 season. Prior to that time the spectators had very little idea of what was going on during the game, as far as individuals were concerned.

Washington and Jefferson gave up the idea, for some reason, after one year and it was all confusion again until 1913 when University of Chicago, under Coach Amos Alonzo Stagg, tried the numbers again. Spectators, newspapermen, and all followers of the sport took to the idea this time. Within a few years it was a general practice.

Opening up of the game by the forward pass also brought about other new ideas in offensive football. Glenn S. (Pop) Warner, who coached at many schools during his long 45-year career, is perhaps most famous for introduction of the single-wing and double-wing formations. For many years the leading teams in the country used one or both of these formations.

John Heisman, coach at Georgia Tech, made the "jump shift" famous around 1916 or 1917. This tricky maneuver would start with the center facing straight ahead and standing up over the ball. The other linemen stood in close formation about a yard behind him with the backs in a tight "T" behind them. While the quarterback was calling signals the center would twist his body and give everyone the shift, or "jump," signal. Then, as he turned again to the front and started down over the ball, the other ten men would jump into single-wing formation to the right or left, pausing the briefest of moments there before starting the play.

Around this same time Coach Knute Rockne introduced the Notre Dame shift from a box formation—a maneuver that was very similar to Heisman's jump shift and carried with it the same element of surprise. Rockne's great success at Notre Dame helped popularize this formation and it soon became almost as widely used as Warner's single and double wing.

Strangely enough, very little was written or heard of defensive maneuvers during this period. Gradually the game was becoming more open and spectacular, with the forward pass increasing in popularity. Just when it seemed that the offense would get a real advantage, coaches began to concentrate more on defense. Changes soon became just as evident in methods of stopping the attacks as they had in the advancement of offense and the game reached its normal balance. Rule changes were also factors in giving the offense or defense temporary advantages through the years, but always new ways were found to nullify these advantages.

Through the 1920's many rule changes were put into effect that affected the game. Some of the more notable ones were the coin toss before the start of each game, the winner to have choice of kicking off or receiving; penalty of down and loss of five yards imposed for incompleted forward passes after first one (later rescinded); goal post set ten yards back of goal line; time limit of thirty seconds placed on putting ball in play after it was ready for play, and limit of fifteen seconds placed on time permitted in huddle; run with fumble recovered by opposition prohibited; backward passes and fumbles going out of bounds between goal lines awarded to last team touching the ball.

These rule changes, and ones that came in more recent years, were usually motivated by a desire to curb or help the offense, or for safety reasons.

Most important thing that happened during the 1930's was introduction, or "re-introduction," of the "T" formation in football. This formation, with many inovations, proved to be a real turning point in the game. As teams all over the nation began to use the "T" formation with great success on offense, the defensive experts rose to the occasion to meet the challenge. Soon players in many schools were forced to learn almost as many defensive signals as offensive ones. A player had to be thinking all the time to play at any position on a modern football team and the days of sheer brawn were gone forever. Speed, brains, and quick reaction became the prime requisites for the prospective college football player.

So from its wild and brutal beginnings football has progressed to the game as we know it today—a game which blends initiative and teamwork, teaches loyalty and leadership, promotes fair play and fortitude.   Football has become an American way of life.

2

Football Is a Game

BECAUSE of the great public interest in football, and the subsequent desire of all schools to have a winning team, the temptation is great for coaches to forget that football is a *game*. Free and easy practice sessions have disappeared from many, many campuses. Drudgery from Monday through Friday has become commonplace for football players at a great number of our colleges—particularly those playing a so-called "big-time" schedule.

It is my belief that such drudgery not only is distasteful to the players, it also is extremely harmful to the effectiveness of the squad as a football team.

Perhaps the Georgia Tech philosophy of football can best be summed up by quoting two articles written during our undefeated and untied 1952 season.

After visiting our campus the week before Tech's important

game with Duke University (also undefeated at the time), assistant sports editor Benny Marshall wrote in the *Birmingham News* of October 29, "Football is a game at Georgia Tech, and the men who play it enjoy it. They're glad they came."

Later the same season, before an equally important game, a November 24 *Time* magazine article declared, "At Georgia Tech they come as close as any big-league squad can to playing football for fun."

I have tried to follow a very simple philosophy in coaching and have been very fortunate with it. I believe in coaching football players exactly as I would have liked a coach to have coached me, or as I would like to have my son coached.

I was fortunate in both high school and college in having good player-coach relationships, and I have tried to carry this on in my work. My college coach, General Bob Neyland, at Tennessee, had great ability in handling men. This impressed me as being the most desired characteristic for successful coaching and I have always tried to develop that characteristic in myself.

I believe it is important to keep always in mind, under all conditions and circumstances, that football is a *game*. Try to permit your players to have as much fun and enjoyment out of practice as possible, and at the same time give them adequate coaching. The problem we all face is to develop a good football team without making practice a complete drudgery. There are certain principles involved in accomplishing this:

1. *Do not have extremely long practice periods.* Plan every minute—yes, every second—of your practice sessions and then follow your schedule to the second. Don't run overtime because your players seem to be having a "bad day." Usually they will only get worse, which will be discouraging to the players as well as to yourself. Better to cut the practice off at the planned time and start fresh on the next day.

2. *Do not keep a player doing the same thing over and over again until it becomes monotonous to him.* Plan your practice from an individual as well as a general standpoint, actually writing down the names of the players who will participate in different phases of the practice so you can be sure that no one player will be repeating monotonous drills.

3. *Make every practice, and every segment of practice, as competitive as possible since competition appeals to most every boy.* See who can bat down the most passes on defense; which backfield group can run the most plays in succession without a mistake; which of two teams on offense can complete the most passes, and so on.

4. *Have certain periods of practice that are definitely outlined as relaxing and fun.* This ties in somewhat with number three above, but it is also well to plan at least one practice day a week that is devoted almost entirely to relaxation.

I do not believe in scrimmaging your top players, with special exceptions, after the season starts. My theory on this is that you will lose more by players getting hurt in scrimmage than you will gain by the scrimmage itself. Then, too, your varsity man isn't going to get the reaction from a B-team player or freshman that he will get from the good players he will be asked to face on Saturday. So, why waste your time?

Now, I do not want to mislead you into thinking that I believe a football team can get into shape for a rugged schedule without hard work. The point is that *you can get the necessary running and hard work into practice without the drudgery.* And you will find it is just as important to insert enough relaxation to keep your team from going stale and losing the desire to play. Many a football game is lost on the practice field Monday through Friday, leaving the players too banged up or too tired to do their best at game time.

Mondays and/or Fridays are particularly good days to break

the practice routine with "fun" for your players. Those are the days you may find it helpful to keep the boys in shape and happy at the same time with touch football games, volleyball games played with a football over the crossbar at the goal posts, impromptu foot races, punting games, touch pass scrimmage, and other such contests.

Do not forget that linemen enjoy punting and passing the ball, something they never get a chance to do in a game when the backs have all the limelight. Give linemen a chance to show themselves off as much as possible on your relaxing days, or better still, design a play that will terminate with a lineman receiving a lateral pass. You may never use this play in a game, but it certainly will build up the morale of your linemen.

If you have a natural comedian on your squad, and almost every squad has one, encourage his talents. He'll come through for you in many important tense moments.

While we are discussing morale of the squad and individuals on the squad, I am sure that there is one more important factor that should not be overlooked. Encourage all members of your squad to attend church regularly. Do not attempt to take them in a group to any one church, but urge them to attend regularly the churches of their own choice. There is no substitute for the spiritual uplift a boy receives through church attendance and church work. And as a coach you will find you are actually helping yourself by setting a good example in this respect.

Do not adhere to a great number of strict training rules. Try to live by the old rule of working hard while you work, leaving enough time for play and relaxation. Do not ever forget that football is a *game!*

3

Analysis of Athletic Coaching Failures

BEFORE the idea of this book became a reality, I contacted Professor A. W. Hobt, head of the Department of Physical Education at the University of Tennessee. Professor Hobt is one of the foremost men in his field and has had a tremendous amount of influence on my thinking in my coaching career. One statement he made has stayed with me until this day and still holds true—"It's not what you know, it's what you teach." He has given me some vital information on the reasons for athletic coaching failures that have helped me and, I am sure, are worthy of a prominent place in this book. So, with his cooperation and permission, I would like to give you a brief analysis of common athletic coaching failures.

14

The following is an effort to list the more common causes of athletic coaching failures. Many of these failures are due to carelessness or thoughtlessness on the part of the inexperienced or untrained coach, and merely by calling the failures to his attention he may avoid making the same errors again. To this extent, he will make a greater contribution to his school and community, and his tenure of office in athletic coaching should be longer. For the purpose of this discussion, seven separate areas of failure are listed, although it will be seen immediately that these areas are often closely related and react upon each other.

1. The athletic coach is sometimes accused of lack of effort and interest

Success in athletic coaching goes hand in hand with hard work. Over a period of years it cannot be considered a matter of luck. Too frequently the inexperienced coach does not comprehend all the duties and responsibilities of his work and, due to this fact, he creates the unfortunate impression in the community and among his players that he is lazy and indolent. The duties and responsibilities of an athletic coach include:

A. *Reading and study of books on coaching, athletic conditioning, first aid, physiology of exercise, psychology, education, and the like.*

B. *Detailed and business-like organization of that part of the program assigned to him for administration.* This may include any or all of the following: organization and administration of the budget; purchase, repair and care of equipment; supervision of ticket sale; general publicity and special game publicity; seating and comfort of spectators; automobile traffic and parking; arrangements for officials, etc. Space prohibits detailed discussion of the elements of organization. Needless to say the alert and conscientious coach will spend the time and energy necessary to carry out efficiently any administrative duties he undertakes.

C. *Study and analysis of strength and weaknesses of his coaching system and of other systems in order to plan intelligently for the season of coaching.* It is not the coaching system that determines success but the thoroughness and efficiency with which the system is taught. Young coaches should hesitate to change from the system they know best and, instead, should concentrate on thorough teaching of the better known system.

D. *Study and analysis of the playing strengths and weaknesses of the members of the team.* Individual instruction should be given to overcome weaknesses and to take maximum advantage of playing strengths.

E. *Outline of a daily plan of practice before the practice session begins.* Lesson planning or practice planning is essential to success in the coaching profession. Also, the coach will find that an occasional unprejudiced introspection of his own efforts will be helpful.

2.   Below average and inexperienced players constitute a common coaching problem

Although it is generally agreed that there are factors of good and bad fortune connected with the playing strength of every athletic squad, the energetic coach will have several legitimate methods at his command by which he can improve both the quality and size of his squads:

A. The coach should make friends with promising elementary and junior high school athletes and should encourage them to remain in school.

B. The poor students of the squad should be helped with their studies and encouraged to set up some plan for their adult life that includes graduation from high school and university.

C. A pre-season canvass of all boys in the school should be made and they should be invited personally by the coach to try out for the team. In this connection it is frequently necessary to see the parents to get parental consent.

D. The athletic coach should promote modified intramural athletics in elementary and junior high schools and should co-operate with the school authorities and Parent-Teacher Associations in providing sports supplies and equipment for use by these younger players.

E. Junior varsity teams should be organized for younger and smaller players. Unpaid coaches can usually be secured from among recent graduates, and a schedule of intramural play can be arranged either to precede varsity games, or to be played during intermissions. In another year many of these young players will be of varsity size and physique and the previous playing experience will be of real value to the next year's varsity squad.

3. Poor physical condition on the part of the players is a frequent cause of failure

As a general rule, the athletic coach is held responsible for injuries and poor physical condition of his squad members. He has the following procedures to help and protect his players:

A. A medical examination *must* precede active participation in strenuous competitive athletics. An examination of the heart and lungs, a test for hernia, and a check of recent illness and operation are the important items here. This service can be obtained either free or at a nominal charge by a physician who is interested either in the school, or sports, or both.

B. In the absence of a qualified trainer, the coach should secure the needed technical knowledge to apply first aid, and he should treat minor injuries promptly. Minor injuries that are ignored frequently become infected, the result being that the injured player is prohibited from playing for from one to several weeks. Of course, the danger to health is even more important.

C. The athletic instructor should work to condition his squad so that they will be physically fit to play an entire game at top speed. Conditioning results from exercise taken daily over a period of several months. There is no short cut to physical conditioning and endurance. Successful coaches attempt to measure the amount of physical work included in each practice session to the point where the participants definitely feel the tiring effects of the work, but practice should be stopped each day before harmful fatigue or exhaustion sets in. Adequate focus on conditioning is a frequent omission of coaching duties and must not be overlooked.

D. Except with the approval of a physician, the coach should not run the risk of playing a boy in a game when he is injured and when he might receive a permanent physical defect as a result.

4. Inefficient teaching methods result in mistakes by players

The athletic instructor should plan all practice periods and teaching procedures intelligently. There are many accepted principles and psychological laws of learning that have practical application in the field of athletic coaching.

A. In general, we may think of athletic coaching as the teaching of motor habits. These complex motor coordinations are learned slowly. Drill, practice, and more drill are necessary parts of this learning procedure. Explanation and demonstration by the coach are important elements, but there is no short cut to learning. Nothing will take the place of participation by the learner. These drills should be made as interesting as possible to the participants—but regardless, the practice must be carried on.

B. A few fundamentals (blocking, ball-handling, footwork, etc.) well taught are more conducive to success than having all skills explained but none habituated. The coach should work for perfection of execution and focus on attention to detail.

C. It is not what the athletic instructor knows that determines his success—it is what he teaches. The correlation is not always a positive one. This psychological principle of teaching should give confidence to the coach who was not a regular on his college team and should serve as a warning to the former college star.

D. Performance is more important than form. The coach should hesitate to require detailed mechanical movements of a player if his present performance is highly effective. Remember there are many football punters ruined by coaching for every punter helped by it. Also, it is absurd to see ten different university basketball squads using ten different mechanical techniques in foul shooting with every boy on each squad carrying out the detailed mechanical method prescribed by his particular coach. It would seem that at least nine of these ten coaches must be teaching inaccurately. However, the coach should make an accurate measurement of performance before he permits unorthodox execution.

E. The well-known, widely accepted and little used psychological laws of cause and effect have most important applications in athletic coaching. The wise coach will keep them uppermost in his teaching focus. These laws tell us that a habit to be made lasting should be followed by satisfactory results and a habit not to be lasting should be followed by unsatisfactory results. As a general rule, praise of effort is more effective than criticism.

F. Constructive criticism is necessary; destructive criticism is harmful and demoralizing. Do not tell a player he is poor —tell him how to correct his inaccuracies.

G. Teaching effort and energy should be directed to the end that the coach may expect his team to win from those opponents who are potentially just as good or a little better than his own team.

H. There are individual differences in learning capacity. Be patient with the slow learner. A team is no stronger than its weakest player.

5. Poor team morale spells failure in coaching efforts

This is a phase of coaching that can be analyzed and developed intelligently. It is possible to provide an intelligent analysis of the causes of poor morale in any athletic squad. Here are suggestions for improvement of morale:

A. When the team is losing, it needs encouragement and not destructive criticism and sarcasm. The coach should take the blame for any game that is lost and should point out to his squad an encouraging analysis of the defeat as soon after the game as possible. When the team is winning, it may be best to assume an unsatisfied and critical attitude—but give the players the credit for the victories.

B. Require group loyalty. Prohibit criticism, wrangling, and jealousy within the squad at any cost. There must be a feeling of all for one and one for all. The first indication of criticism, wrangling, or jealousy among teammates must be dealt with promptly, fairly, and in a friendly but business-like manner.

C. The athletic coach must be loyal to his team at all times. This is necessary if he expects the players to be loyal to him. He should criticize the player to his face, and not when the player is absent. He must defend the player against criticism when the player is not present. (If the drug store "cowboys" are capable of respecting anyone, this action will cause them to respect the athletic instructor. Also, the player defended will hear of the defense by the coach and will feel friendly toward the coach.)

D. The athletic coach should try to treat all players fairly. He must be tolerant to the extent that he will not permit a known feeling of hatred toward him on the part of one of the players to interfere with a just selection of his team on a strict basis of playing ability. The coach must remember that this feeling of hatred may, and frequently does, change to one of respect and friendliness within twenty-four hours. Also, the coach should remember that the antagonistic feeling on the part of a player is most frequently due to some treatment by the coach that the player interprets as unfriendly or unfair. In such cases, a friendly conference will erase the misunderstanding and establish a feeling of friendliness between the two individuals. In this, the coach must take the initiative.

E. The athletic coach must feel friendly and kindly toward every boy on his squad. When he has this feeling it will be found that the boys generally have a similar feeling toward him, and a feeling of harmony will soon develop throughout the entire squad. Again, the coach must take the initiative. A thoughtful coach will soon realize that this group feeling comes from the heart, not from the mouth, of the athletic instructor.

F. The athletic coach should be friendly with all of his players, but not too familiar. He should not be friendly toward some and sarcastic, critical, and domineering toward others. This latter attitude will soon lead to friction and poor team morale.

G. The coach may prevent inferiority complexes on the part of young second-string players by talking with them, pointing out to them their playing strengths and weaknesses, and encouraging them in their efforts to improve. To ignore or unduly criticize a substitute player will generally break his confidence and ruin him as a player. Criticism should be made in keeping with the potential abilities of the individual criticized. If this policy is made known to the players, they will welcome criticism. To attempt to show off by directing harsh criticism at an awkward, unskilled player is an act unworthy of any athletic coach.

H. In dealing with each disciplinary situation, the following procedure is suggested: do not speak until there is absolute quiet; then, talk with a low tone of voice; do not say too much; be sure a penalty can be enforced before it is announced; and do not hold any malice afterward—treat the incident as closed.

6. **Athletic coaches are frequently accused of failing to cooperate with the academic faculty and other extracurricular agencies of the school**

In the majority of cases, these accusations are either unwarranted, or are caused by carelessness, thoughtlessness, or shyness on the part of the coach. Men in the athletic coaching profession should show an interest in all other phases of school work and should go out of their way to cooperate with people in these fields. To eliminate these accusations, the following additional points are suggested:

A. A friendly cooperation regarding the use of school and community facilities, supplies, and equipment reacts favorably upon the athletic program.

B. In like manner, a fair, unselfish, cooperative attitude toward the use of school appropriations and athletic funds for other school projects indicates a desirable character trait of the athletic coach.

C. The avoidance of criticism of co-workers, employers and townspeople indicates cooperation. It is important to remember that even a door knocker is always on the outside of the door. Boosters are usually accepted in a social group; knockers or critics are usually regarded as small, social outcasts.

D. The ability to accept adverse decisions and criticisms gracefully is important. In order to develop professionally, it is wise, but difficult, to take the attitude that they are given in a spirit of helpfulness. Then, the coach should analyze the criticisms factually, and revise conduct or policies in keeping with the factual analysis.

7. Lack of community respect can reduce tenure in athletic coaching work

In this connection, the athletic instructor should dress appropriately; guard his reputation zealously; be mannerly, not boisterous and rowdy; choose his friends carefully—avoid the "tin-horn" element and make friends with the better element of the community by showing an interest in them, in their work, and in their recreations. He should take an interest and active part in community affairs; refrain from criticizing people or projects—instead, be an optimist and a booster; prohibit swearing, gambling, drinking, questionable stories, and other unsocial actions on the part of the players, and the coach must avoid these same acts himself.

4

Personnel

EVERY coach has a big decision to make in where to play a boy. This judgement in itself may reflect on a coach in the final score of the game. It is of utmost importance to be able to adjust your offense and defense to your available material; conversely it is equally important to adjust your personnel at hand to your offense and defensive strategy.

There can be no set rules in selecting boys for various positions. The main requirement is to recognize ability. Be sure you are playing the best boys. Remember, ability may come in any size. Never completely overlook any boy because of his physical requirements, either height or weight. The small back may have more spring and ability to play a forward pass at its height than a taller boy. There have been may small boys, in the line and backfield, who have played brilliantly here at Georgia Tech—the reason being that every boy is given an equal chance to play at his position.

Personnel can be broken down into the various positions; at the same time there are three basic groups to discuss—ends, backs, and linemen.

BACKFIELD PERSONNEL

Quarterback

The quarterback of a football team should be the first player to be considered by the coaches in making their plans for a successful team.   He is the key man in any offense and, therefore, more important than any other member of the squad.   He is important not only because he has his own assignments to carry out, but he also has the added task of directing the play of ten others.

Here are some important things to consider when choosing your quarterback.   First, you will select him from those candidates who are your best football players.   He must be cool and confident.   He must gain the confidence of his teammates through his ability.   If he fails to have confidence in himself, it is ridiculous to expect his teammates to have faith in his judgement.   You will want an intelligent boy.   He should be clear-headed and inclined to do a good job of thinking.   The classroom records do not always help you to judge the boy's mental ability, because many smart boys fail to make quarterbacks.   Also, you will want a boy with personality, one who is full of pep and enthusiasm, who is liked by his teammates and who will make a forceful leader.

The quarterback must be willing and capable of learning the duties of every man in every play.   He must be able to recognize his opponents' weaknesses and take advantage of them through knowledge of his offense.   He must have a good, commanding, rhythmic voice.   The quarterback who calls signals in a weak, irregular manner, beside being difficult to hear, will tend to destroy the timing and co-ordination of plays. A clear, snappy and incisive voice will help give a team the precision and dash necessary in its offensive movements.

A quarterback must be thick skinned to outside criticism. All quarterbacks make mistakes, and there will always be some-one ready to criticize. However, the quarterback must try to profit by his mistakes instead of worrying about the grandstand coaches and letting them get his goat. He must conduct him-self as a gentleman on and off the field. And last, the boy must have personal ambition to become a great field general.

Halfbacks

Play in the backfield requires a more active type of man than is necessary for the line. Speed, balance, and timing are very essential for a good halfback. Basically, there is no substitute for speed in any position, and this is true for the halfbacks more than any other position. Boys with high knee action, and who run with feet spread slightly apart, will usually be the best ball carriers.

In the "T" formation, size at the halfback positions is of little importance. The halfbacks as a general rule are asked to do very little blocking. In selecting the halfbacks, it is important that they be good pass receivers. Many of the best pass routes are to the halfbacks in the flat or deep. Also, the halfbacks should be able to throw a running pass. This does not take an accomplished passer. But, with a little work they will be able to do this and put additional pressure on the defense every time they start around end.

Fullbacks

In selecting the fullback, pick the tough, rugged boy. It is nice if he has break-away speed, but not as necessary as at the halfbacks. He should be the most dependable back. He has got to make the tough yardage inside when needed. Also, it is necessary for him to be an efficient, willing blocker. Upon him will fall the responsibility of protecting the passer and blocking for the halfbacks on runs.

ENDS

Height and weight: The offensive end should be of average height (five feet ten inches) or more. Tall ends, as a rule, enjoy an advantage over short ends in pass receiving, but extreme height is not a fundamental factor. The average weight of the offensive end should range between 180 to 195 pounds. This is in view of the fact that the end is called upon to block defensive tackles and linebackers who are the heavier men of the defensive team.

Age and experience: Age and experience are beneficial to mental and physical maturity; a fundamental factor that contributes greatly to individual ability. However, in a game, age and experience contribute only to those who have acquired the faculty of perfecting the techniques of end play.

Ability: Natural traits of speed and agility are desired in candidates for the end position. The end position demands from the player skills in blocking and tackling as well as in catching and running with the ball. Each of these basic fundamentals demand skills which must be perfected. It is important that natural traits in ability be augmented by adopting those traits to the desired technique.

Attitude: A well-rounded attitude must be developed in relation to the game of football. The mind must be conditioned to accept exacting demands with a spirit of cooperation and competition. Physical co-ordination governed by a healthy competitive attitude permits the utilization of muscles more freely and the manipulation of them at will.

LINE PERSONNEL

Tackles

The type of defense you play will have a definite bearing on personnel in this position. If you use the type of defense that is outlined in this book you will need tackles with speed and reaction. They do not have to be giants to play tackle in the modern game of football. You certainly want the big boy who can move and react, but if you don't have the big boy you must move down the scale and take the boy who can move and has good reaction. Without speed at this position you can get into trouble sometimes without knowing why. Weak tackles can put so much more pressure on the ends and linebackers that you might even think they are doing a poor job.

Tackles certainly should be the "meanest" men on the team. They should love contact and should be an inspiration to the rest of the team without saying a word. Remember the old adage, "By their deeds ye shall know them." Tackles should be selected first for defensive ability. If they can play defensive football they can play offensive football. With their speed they will be a great factor in playing to the other side of the line and can help the secondary stop long runs. It should be an honor to boys to be allowed to play the tackle position.

Guards

Guards can be the weakest personnel in the line without impairing the team's efficiency. Here is a spot where you can play the small boys who have a great desire to play. This is often the place for the boy about whom coaches will often remark, "It is a shame the boy is too small to play. He certainly has more desire than anyone." Take this boy and put him at guard and you will find added strength because guards have more protection than any men on the line of scrimmage.

The first requirement is that the guard should have good lateral speed. They must be able to pull out and make offense field blocks. On defense they must be able to help out in pursuit on every type of play to their side. They can be weak right under their position and still be an asset to the team through their speed in pursuit The wedge or power aimed at the guard position is one of the slowest ways to win a football game.

The guards can be the shortest men on the line of scrimmage. They can take advantage of their stature on offense, going straight ahead, or pulling out to block. A stocky boy has more body balance and can turn up into offensive holes better than taller boys. They can come up into defensive men with more power. On defense they can use this advantage because they are lower and harder to get under to be removed completely from a play.

As tackles are primarily picked for defense, guards may be picked because of a natural ability for offense blocking. A team's value may improve your offense team's strength without hurting the defense.

Guards should be the "cheer leaders" on the line. It is necessary and very important that you have "leaders" on every team. Every good team will have at least three leaders—boys who will talk and keep up the morale. Often you will see a team that seemingly is playing consistently better ball than their natural ability would indicate. If you will analyze such a team you will find that there are an exceptionally large number of leaders. These leaders can inspire teams to play up to and over their natural ability. The guard's position is a good place to put those players with leadership qualities, although sometimes you must sacrifice ability to do so.

Center

The center is one of the most vital positions on any football team. The center must be selected with utmost care. He is a man who starts every offensive play, and should be the logical man to call your defense signals. He very definitely should be one of your leaders. This is one position where leadership is a prime requisite.

The center must be a smart player. He must be able to think under pressure. He has as much responsibility in calling defense signals as the quarterback has in calling offense signals. Because the center is directing eleven men's responsibilities on defense you can see that he is more than just a lineman and must be picked for more varied qualities than other line personnel. With work any boy can be taught to snap the ball to quarterback or tailback, so don't give up if it looks like the boy who should play center has never snapped the ball. This is one of the minor functions of this position; although it is of major importance, it is an ability that can be coached.

The center must be a good tackler. Linebackers figure in more tackles than any other men on the team. The tackles they must make are more important because usually if the runner gets through to the linebackers he has an excellent chance for a long run. Centers also have the added responsibility of playing pass defense. They figure more prominently in the short passing game.

In selecting a center there is no particular size to look for. The center may be any size if he meets the position's qualifications. He must be:

1. A leader
2. Football smart
3. A good open-field tackler, and
4. Able to play pass defense.

5

Fundamental Offensive Play

IT IS in the offensive line that we find the unheralded and unsung heroes of any football team. The first downs and touchdowns of legendary halfbacks would never have come to pass but for the "blood, sweat, and tears" of an offensive line. *Offensive line play can't be faked.* Wedges must be formed, traps executed precisely, and secondary defenders removed, before yardage can be accumulated. So closely related are the functionings of offensive linemen to the glamorous exploits of the backfield that today the average fan is just beginning to realize that great halfbacks are a reality only because great offensive line play is an actuality.

BASIC OFFENSIVE LINE PLAY

Since these facts are self-evident, let us see how offensive linemen go about their business of protecting ball carriers, passers, and punters.

To do an efficient job on the line of scrimmage, an offensive man must first assume a position or stance that will give him every advantage possible over his opponent.   There are five major factors necessary to any good offensive stance.   Listed in order they are: (1) Leg spread, (2) Foot stagger, (3) Arm position, (4) Plane of hips, back, and head, (5) Weight distribution.

1.   Leg spread

Here, as in the foundation of any structure, it is essential that the upper structure not over-balance the base.   Consequently, it is found that a leg spread that keeps the feet at shoulder width proves to be most efficient.   When the feet are brought closer together, the offensive man commands only a minimum amount of the balancing power necessary to perform his tasks. At the same time, the narrow stance tends to cause a much deeper foot stagger, which is not desirable.   A leg spread in which the feet are wider than the shoulders will cause the offensive man to have to collect himself before releasing, thus causing the loss of valuable time.

2.   Foot stagger

Here again, as in the "leg spread," we are concerned with the base of a structure, so that once more we look for stability and balance as well as efficient and quick maneuverability.   Consequently, it is found that a *heel and toe* foot stagger is the most desirable.

The best weight distribution and maximum maneuverability are attainable when the toes of the staggered foot come no farther forward than the heel of the lead foot.   When both feet are on a line, parallel to the line of scrimmage, the offensive man has less balancing power and protection from the sharp thrusts of a quick and aggressive defensive man.   It is also found that when the feet are staggered more than the heel and toe position allows for, there is a tendency to drop the hips below the desired level. At the same time the staggered knee is dropped so close to the ground that only the barest minimum of driving power is realized from the leg and knee.

3. Arm position

Indifferent placement of the extended arm in assuming the tripod stance can easily offset the advantages acquired through proper leg spread and foot stagger. Improper positioning of the extended arm on the ground may cause the offensive man's stance to point "inward" or "outward." Since linemen are admonished at the very outset of their training *never to point on the line of scrimmage,* such carelessness on the part of an offensive man quickly dooms his efforts to mediocrity.

The extended arm (if the right arm) should be on a line with the right knee or just inside the right knee, and perpendicular to the line of scrimmage. This position readily squares the offensive man with the line of scrimmage. Now, with the proper weight distribution as well as correct plane of hips, back, and head, our offensive man is ready to explode into his opponent.

The other arm is carried in a relaxed but ready position across the thigh of the adjacent leg. The blocker is always ready to bring either forearm up into his block (though only as allowed by the rules). Failing to do so sharply minimizes the blocking surface employed by the offensive man. Remember, too, the offensive man's shoulders should be on the same plane and parallel to the ground.

4. Plane of the hips, back, and head

Here, we are concerned with certain idiosyncrasies of coaches, players, and fans that have brought about endless

argument, discussion, and debate. Yet, in coaching the "T"
formation style of offensive line play, it quickly becomes evident that when the hips, shoulders, and head are all on the
same plane, the lineman is in a position in which those portions
of the playing field he is concerned with are in ready vision.
He also has freedom of motion to go in any direction with the
greatest speed. Carrying the hips on a plane lower than the
shoulders, in these days of "retreating" and "off the line defenses," causes the offensive man to have to lift his hips before
releasing, thus reducing his speed in making contact with the
opponent. This much time advantage can never be given to
the defensive man without courting disaster.

Caution, though, should be exercised in getting the offensive
man's hips at the desired height. Too often in tending to raise
his hips the man automatically takes all of the cocked power
out of his knees. In seeking to carry the hips high, he assumes
a straight-legged stance. It should be remembered that the
legs and knees generate considerable power when slightly
cocked and help to deliver the tremendous impact necessary
to handle an opponent. Every effective lineman is conscious
of this fact and never assumes a straight-legged stance from
which he can muster little or no leg drive.

5.   Weight distribution

Proper balance is an essential in building any structure.
When the player assumes an offensive stance, it is imperative
that his weight be so distributed between the feet and the extended arm that perfect balance as well as maximum mobility
is afforded from that position.

It is to be remembered that the offensive lineman, much like
the sprinter on the track team, needs to get away from his
original position on the line of scrimmage with the greatest
speed. Does it not then naturally follow that the weight for-

ward idea, combined with the tripod stance, affords the offensive man the simplest, yet most maneuverable stance from which he can explode into his opponent with the greatest force?

Placing all of the weight on the extended arm doesn't allow for effective blocking of loose or retreating men because it definitely tends to over-balance the offensive man as he seeks shoulder contact with his opponent. Carrying most of the weight back at the hips causes the offensive man to lose valuable time collecting himself before being able to release from the line. Giving the defense these advantages is seeking defeat. Therefore, when the offensive man carries only a portion of his weight on the extended arm, he assumes a stance most advantageous to himself so far as comfort, maneuverability, and speed are concerned.

The legs are spread so that the feet are shoulder wide and staggered to a heel and toe distance; the extended arm is just in front of the knee of the same side of the body, or just to the inside of that knee. The other arm is carried in a ready position, resting on the thigh of the adjacent leg. The hips, shoulders and head are on the same plane parallel to the ground, and the weight well forward on the extended arm. The offensive man is now ready to release into his opponent with all the speed and viciousness at his command.

For some time now, coaches, as well as players, have been recognizing the value of seeking naturalness in a man's stance, as well as comfort and maneuverability. Any attempt to stereotype a particular stance for offensive linemen, without regard for certain physical deviations as to length of arms, legs, and body, is committing a cardinal sin in this phase of coaching. What holds good for one particular man need by no means be the best stance for another man. Consequently, great care should be taken in adjusting a man to the stance described in the preceding paragraphs.

It should be noted at this point that we have been most positive in all our statements relative to the offensive lineman's stance. No exception was made for any of the four inner offensive positions on the line of scrimmage, not even in the case of the center. Since "T" formation centers are expected to do all that other offensive linemen are called upon to do, as well as to snap the ball, should it not follow then that they assume the same stance the other linemen take?

The center deviates in one way. He has both arms extended since he is expected to snap the ball to the quarterback or one of the other backfield men. The center (if right handed) will grasp the ball at the forward end of the long axis with his right hand, exercising care that neither the pointer finger nor the thumb is extended over the very end of the ball. This latter places the center in an offside or illegal position.

The right hand is an extension of the right forearm. The elbow is straight and is never bent anywhere along the arc of the snap. Most of the center's weight is supported by his arms. This naturally causes the forward point of the ball to be tilted downward as though standing on its end. Caution again should be exercised here in not tilting the ball over too far, thus causing an illegal position. The center's left arm is extended and the left hand placed on the ball at about midpoint of its long axis. The hand is so placed only to serve as a balance and a guide for keeping the path of the ball straight from the center's right hand to the quarterback's hands.

With both arms extended, elbows locked in a straight angle, weight well forward on the ball, the center is ready to execute a perfect exchange with the quarterback and is at little or no disadvantage in carrying out his blocking assignment on the line of scrimmage or in the secondary.

Releasing from the line of scrimmage (getting off on the ball)

Too much accent cannot be placed on this phase of offensive play. The offensive individual or team that consistently gets off on the snap of the ball is certain to have a most definite advantage over the defense. Too many offensive men are defeated, at this stage of the game, without ever having had an opportunity to prove their blocking abilities. Getting the jump on an opponent often means the difference between success or failure on any particular maneuver.

To insure offensive success in releasing from the line, three methods are now being used: (1) The "lunge-out" release, (2) The "step-out" release, (3) The "all-fours and step-out" release.

Of the three releases, the first two are methods that have been in general use and practice for some time. The third method has only recently come into common usage. It will be found though that the idea itself is not new but one that has been used on occasions by many oldtime line coaches.

1. "Lunge-out" release

Releasing in this manner brings the offensive man into contact with his opponent with the greatest speed. From the tripod stance, explained in the preceding paragraphs, the head, shoulders, and upper body portions are thrown across the line of scrimmage at the opponent, as the slightly cocked knees are extended to a straight angle position.

The man should be cautioned that as his feet leave their starting position there will be a tendency to widen his foot base upon making contact with his target. This is to be avoided, since it will cause loss of power and maneuverability.

If, upon regaining ground contact with his feet, it is found that a narrower base has been taken, the man needs to adjust the width of his feet immediately, because in this position he sacrifices considerable balance. It must be remembered that upon making contact with the head, shoulder, and forearm, the lineman immediately starts with short, digging steps to drive his opponent in the desired direction. This method is most effectively used when the opponent is head on and playing "tight" on the line of scrimmage.

2. "Step-out" release

Releasing in this manner, the offensive man takes a short, jab step at the same time that he seeks contact with the head, shoulder, and forearm. This step (six to eight inches) affords a well balanced base. Should the defensive man be retreating or playing off the line of scrimmage, the offensive man will not have the tendency to slide to the ground and thus lose his man completely.

Since this method of releasing is just a fraction slower in contacting the defensive man, there will be certain disadvantages to using it compared with the "lunge-out." The effective offensive lineman, though, will have in his repertoire both of the methods described and will, also, be proficient in the use of the third when the occasion demands such a release. Remember when using the "step-out" release that we are expecting the defensive linemen to be playing a loose, retreating, or off-the-line defense.

3. "All-fours and step-out" release

Though not the most popular, this method of releasing has certain advantages. It is especially effective against a defensive man who plays low and uses his hands well, since it affords the offensive man good balance as he goes under his opponent's hands. Should the defensive man be playing "loose" or "off the line," the blocker is still in excellent position to carry out his intention. In obvious wedge-blocking situations, it is almost a must.

From the tripod stance, the blocker takes a short jab step with the desired foot as the body lunges across the line of scrimmage. Leading with the head, which goes under any defensive hands between the blocker and his target, the blocker extends his arms and he ends up in an "all-fours" position upon contact. As contact is established the arms are retracted to the chest and the forearms raised as extensions of the shoulder blocking surface. At the same time, the blocker starts a lifting action with his head, neck, and back, and begins using short driving steps to move his opponent. At the conclusion of the block the offensive man is in a high position, face to face with his opponent, between his man and the ball.

FUNDAMENTAL BLOCKS

Unless the blocking phase of the game is well taught and drilled, as well as precisely incorporated into the offensive system, the game becomes a tugging, stumbling, shoving mass of uncoordinated offensive maneuvers that is dependent on the *"pray-and-hope"* method of advancing the ball.

Over the years, coaches and players have devised any number of different offensive blocking techniques by which the defensive man was to be rendered useless on any one particular play. No attempt will be made here to cover all of these methods. There is no doubt but that certain methods omitted from this discussion have their place, but it is believed that the following blocks must be taught and practiced to make an offensive lineman productive:

1. Straight shoulder block
2. Reverse block or cross shoulder
3. Cut-off block or crab

4. Post block   ⎫
5. Drive block   ⎬ double team block
6. Trap block   ⎭
7. Fan block
8. Roll-up block
9. Pass protection blocks
   a. Aggressive
   b. Passive
   c. Screen
10. Punt protection block

1. Straight shoulder block

The straight shoulder block is the first and most important block the offensive lineman must master. Linemen displaying a weakness here should not be allowed to substitute another block without risk of poor offensive execution. Some "can do," some "can't do." It is in teaching the straight shoulder block that many "can't do" folks are separated from those who "can do."

Employing the tripod stance and any one of the three releases, the offensive man makes contact with the desired shoulder and forearm. His hips now are slightly lower than the shoulder level. The neck is set so that the head is locked and used to exert pressure against the opponent, thus keeping the opponent in a vice-like grip of head, neck, and shoulder.

As contact is made with the shoulder, the legs begin their churning action to carry the opponent in the desired direction. It must be remembered that, upon contact, the upper body starts a lifting action. This causes the hips to sink even further, seeking the power generated in the legs and knees. This lifting action tends to set the defensive man well in the vice created at the shoulder and "takes away" the opponent's legs, so that he is rendered helpless.

As the opponent turns with the original contact or immediately after the contact, the offensive man's hips are swung around so that he has his whole body between his opponent and the path of the ball. The opponent is then driven laterally down the line of scrimmage.

2. Reverse block or cross shoulder

Some coaches are prone to teach two versions of the reverse or cross shoulder block. In reality there is but one basic principle involved, and, consequently, we are concerned with but one block. The defensive alignment and the offensive intention determine the variation to be used.

a. *When defensive man lines up head-on the offensive man.* The offensive man desiring to contain his man on the line of scrimmage without allowing him any penetration will contact his opponent with his head. The head is used as a ramming rod and driven straight into the opponent's midsection. This assures the offensive man that his opponent will not penetrate. Upon making contact, the arms are extended downward and as they touch the ground, the offensive man swings his hips around to the desired side of his opponent with his legs ready to cut off any lateral motion on the part of the defensive man. The hips are carried high and in tight contact with the defensive man.

b. *When defensive man lines up on the inside of the offensive man, or when head-on and charge is to the inside.* Since the defensive man is already at an angle (or it is known that he intends to charge at an angle), allowance must be made for the time element involved before the offensive man actually comes in contact with his opponent. Realizing that his opponent is farther away (lined up inside) or will not be there (head-on but slanting to inside) the offensive man has but one thought in mind: "The defensive man must not be allowed to penetrate into the offensive backfield." Therefore, he throws his body across the path to be taken by the defensive man, contacting his opponent with his own outside shoulder. The hips then are swung into the defensive man and carried high from an all-fours position. When this crab-like position is maintained and the hips kept in contact with the opponent there can be no lateral movement to the outside on the part of the defense.

Remember that this block is used only when control of the line is desired and defensive men are to be contained—*never* when a hole is to be made or a man is to be removed from an area.

3. Cut-off or crab block

The cut-off or crab block is used only when it is desired to keep a defensive man from making any lateral movement to one particular side. On wide plays around the defensive ends, offensive linemen often find it impossible to drive opponents away from the path of the ball. Consequently, an effective yet less tedious block such as the cut-off or crab can be used. Then, too, the defensive man might be aligned so that he is well outside the offensive man and it would be a physical impossibility to drive him in. Therefore, the use of the cut-off or crab block is readily acknowledged as being good standard equipment for offensive use.

Should the defensive man be head-on to the offensive man, stepping out at a 45-degree angle with the outside foot will place the offensive man's body outside the defensive man. With this motion, the arms are thrust forward and beyond the opponent. As the outside foot contacts the ground the inside leg is brought up between the opponent's legs.

With the inside leg and upper body portions forming a lock on the defensive man's outside leg, the hands are allowed to sink to the ground, thus placing the offensive man in a crab-like position around the defensive man's leg. The offensive man immediately crabs around his opponent, keeping his inside foot stationary but digging with his outside leg so that his feet end up perpendicular to the line of scrimmage.

This situation affords the defense only one avenue of escape. By making use of the "roll-out," he can escape to the inside, which is where you would have him. Lateral or backward motion by the defense is impossible if the offensive man brings up his outside leg perpendicular to the line as he should.

Should the defensive man be lined up outside the offensive man then it is necessary to step laterally down the line of scrimmage at a 180-degree angle to a head-on position before throwing the inside knee between the opponent's legs.

4. Post block

In executing the post block the offensive man is usually working in conjunction with another offensive lineman. It is one portion of the double-team block. Formerly a single-wing maneuver, the post block is now coming into wide usage among "T" exponents because of the desire to create more blocking power at the hole.

The offensive man who is to be the post on a double-team releases from the line of scrimmage with a short jab step (six to eight inches) with the leg nearest the "drive" block man. At the same time he brings the forearm nearest the "drive" man up to shoulder level. This latter movement gives an extended blocking surface and at the same time affords the blocker protection for his face from his teammate's forearm.

If the defensive man is charging, the post blocker must make substantial contact with his head, shoulder and forearm. When the defensive man is trying only to hold his ground and remains stationary, hard contact with the head and shoulder is not necessary for it tends to drive the defensive man back-ward, which is not desired. As soon as the "drive" man makes his contact, the post man swings his hips toward his teammate, slides his head to the outside while containing the opponent on his inside shoulder, and begins driving the defensive man later-ally down the line.

Post men must be ever on guard for defensive men attempt-ing to get under them. It is the posting man's responsibility to keep the defensive man from submarining or getting so low that the double team fails. Knowing the snap count, the of-fensive man is always ready to fire his head under any opponent showing a desire to go under. From an all-four position, the postman, using his head and neck as a brace, starts lifting the opponent with his head and shoulders so that his teammate can execute his "drive" block.

5. Drive block

The drive block is the second portion or "business end" of the double-team block. The driver's forearm and shoulder nearest his teammate are thrown into the defensive man as he steps in with his inside foot. As good solid contact is made, the hips are swung outward, thus placing the offensive man's body between the defensive man and the path of the ball.

It must be remembered that the opponent is driven laterally down the line of scrimmage, not back from the line. As the impetus from this contact and follow-up move the defensive man past the post blocker, he in turn swings his hips into the drive man and the double-team carries the man out of the area.

Should the drive blocker find the defensive man under his post blocker and thus unable to lift the opponent, he can assure some measure of success in keeping the defensive man from interfering with the ball carrier by "smothering" him. This is done by covering the submerged defensive man's body with his own to keep him stationary or to keep him from reaching with his arms after the ball carrier.

6. Trap block

The trap block involves pulling linemen out of their original positions, with the snap of the ball, to block at another point along the line. Two schools of thought prevail regarding this offensive function of getting out of the line: (1) the drop-step method, and (2) the pivot or cross-over method.

a. *The drop-step method.* The offensive man pushes hard off the ground with his extended arm. At the same time he drops his foot, on the side to which he intends to pull out, diagonally backward so that upon contact with the ground his foot is at a 45-degree angle to the line of scrimmage. Without raising his body any higher and with his head up, he then swings his other leg across, pivoting on the dropped foot so that he is facing down the line.

b. *The pivot or cross-over.* This method of pulling out is the faster but since it necessitates a quicker and more agile lineman many line coaches have discarded it for the drop-step method. The offensive man pivots on the foot on the side to which he is going, at the same time that he pushes off on the extended arm. Without raising his body, he crosses over the pivoting foot with the adjacent leg and is now facing down the line.

Eliminating one foot movement, this method, though faster, has one feature that at times becomes a disadvantage. In swinging over the pivot foot, some linemen turn out so far that actually they are facing into their own backfield. This causes the man to run an arc in getting to his opponent rather than a straight line. This loss of time most always means defeat for the offensive man.

Having executed either pull out, the man is now ready to go

after his opponent.   Quite naturally there is always some reason for the assigned path the trapper uses in getting to his man. The paths shown in Figures 1 and 2 insure greater success against the different situations that might arise than any others.

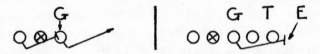

Fig. 1 (*left*).   Guard trapping guard in 6-man line.
Fig. 2 (*right*).   Guard blocking (trapping) end out in 6-man line.

It will be noted that in both illustrations the trapper goes into the line in going after his opponent.   This path, rather than the one parallel to the line of scrimmage, affords success against the defensive man who tends to pinch or play the inside.

Since the defensive man may act in any of the four following ways, the offensive man must always be in position to handle him.

1. When the defensive man is pinching in (see Figure 3), the trapper must go down into the line, or the hole will be blocked.   Using a drop step, the offensive man now pushes off of his dropped foot, taking a path over the far hip of the center.   (The pivot is never used when pulling out behind the center.)   This type of defensive player must be met head-on with maximum power and drive since he is moving into the area the ball carrier is approaching.   If the defensive man is driving in submarine fashion and the trapper cannot get under him, the defensive player must be smothered so that he cannot body block the ball carrier or trip him with an arm.

2. When the defensive man is slanting out (Figure 4), upon getting into the hole the trapper can see immediately any linebacker rushing in to replace the man slanting out.   This line-

backer must be taken as though he were the original man at the spot. He is met head-on and turned to the outside. Should no linebacker or other defensive man be coming in,

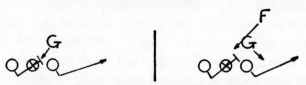

Fig. 3 (*left*). Defensive guard pinching in.
Fig. 4 (*right*). Defensive guard slanting out.

the trapper does not follow the slanting man but continues down field for a secondary defender.

3. When the defensive man is coming across hard (Figure 5), the trapper finds his task quite easy. Intent on getting to the ball carrier, the defensive man doesn't see the trapper and at the time of contact is in the most advantageous position for the offensive man to handle. The trapper, driving across, contacts his opponent with his shoulder so that his head is on the downfield side and drives through his man. Going to the knees or stopping at the point of contact has ruined more trap plays than any other single thing. If the defensive man has penetrated well across the line, the offensive man resorts to a driving body block, thus getting his opponent's legs out from under him so that there will be no base from which to seek support. This block assures the offensive man that his opponent won't be arm tackling the ball carrier.

Fig. 5 (*left*). Defensive guard coming straight across hard.
Fig. 6 (*right*). Defensive guard feeling his way.

4. When the defensive man is feeling his way across the line (Figure 6), the trapper must be on guard against the defensive

man's hands and forearm.   It is when playing this way that the defensive man makes best use of these weapons and the trapper must be sure that on approaching his target he dips low enough to get under the hands or forearms thrust at him.

Above all, and regardless of the defensive movement, the trapper must remember to work fast, hit hard, keep his feet, and to keep driving.   The opponent must be moved and unless the trapper drives hard and stays on his feet the maneuver will fail.

7.   Fan block

Good fan blocking is a quick way to assure touchdowns. Unless secondary defenders are removed, even the most talented halfbacks find it difficult to cross goal lines.   Actually the fan block itself is anticlimatic so far as this discussion will go, for it might be a straight shoulder block (when used on a linebacker) or a roll-up block (when used on a defensive halfback).

Of prime importance is the release from the line and the path the offensive man runs to get position on his opponent. No secondary defender can be removed successfully unless the offensive man first positions himself so that his job can be accomplished.

The first factor to be considered in this regard is releasing from the line.   The offensive man must bear in mind one thought: *I cannot be held up.*   This he can assure by varying his release and also by varying the split between himself and his teammates.

The next factor, and most important, is for the offensive man to run a course in the secondary that will get him where he wants to go in the shortest time, and that puts him in the most advantageous blocking position.   Many fan blockers disregard their routes and as a consequence would have enjoyed the game more as spectators.

There are two ways fan blocks are culminated: (1) Fanning back on a linebacker, and (2) Fanning across for a halfback.

1. *Fanning back on a linebacker.* The center or either of the weak-side offensive men can be assigned to this task. On releasing from the line, the blocker takes a path laterally through the secondary that will put him deeper than and beyond his opponent. This path, naturally, will vary with the type play and the timing. Having reached the farthest point of this route, the blocker turns back on the linebacker and with a good shoulder block drives him from the ball carrier's path (Figure 7).

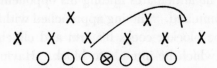

Fig. 7.   Guard fanning on linebacker.

2. *Fanning across for a halfback.* Here, the blocker must have speed and a good sense of direction. Coming across the field after a man who has considerable area to maneuver in, the blocker must first choose the shortest route and then, moving at full speed, execute an effective roll-up block to eliminate him (Figure 8).

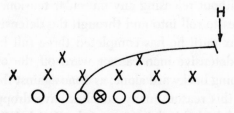

Fig. 8.   Guard fanning across for halfback.

8.   Roll-up block

The roll-up block is used by offensive men when removing secondary defenders downfield. Defensive safety men and halfbacks, having considerable territory to maneuver in when warding off offensive men, are difficult to handle unless blocked in a manner whereby their escape techniques are rendered useless. *The most efficient method used by the offensive man in doing this is the roll-up block.*

The roll-up is a block that can be executed while the offensive man is running at full speed. This one factor is responsible for the increase in popularity of the block. In fanning downfield the offensive man runs directly at his opponent, or to the spot at which he anticipates finding his opponent, with all the speed at his command. Having approached within three yards of his man, the blocker cocks his arm and clinches his fist on the side with which he intends to block. Having cocked the arm, the fist is now thrown past the defender's midsection and chest, as though the blocker actually intended to strike the defensive man a blow.

Throwing the arm out thus, and meeting no resistance, while traveling forward at full speed, the back of the blocker's shoulder comes into contact with the defender because of the offensive man's forward motion. The offensive man's body, legs, and arms are extended to their full length at the time of the contact. Without releasing any muscular tension, the blocker now continues to roll into and through the defensive man and does not relax until he has completed three full body revolutions. The defensive man cannot ward off the offensive impact by stepping backward alone, as done against the high body block. For this reason, many coaches have dropped the use of the old high body block in favor of the ROLL-UP block when working on men in the secondary.

9. Pass protection block

The pass protection block, an important offensive maneuver, has taken on new significance during the past ten years. With teams throwing the ball much oftener during the game, pass protection now is a regular assignment, not just a task undertaken in an effort to surprise the defense.

Three different pass protection methods are in common use today: (1) Passive blocking, (2) Aggressive blocking, and (3) Screen blocking.

1. *Passive blocking.* This method is used when the offense has no particular desire to surprise the defense with a forward pass. The offensive linemen, by their movements, show immediately that the play is going to be a pass. The blockers drop step with the outside foot (six to eight inches), as they pivot on the inside foot and then drop step the pivot foot. They maintain a low, crouched position, waiting for their opponent to show his intended path.

Should the opponent come across the line along a path outside of the blocker, the offensive man drives into him with a shoulder block (head between the defensive man and the passer) and allows forward progress but along a path that will place the rusher behind the passer. Since the action is passive, the offensive man must remember that he cannot be completely relaxed so that the rusher's momentum carries the blocker back into the passer. The rusher is never allowed straight line progress that leads directly *to* the passer, but only penetration along an arc that ends up *behind* the passer.

Should the rusher change his path and rush to the inside of the blocker, the offensive man no longer remains passive but with an aggressive shoulder block (head between passer and rusher) drives the defensive man into the center. A good offensive line adheres to one pass protection maxim, *"They will not touch our passer."*

2. *Aggressive blocking.* This type of pass protection is used on short passes, just over the line or into the flat when the offense wants to assure no defensive penetration and desires to surprise the defense with a pass. Since the defensive linemen are engaged immediately and most aggressively, they (the defense) have no time even to consider helping to defend against a forward pass.

One caution here for the offensive linemen—their blocks must be kept low so that the defense will not be countering from high rushing positions. Too often well-directed passes have been deflected by the outstretched arms of a tall, aggressive rusher, only because the offensive man's block raised the defensive man to his maximum height.

3. *Screen blocking.* When efficiently executed, screen blocking is the most discouraging offensive maneuver that defensive men have to contend with. By the same token, defensive rushers who are released too soon by screen blockers prove to be equally discouraging to the offense. Proper timing when blocking for screens is a most vital factor.

The linemen comprising the screen use the same movements employed in passive pass protection, except that they work in a higher position. A short drop step is taken with the outside foot and then the inside foot, in turn, is dropped backward about half as much to square the blocker with the line of scrimmage. The opponent's penetration is stopped with a high shoulder contact and maintained for a designated time. Upon releasing the rusher, the offensive blockers move laterally down the line and establish a new line of protection for the receiver. Naturally, in screens over the middle, the blockers would release their men and remain stationary until the ball was caught by their receiver.

10. Punt protection block

The punt protection block is one block coaches will not tolerate having poorly executed or being missed. Loss of the ball due to a blocked punt means such a substantial loss of yardage that the outcome of the game might easily be determined by this single factor.

In protecting the punter, whether in the tight line formation or the spread, the offensive linemen execute the same basic movements. One rule must be adhered to: *"Never be the aggressor."*

The defense is made to show their intention. A short drop step is taken (when in the tight line), and, as the opponent shows which way he is going, the offensive blocker picks him up with a high shoulder block. The block is maintained until the ball is kicked, then the offensive man follows an assigned path downfield to make or assist in making the tackle. The blocker must always be on guard against releasing his man to the inside. Whenever the opponent charges to the inside, the blocker immediately becomes more aggressive and drives him into the center of the line.

Men protecting the kicker must never go to the ground when blocking. Two very good reasons necessitate this caution: (1) The opponent when released too soon will block the punt, and (2) The blocker will be late getting downfield to make the tackle.

When protecting in the spread formation, the defensive alignment might necessitate a diagonal step, by the offensive blocker, behind the line to cut down the area his opponent has to maneuver in. This is the only time the blocker will go "after" his man.

Extra point and field goal protection

The blockers here follow the same rules as in tight punt protection, with these stipulations: The guards must always be conscious of any defensive attempt to "gang up" on the center or to pull him laterally so that some fast man can rush up the middle to block the kick. The offensive linemen must never go to the ground since an opponent coming over them might easily block the attempt.

Remember the offensive men must be ready to tackle any ball carrier should the opponents try to run back an attempted field goal that is short of the cross-bar or to one side of it.

Offensive line spacing

Linemen must remember there are two basic concepts underlying the many different defensive line deployments employed today: (1) Maintaining a given distance between self and teammates, and (2) Playing assigned position in relation to opponent and disregarding the offensive splits. With this knowledge, an offensive man can gain considerable blocking advantage over his opponent, once he determines which of the two defensive principles is being adhered to.

When the defensive man will yield only a given distance between himself and his teammates, blockers can always gain a blocking angle by splitting wider than the defensive man will go, or by moving in after lining up split. The same is true when the opponent plays an assigned position in relation to another offensive man.

Intelligent use of splits in the offensive line can nullify the efforts of the best of defensive lines. Offensive men must remember that taking a split on the line of scrimmage for no particular reason, other than to be splitting, can bring about blocking failures that could easily ruin the whole offense.

Common offensive line mistakes

The center. The introduction of the "T" formation brought about a new day for the left-handed center. These unfortunates were usually converted to some other position or had to watch the game from the sidelines. Since the ball snapped by the left-hander spiraled in the opposite direction from that of the right-handed center, it was believed that such a snap was harder to hold. The fumbles that might or might not have been the result of this reverse spin certainly pointed the finger at the left-handed center and he became a doomed man unless he was able to master the right-handed snap. The hand to hand exchange employed in the "T" formation has eliminated this biased feeling toward the southpaw.

Since no offensive play can get underway without preliminary effort on the part of the center, he assumes a most important position in the offensive plan. Unless he starts his snap at just the right time and delivers the ball to the "T" quarterback or to a halfback, setting back of the line, in just the right spot, even the best designed offensive play will fail.

The exchange (snap). Some "T" formation people still labor under the fallacy that the ball "can't be snapped too hard by the center." This mistake has been made too often in recent years and offensive units have suffered much embarrassment because quarterbacks were unable to handle the ball.

The pass from the center to the quarterback must be quick, direct, firm, smart, but *never with all the center's strength.*

Beside possessing a fine sense of timing and rhythm, the center needs to be a "holler-guy" and full of enthusiasm for his assigned task. Above all, the center must remember, his snap comes first and then any other assigned tasks follow.

There are three common mistakes made by centers: (1) Snap made too late, too early, too hard, too slow; (2) Not moving out with the snap; and (3) Going to ground after contacting opponent.

The guards. These vital offensive positions should be manned by quick, agile individuals who have the speed of halfbacks and a keen desire for body contact. Used as prime "interferers" along the line of scrimmage, they must be physically rugged enough to handle even the biggest of defensive men. Since they are often asked to pull out of the line to lead ball carriers along assigned paths, it is essential that guards have enough speed so that when synchronized with the backfield maneuvers there will be no delay in getting the ball to the point of attack.

Six common mistakes are made by offensive guards: (1) Cheating on weight distribution when pulling out of the line, (2) Switching stagger of feet when pulling to opposite side, (3) Raising straight up to pull out of line, (4) Running arcs instead of straight lines behind the line of scrimmage, (5) Going to the ground on trap blocks, and (6) Looking back at ball carrier when working in secondary.

The tackles. Without good blockers at the tackle positions, the "T" formation attack is like the baseball pitcher without a curve ball. It is around the efforts of these key blockers that the "T" offense builds its system of operations. Not only are the tackles called upon to control the line of scrimmage at the most popular point of attack but they are also assigned key blocks on opponents in the secondary. These latter blocks often make or break touchdown runs.

At times tackles are assigned "pulling out" duties. These must be carried out with the speed and agility of guards.

Few passes will be completed by the offense when the tackle spots are manned by mediocre blockers.

Common mistakes made by offensive tackles: (1) Driving defensive man backward instead of laterally down line, (2) Indifferent use of split between self and teammates, (3) Showing intent to pull out of line, (4) Taking too deep an angle when fanning across field, and (5) Varying stance when protecting the passer.

OFFENSIVE LINE COHESION

Unless the functions of the individual members of an offensive line are well co-ordinated and synchronized to the backfield movements, advancing the ball is an impossible job. Since the line is called upon to retain, support, defend, and to provide passage for halfbacks, it can readily be likened to the wall of a building. When carelessly or indifferently constructed, a wall doesn't perform the functions expected of it. The same can be said of an offensive line. When runners can't advance the ball, passers don't get away their throws, and punters have their kicks blocked, the trouble will usually be found up front in the line.

To do the job expected of it, an offensive line must first master the different blocks to be used. Next, it is imperative that each man learn perfectly the rules or assignments pertaining to his position. With this background, the blockers must next "get off on the ball" or "with the ball." An aggressive and well synchronized offensive line can make ball carrying an easy task.

Remember, the cautious offensive line never defeated its defensive equal.

QUESTIONS ON BASIC OFFENSIVE LINE PLAY

1. What are the five major factors of an offensive lineman's stance?

2. List three different methods of releasing for an offensive block.

3. Tell how an intended straight shoulder block might end up as a reverse or cross shoulder block.

4. What two methods are used in pulling offensive linemen out of the line?

5. What five blocks will a good offensive lineman master for use on the line of scrimmage?

6. Name three different methods of protecting the passer.

7. On attempted field goals, what must members of the kicking team always be on guard for?

8. What four different defensive maneuvers might trap blockers be confronted with?

9. What two basic defensive theories must offensive linemen, who use splits, understand?

10. Give two reasons for not going to the ground when protecting the punter.

TRUE–FALSE QUIZ

1. (*T–F*) A lineman who is a poor shoulder blocker should resort to using a body block.

2. (*T–F*) Linemen who pull out should carry all of their weight back at the hips to make the pull-out faster.

3. (*T–F*) When a defensive man is using his hands effectively, the offensive blocker should line up off the line to handle him.

4. (*T–F*) The reverse block is used to contain an opponent on the line of scrimmage and to allow no penetration.

5. (*T–F*) Double-team blocks are strictly single wing maneuvers.

6. (*T–F*) The lunge-out release should never be used when the defensive man is playing loose or retreating.

7. (*T–F*) The drive man of a double-team combination is responsible for keeping the opponent from submarining.

8. (*T–F*) The pivot method of pulling out should not be used when pulling behind the center.

9. (*T–F*) Linebackers can detect pull-out men who change their weight distribution when not charging straight ahead.

10. (*T–F*) When blocking for extra points, offensive linemen must be most aggressive to keep rushers away from the kick.

11. (*T–F*) The reverse block and the cross shoulder are the same type of blocks.

12. (*T–F*) Screen blockers should move downfield just as soon as they have released their men.

13. (*T–F*) Aggressive pass protection blocks should be kept high in order to hide the passer's movements.

14. (*T–F*) Splits are taken in an offensive line only to gain blocking angles.

15. (*T–F*) Offensive linemen should strive to drive their opponents laterally along the line of scrimmage, except when wedging.

16. (*T–F*) A defensive man rushing straight and hard across the line of scrimmage is easiest to trap.

17. (*T–F*) An offensive lineman should govern the height of his own stance by that used by his opponent.

18. (*T–F*) Varying the type of release used assures offensive linemen of getting off the line of scrimmage when blocking in the secondary.

19. (*T–F*) The defensive man who waits on the line of scrimmage is easiest to trap.

20. (*T–F*) "T" formation centers can and often do snap the ball back to the quarterback too hard.

FUNDAMENTAL END PLAY

The end commands a position of strategic importance on the flanks of the offensive line.   He has a vantage point from which he can observe certain elements of the defensive alignment. Because of his flanking position, the end is called upon to execute certain duties that in their nature differ from those of the remaining linemen.   The flankmen are therefore selected for their highly specialized duties from available players who can maintain a high degree of proficiency throughout the football season.

Stance

The stance should accomplish an individual purpose relative to an individual duty.   Unlike the other positions in the offensive line, the end must assume a certain position to gain power in his blocking; in releasing for a pass, he should not vary his stance.

A consistency in stance should be achieved to guard against possible tip-offs to the defense as to which duty the end is going to perform. To develop a stance with some degree of consistency, the parallel stance is suggested. The parallel stance pictured in Figure 9 shows the toe of the staggered foot on an arbitrary line with the heel of the opposite foot.

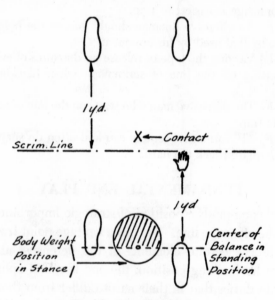

Fig. 9.   Parallel stance.

The parallel stance should give the player the following: (1) Relaxation, (2) Balance, (3) Vision, (4) Position for power, (5) Position for speed.

The stance should be a position in which the body can relax and maintain a well-balanced base, and should give a head position that enables good vision on and beyond the line of scrimmage.

The following procedure is employed to assume a parallel stance:

1. From a standing position, place the feet parallel and as wide as shoulders.

2. Relax the body, letting the knees bend forward with the buttocks dropping to a squatting position.

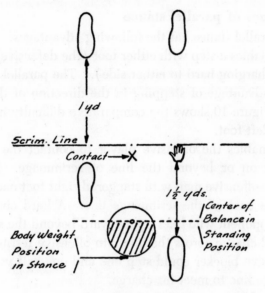

Fig. 10.   Staggered stance.

3. Extend the right hand and arm to the ground in front of the right knee, the left arm resting on the adjacent knee.

4. Lean forward upon the balls of the feet, lifting the buttocks to the level of the shoulders.

5. Shift body weight slightly forward. A minimum of 51 per cent of the weight should be forward on the extended arm.

6. Keep the head up, eyes looking straight ahead.

How to assume stance for speed and power:

1. Repeat steps (1) through (6).

2. Shift a minimum of 51 per cent of body weight to the left leg to free the right leg for quick movement.

3. Extend right arm, and lock it for powerful backstroke on start.

4. Drive off left leg, taking maximum step with free right leg.

Advantages of parallel stance

The parallel stance has the following advantages:

1. It enables a step with either foot (the defensive opponent may be charging hard to either side). The parallel stance offers the advantage of stepping in the direction of the desired drive. Figure 10 shows the comparative difficulty in stepping with the left foot.

2. It enables the offensive player to contact the defensive opponent on or beyond the line of scrimmage. Figure 10 shows the offensive man with staggered right foot one and one-half yards back of the scrimmage line. A hard charging defensive opponent who lines up one yard beyond the scrimmage line could charge across the line into offensive territory before the offensive blocker could step one and one-half yards to the scrimmage line to meet his charge.

3. It enables a longer initial step. In stepping off on a pass route, a long, quick, first step is desired to enhance the end's chances of clearing the line and of getting quickly into the open to receive the ball.

4. Body weight can be shifted to either foot. Figure 10 shows that it would be difficult to shift body weight to left foot. This fallacy in stance often prompts the end to raise up on starting, giving the defensive opponent an advantage in balance as well as in leverage.

5. It provides a more balanced base. Figure 10 shows the center of balance is back of the line of equal weight distribution. The parallel stance insures that a minimum of 51 per cent of body weight will always be forward.

Blocking

The end, in carrying out his specialized duties as a flankman, must be able to block on running plays. He gains a tactical advantage on passing plays because of his flanking position on the offensive line, only to lose this advantage on running plays. The inner linemen are flanked on both sides by potential blockers, while the end is flanked only on his inside, which leaves a wide margin for error to his outside. This relative disadvantage to the end in blocking presents an approach to line blocking which is different in many respects from that of the inner linemen.

It has been said that blocking is 90 per cent desire and only 10 per cent know-how. The viewpoint to be expressed here is one that deals primarily with the fundamental steps used in individual blocking technique.

Cut-off block

The cut-off block is employed on all plays run to the outside of the end position. On varying defenses the end will be called upon to block the defensive tackle, linebacker, or defensive end out of the pattern of play. To the end, the cut-off block becomes one of the most important blocks in his repertoire, and must be executed with skill and tenacity to obtain the desired results.

Because of the wide area to the end's outside, the approach to the cut-off block is dealt with in this connection. The amount of force used in the cut-off block is directly related to the width of the area between the end and the sideline.

1. *Cut-off block on tackle* (Figures 11 and 12):
 a. Get off *with* the ball.
 b. Do not drive into the target, but *away* from it.
 c. Cross-step toward line of scrimmage with inside foot,

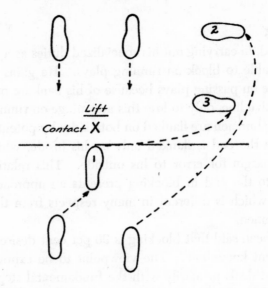

Fig. 11.   Cut-off block on tackle.

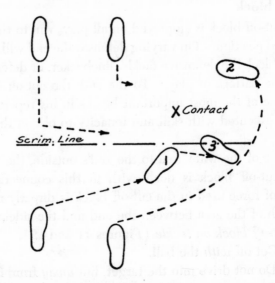

Fig. 12.   Cut-off block on tackle charging to the outside.

touching the ground with the hands as far away from target as possible.

d. Use the inside foot as a pivot and swing the outside foot in a wide arc into a position parallel to the line of scrimmage.

e. Final position should place the body between target and hole, knees slightly bent for balance, back and head straight.

f. Be passive at this point; do not go after target, let target come to you. Let body remain as a buffer between target and outside area.

2. *Cut-off block on linebacker* (Figure 13):

a. Get off *with* the ball.

b. Drive with controlled speed at 45-degree angle toward a point opposite to and outside of linebacker's position.

c. Keep eyes on the target at all times. Be ready to turn back to the inside if target charges to the inside.

d. Final position should be with feet spread well apart directly in path of linebacker's charge, knees slightly bent, back and head straight.

e. Do not try to contain linebacker in one final effort. Be passive and let target come to you. Remain as a buffer directly in linebacker's line of charge. (See Figure 13.)

3. *Cut-off block on end:*

a. Line up with head and eyes straight ahead.

b. Shift body weight to the driving foot, freeing near foot for a quick step.

c. Step with near foot straight down line in front of defensive end.

d. Do not throw into end or try to hook him at this point. Remain as a buffer keeping him from penetrating the line of scrimmage.

e. Fight down line of scrimmage, maintaining good balance by keeping feet well spread and staying low by bending at knees.

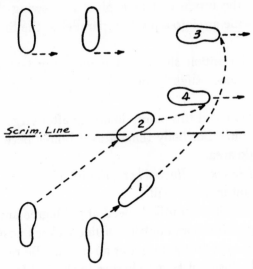

Fig. 13.   Cut-off block on linebacker.

f. With the help of the runner faking inside or outside position, the offensive end should be able to block the defensive end out of the play.

Drive block

The drive block is used in blocking defensive opponents lined up directly in front of the end's position.   This situation presents itself on all plays called to be run over the end's position, or off tackle.

1. *Execution of the drive block* (Figure 14):

a. Line up as close to target as possible (to cut down margin of error).

b. Get direct eye contact with the target and hold.

c. Approach target with the head and shoulders higher than the desired point of contact.

d. Step toward the target with either foot, disregarding right or left position.   Let the target show his direction of charge.

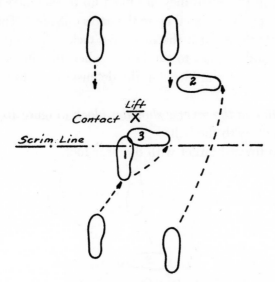

Fig. 14.   Drive block.

e. Prior to making contact, drop the head and shoulders to a lower point than initially indicated, then lift by extending the near leg.

f. Carry the whole body along with the initial step by pushing the leading foot forward with the body.   This insures full body weight behind the contact.

g. If target charges to the left, let the head slide off to the left and reverse body.   If target charges to the right, let the head slide to the right and reverse the body.

h. Follow through by bringing up the free leg for stability.

Reverse shoulder block

The reverse shoulder block is to be used in blocking opponents to the inside when they are lined up to the end's inside, and outside opponents lined up to the end's outside. This situation presents itself when the defensive tackle lines up to the end's inside and charges to the inside, when the linebacker is to be blocked out, or in blocking the defensive end to the outside.

1. *Execution of the reverse shoulder block* (Figure 15):

   a. Get off with the ball.

   b. Step toward target with the near foot.

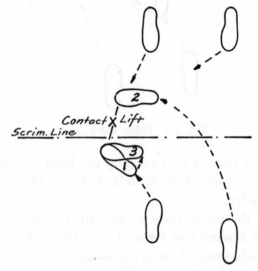

Fig. 15. Reverse shoulder block.

   c. Drive the head and near shoulder in front of target making contact with outside shoulder and forearm.

   d. Assume a low driving position, with both hands on the ground as in the bear crawl. The near foot is extended with head and thorax well over the extended knee.

e. Lift off the extended foot, bringing the free leg up immediately to the outside of target for driving purposes. Use the free leg to hook target if necessary.

f. Drive target down line away from route of the ball carrier.

Downfield block (extended)

The downfield or extended block is to be used on all blocks executed by the end beyond the official scrimmage zone.

1. *Execution of the downfield block* (Figure 16):

a. Get off with the ball.

b. Get clear of the line.

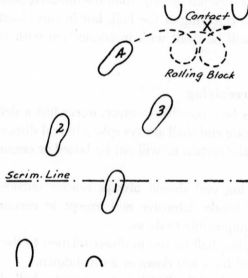

Fig. 16. Downfield block.

c. Approach target under controlled speed.

d. Close to within striking distance of target (about one yard).

e. With eye on target drive the head in front of target,

throwing off the opposite foot from the nearest shoulder to the target.   Roll body as in barrel roll.

f. Repeat roll three times.

RECEIVING

The forward pass is an important phase of the offensive technique, and must be dealt with as an integral part of the offensive scheme.

The forward pass, however, cannot be treated as a separate maneuver concerning only the passer and the receiver, but must be considered a team effort requiring maximum efficiency from every member of the offensive team.   The success of the forward pass depends greatly upon the offensive maneuver that precedes the throwing of the ball, but in this chapter the forward pass will be dealt with in connection with the receiver only.

Rules of receiving

1. Always be a possible receiver, never just a decoy.

2. Receiving end shall always split a liberal distance from his tackle to make certain he will not be boxed or crammed by the defense.

3. Receiving end should always release outside defensive tackle, and inside defensive end except in certain instances where it is impossible to do so.

4. All routes shall be run in direct relation to the number of yards needed for a first down or a touchdown.

5. The length of the first leg of any route shall always be in direct relation to the depth of the passer, or to the time it takes for the passer to get set to throw.

6. Know at all times the duties of the weak-side end and perform accordingly.

It has been found that the majority of all incompleted forward passes result from the receiver's inability to gain a vantage point over the defenders, while a high percentage of all completed forward passes result from a properly executed maneuver that enabled the receiver to gain an advantage over the defender. Major emphasis, therefore, will be placed on the receiver and on the techniques used to make the act of catching the ball a more simple and easy task.

The art of receiving may be divided into three parts: (1) Releasing, (2) Maneuvers, and (3) Catching.

Releasing

There are many methods available to get the receiver clear of the scrimmage line for a pass. Yet, in executing his duties of blocking, receiving and covering kicks, it remains for the individual to choose the most effective technique with which to combat the defenders. Many times throughout a game it is expedient that the end clear the line to receive a pass, or to execute a strategic block or tackle.

Whenever possible the tight release should be employed to clear the line for a pass; that is, the end should line up in a relatively close position to the offensive tackle. This should guard against telegraphing to the defenders that a pass has been called. The successful execution of the release enables the receiver to exploit more fully the element of surprise, and to enhance his chances of getting in the clear for a pass. Conversely, a release from an extended position tends to serve as a tip to the defenders that a pass is to be attempted. (It should be explained that the above statements refer to first and second downs of the series as opposed to third downs, which are obvious passing downs.)

In attempting the tight release, the end should experiment with the opponents opposite his position. In doing so, he will be able to learn each of their responsibilities according to the defensive alignment that has been deployed; i.e., a five, six, or seven man line. This will enable the end to vary his split from the offensive tackle according to the range of responsibility of the opposing linemen. For example, if the end takes a one-yard split from the offensive tackle, the defensive opponent may move out with him and little is gained. However, by extending the split to one and one-half yards, the end may be out of the opponents' defensive range of responsibility, which leaves him free to release.

On obvious passing downs (first, second, and third downs when behind and a score is needed, second and third downs when long yardage is needed for a first down) a favorite defensive maneuver is to "jam" or "box" the receivers in the line. This maneuver involves two defenders converging upon the receiver from right and left position to form a wedge.

In order to meet this situation the receiver must resort to the following tactics: (1) release in a low driving manner for leverage and balance, (2) choose only one of the defenders and employ a running play block (this method is suggested because of its psychological effect upon the defender). When being blocked on running plays, the defender strives desperately to get clear of the blocker. The same effect may be achieved by the receiver by faking a block before attempting to release. Remember the defenders must respect the possibility of a run on obvious passing downs.

When three defenders join to hold the receiver in the line (tackle, linebacker, end) the receiver should employ an extended release by taking a greater split from the offensive tackle to gain more territory in which to maneuver.

Maneuvering

Defensive football may be explained by the following axiom: *For every action by the offense, there must be an equal and opposite reaction by the defense.* This means that the offensive end must realize that the moment he releases from the line of scrimmage a defensive opponent immediately reacts to his action. The chance, therefore, is small that he can run a straight course to a predetermined spot without being detected and countered by the defense. In order to deceive the defender and create a favorable situation in which to catch the ball, the receiver must employ all the tricks of the trade, which include the exploitation of any defensive weakness as well as the utilization of his own physical, psychological, and tactical advantages.

Maneuvering is controlled use of the body. The eyes, arms, legs, directional movement, and speed play an important part in the total effort to confuse the defensive opponent. In order to utilize these body components most effectively the end must be a good actor.

Upon leaving the huddle the end should casually look over the defending secondary, paying particular attention to the territory in which the ball is to be thrown. By skillfully observing the defensive alignment and noting its special characteristics, he will be able to exploit his tactical advantage of knowing a pass has been called.

As he assumes his stance in the line the end may review in his mind the following coaching aids to the receiver: (1) get clear of the line without delaying the timing of the pass, (2) run the route deep enough for a first down or a touchdown, (3) be satisfied with just catching the ball, don't expect to score on every play, (4) expect the ball to be poorly thrown, high, wide, or low, and be prepared for the ball at all times, and (5) don't worry about complicated footwork; use speed and deception to elude the defenders.

Upon releasing from the line the receiver immediately obtains eye contact with the defensive man assigned to protect the zone in which the ball is to be thrown. "Eye contact" here means seeing the whole man and observing his initial reaction to the start of the play. It is advantageous to the receiver to know if the defenders have recognized a pass is to be thrown.

If the defenders are taken by surprise and play for a run, certain areas in the defensive territory will immediately open up to the receiver. The end should recognize quickly this advantage and exploit it by getting into the exposed area as soon as possible, and look for the ball to be thrown much sooner than originally anticipated. In order to take full advantage of any defensive peculiarities, the offensive end must be on guard at all times to protect against any tip-offs to the defense that a pass has been called.

Upon approaching the defender, the receiver should try to obtain eye-to-eye contact. The eyes of the receiver become the focal point of the defender's interest, and seemingly the only part of his body he actually sees. (It may be explained that the defender sees the whole body of the receiver, but in an effort to predetermine the receiver's actions, he must focus his attention upon the receiver's eyes for tip-offs of future maneuvers.)

In some cases the defender is taught to disregard the action of the receiver and watch only the point of the ball, yet in most cases in contests involving defender versus receiver the struggle becomes a personal issue letting certain psychological factors take over that favor the receiver. For example, the defender must keep the receiver in front of him at all times and watch the point of the ball. The receiver has only to indicate a determined effort to get behind the defender, which results in his gaining all the territory in *front* of the defender in which to catch the ball. Therefore, the receiver must "lead with his eyes" and manipulate them in such a manner that they will create a false impression tending to confuse the defender and render him susceptible to the efforts to deceive him.

Since the eyes become the focal point of the defender's interest, it should be added that facial expression contributes much to the strength of the impression the eyes make upon the defender. The receiver's face should become a mask of determined effort, which creates the illusion that he is operating under maximum conditions.

The arms and legs of the receiver must also play their part in deceiving the defender. The arms working with the legs give impressions of different rates of speeds. One of the most valuable assets a receiver may have is a change of pace technique that gives an illusion that he is running at half speed when in reality he is running at full speed. To the defender this illusion becomes confusing and adds to the detractive measures he faces in covering the receiver.

Speed is the most important single factor that contributes to the success of the pass receiver. In order to compete on an equal basis with the defenders, a receiver must constantly work on a quick start, change of pace, change of direction, and, finally, a tremendous finish.

Most pass routes are run by starting fast, then easing up to execute deceptive maneuvers, and finishing with a final burst of speed. This lends authority to the fact that an end should be able to run further, faster, and more consistently than any other member of the team. His ability to outmaneuver the defenders may well decide the outcome of the game, and his speed is certainly a deciding factor in the completion of the forward pass.

Catching the ball

No one particular method is required to catch the ball. A forward pass is successful only if the receiver gains possession of the ball. In the process of gaining possession of the ball, the receiver reserves the right to catch the ball the easiest and most natural way. In the act of outmaneuvering the defense the receiver may find himself in many peculiar and awkward positions that tend to make the catch more difficult to perform. There is always the possibility of a poorly thrown pass for which the receiver has to leap high into the air, bend to the ground, or stretch to either side. Therefore, it is safe to assume that the receiver in many cases will employ the most natural and most comfortable way to catch the ball. However, in view of the many difficulties which may be encountered in catching the ball, certain aids to the receiver are offered.

1. Try to relax the whole body momentarily before catching the ball.

2. Be oblivious of all men around you and watch nothing but the ball.

3. "See" the ball all the way into the hands, and while tucking it away.

4. When facing the passer try to catch the ball with the thumbs pointing toward the chest.

5. When facing away from the passer, catch the ball with the thumbs pointing out.

6. Don't think about running with the ball until the ball is tucked away.

7. After the ball is tucked away, assume a low driving position to sustain any tackling blow from the defense.

RUNNING THE ROUTE

The end should learn to run pass routes in relation to the whole route—an example of the "whole" theory of learning. The routes should be divided into three parts called "legs." The first part is the *running leg;* the second, the *maneuvering leg;* and the third, the *target leg.* In learning to execute the route each of its legs should be treated as a complete entity.

The running leg has been explained under the heading, "Releasing," and the maneuvering leg under "Maneuvering." The target leg has been partially covered under "Catching"; however, more should be said about its importance to the over-all act of receiving.

The target leg of a route starts at the end of the maneuvering leg and extends to the point where the ball is actually caught. This part is called the target leg because within its area the end can do more to help the passer complete the pass than at any other point. In forming the target leg the end must follow certain rules that tend to form an imaginary periphery into which the ball is thrown:

1. Face the passer
2. Slow to controlled speed
3. Prepare to react to the flight of the ball
4. Relax the whole body
5. Expect a poorly thrown ball.

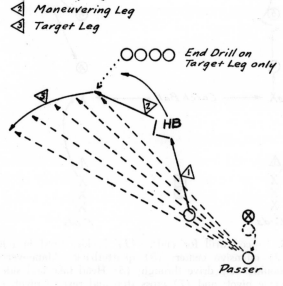

Fig. 17. Pass running drill.

The end is expected to catch any pass thrown within reach inside the target leg, and he is cautioned to expect a bad pass at all times. This tends to help the end catch the bad ones and results in many spectacular catches that otherwise would have been incomplete.

In stressing the importance of the target leg much time and work should be spent in perfecting the following drills: (1) Bad-pass drills, (2) Scramble drills, (3) Reaction drills, and (4) Speed drills.

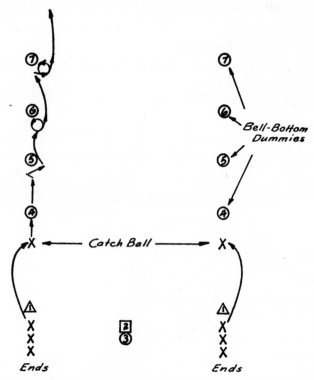

Fig. 18. Speed drill for ends. (*1*) Tackles used in releasing drill; (*2*) offensive center; (*3*) quarterback. Maneuvers: (*4*) Drop shoulder and drive through; (*5*) Head fake and side step; (*6*) reverse pivot; and (*7*) cross step and reverse pivot, ending up in leg raise and stiff arm.

These drills should actually take place within the target area, and game-like conditions can be simulated by starting the ends at the point where the target leg begins and working toward the point where the catch is made. (Figure 17 shows the position of the ends in relation to a proposed pass route.)

The following drills give a sample outline of proposed procedure for a reaction drill and a scramble drill.

Figure 18 shows a speed drill, in Figure 19 a reaction drill is diagrammed, and Figure 20 is of a scrambles drill.

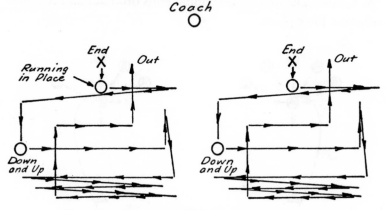

Fig. 19.   Reaction drill.   (*See also* Fig. 100.)

Reaction drill

PURPOSE:

1. To check reaction of individuals
2. As a conditioning drill
3. As a speed and maneuvering drill
4. Alertness

EXECUTION:

1. Ends come up running in place.
2. Coach calls "right," the ends turn and sprint, using full stride toward the right.

3. Coach calls "left," the ends stop, turn, sprint full stride toward left.

4. Coach calls "down," the ends drop to the ground, landing on stomach and toes.

5. Coach calls "up," the ends jump up, running in place.

6. Coach calls "back," the ends run backward, bringing their knees high as possible.

7. Coach calls "forward," the ends sprint forward using full stride.

8. Coach calls "out," the running ends drop out and two new ends take their place.

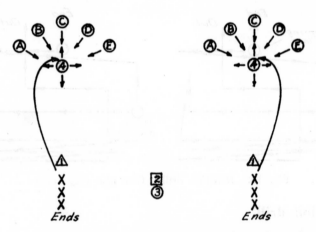

Fig. 20. Scramble drill. (1) Defensive tackle used in releasing drill; (2) offensive center; (3) quarterback; (4) offensive end on spot to catch the ball. A, B, C, D, and E are the defenders.

Scramble drill

The ball is thrown high to an end on a spot. The defenders try to gain possession of the ball. The end has to take the ball away from the defenders. The drill may be used for any pass cut or pattern. The purpose of the drill is to condition ends for going after any type of ball. The ball should be thrown high, low, wide, etc., so that the ends practice receiving all kinds of passes.

6

Offensive Team Play

A STRONG running attack should be an integral part of every team's offensive game. Some teams base their attack on the forward pass, but these teams are greatly outnumbered by teams that use a strong running game as their basic weapon of attack.

The advantages of concentrating on a strong running game are: (1) No fear of rain or unusual weather, (2) Better blocking and tackling (most good running teams are good defensive teams), and (3) It develops the offense's ability to control the ball a greater portion of game by grinding out first downs.

THE RUNNING GAME

A strong running attack should consist of speed, deception, and power (if available). A good running game will enable you to direct the play to any spot along the line of scrimmage.

These plays must be carefully designed to meet any type of defense they may encounter.

Although we are discussing the running game, we are not forgetting the pass. The ideal offense consists of balance between the running and passing game. It is much easier to devise a defense against a team with an unbalanced attack. Certainly, when one is strengthened, the other is automatically strengthened.

Two patterns of running plays

Direct plays involve the back getting to the point of attack as quickly as possible, thus minimizing the possibility of any loss of ground. These plays should be designed to hit quickly with straight blocking. Some of the plays that belong in this pattern are: (1) Straight ahead plays, (2) Slants, and (3) Quick sweeps.

Delayed plays are designed to draw the defense out of position by backfield faking and to allow interference to form in front of the ball carrier.

Delayed plays should be run in series so that they appear identical, yet can hit different spots along the line of scrimmage. Plays that fit into this pattern are: (1) Spinners, (2) Reverses, (3) Fake reverses, (4) Delayed pitch outs, (5) Traps, (6) Split bucks, and (7) Special plays.

Theory of offense

A strong running attack is based on four fundamental principles: (1) Use of maximum speed, (2) Ability to hit any spot along line of scrimmage, (3) Deception by faking close to the line of scrimmage, and (4) Use of optional blocks in the line.

Football is a running game, and the team with over-all speed and quickness has an advantage. The offensive team should

practice to drive out quickly *with* the snap of the ball. The
defense has to react *after* they see the ball moved. The offense
should hug the ball and get the jump on the defense by starting
with the ball. This gives the offense a distinct advantage because it usually allows them to control the line of scrimmage.

Since it is most important to charge out *with* the snap of the
ball, the offense should be based mostly on straight ahead
blocks. On all straight ahead blocks at the hole, the linemen
should take the defensive man in the direction he charges. It
is practically impossible to stop his charge from one direction
and then drive him the opposite way. It is easy to drive the
defensive man in the same direction he charges. This makes
it necessary for the back to run looking ahead and not at the
quarterback, making it possible for him to break on the correct
side of the block. Actually, the path of the back changes very
little.

An example of this is an off-tackle play with the end blocking the man over him. The end's first choice is to block him
to the inside, but if he can't he certainly should be able to block
him to the outside (Figure 21).

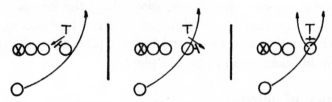

Fig. 21. End blocks on tackle, showing path of back. *Left,*
tackle protecting inside; *center,* tackle protecting outside; *right,*
floating tackle.

In Figure 21, should the tackle play a floating game, the
back runs straight to the end's block and breaks downfield
either to inside or outside. The back should not run at angle
downfield. In cutting behind a block all backs should turn
straight downfield.

Drills for getting off with the ball

All offensive centers should be checked to see if they are snapping the ball at the proper time. If the center is snapping the ball a little too soon, it not only wrecks the timing of the play but gives the defense the advantage of getting the jump. The centers should be checked on this throughout the early season practices until they get the proper timing.

When the centers and quarterbacks first report for practice, have them line up in a straight line and snap the ball. The coach should stand on the line checking to see if they bring the ball up together and at the proper time (Figure 22).

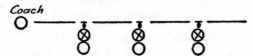

Fig. 22. Drill for snapping the ball.

The offense should be drilled in teams, each day, in getting off *with* the ball. There is no snap count that will insure getting off. Nothing but constant work will improve this from week to week. The best time to concentrate on this is the beginning of team work each day.

A good drill to use for getting off with the ball is to put seven men holding a hand dummy about a yard in front of each of the seven linemen (Figure 23). One or two coaches should

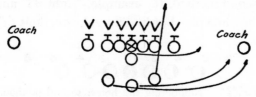

Fig. 23. Drill for getting off with the ball.

stand on the line of scrimmage, similar to a head linesman. The quarterback can call all of the plays with straight blocking and all linemen drive block each dummy. The linemen should really "pop" these dummies at the same time. The coach should check the linemen to see if they are hugging the ball, and see if they are getting off together with the snap. After about three minutes of this, go into regular offensive teamwork.

Numbering system

Since the offense does not know what alignment the defense may have, it is best to designate the holes over the outside hip of the offensive linemen.

There are two popular methods of numbering these holes. In the first method, *odd* numbers are used to designate plays to the *left, even* numbers to designate plays to the *right*, and end runs are given the largest number to each side.

For example, in this method of numbering, "48" and "49" would be the same play but in different directions—right and left respectively. (See Figure 24.)

Fig. 24. Numbering the holes: first method.

The second numbering system that is widely used employs the same numbers for both sides of the line, but "right" and "left" designate the direction of play.

In the second method, for example, "right 98" and "left 98" would be the same play but in different directions (Figure 25).

Fig. 25. Numbering the holes: second method.

The advantage of the second method of numbering the holes is that the offense will have only half as many play numbers to learn.

Offensive plays in series

It is best to arrange offensive plays in groups or "series." This makes it much easier for the quarterback because he can associate the plays in these series and remember the order in which they are called. He knows that when he calls one play he is setting up automatically the other plays and passes in that series.

Example of a series

The ideal series should consist of a play over the middle of the line, a play off tackle, and a play around end with the quarterback handing to one of the backs and faking to the other two, then dropping back as if to pass. Designate the series by calling them "30-series," "50-series," "90-series," and so on.

The "90-series" could be the one in which the halfback fakes up over the 8-hole, the fullback over the 4-hole, and the off-halfback around end. (See Figure 26.)

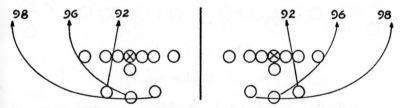

Fig. 26. An example of a 90-series. (This is the one used at Georgia Tech.) Left formation and right formation.

The quarterback either fakes or gives to all three backs. It will depend upon which play is called. To improve faking, in doing group work with the backs let the quarterback call "right 90-series," or "left 90-series," and the quarterback can give the ball to any one of the backs. The backs will get in the habit of faking because they won't know whether or not they are going to get the ball.   The quarterback will learn to associate these plays and passes, from these fakes, and be able to call his plays more effectively.

To get into different flanker "sets," the backs should be lettered.   The most popularly used flanker is the "left halfback set right"; this "set" can be called "A."   The second most used is "right halfback set left"; this "set" will be "B."   Then, "right halfback set right" will be "C," and "left halfback set left" will be "D."   (See Figure 27.)

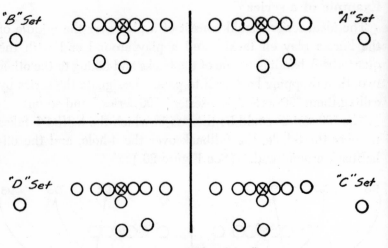

Fig. 27.   Flanker "sets."

To call a 90-series play with a flanker, the quarterback would say: " 'A' set right 92 on '2.' "

The ends should be lettered "X" and "Y."   (See Figure 28.)

The quarterback could spread an end by calling: " 'X' spread right 92 on '4.' "

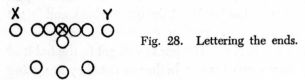

Fig. 28.   Lettering the ends.

Quarterback and Center stance   Fullback stance

Center stance   Halfback stance

Defensive Guard stance

Quarterback grip

Drill for getting off w
the ball. (See pages 8
86.)

e "roll out." *(See pages 6–187.)*

Above: The "forearm shiver" *(see pages 182–184).* Below: Tight punt protection line up. *(See pages 256–259.)*

Punt mechanics.
*(See pages 248–252
for complete discus-
sion of principles in-
volved.)*

Left: The quarterback taking the ball from the center in "T" formation. Note the right guard pulling to lead interference, and the quarterback turning for the hand off. Right page: Two "T" formation line ups.

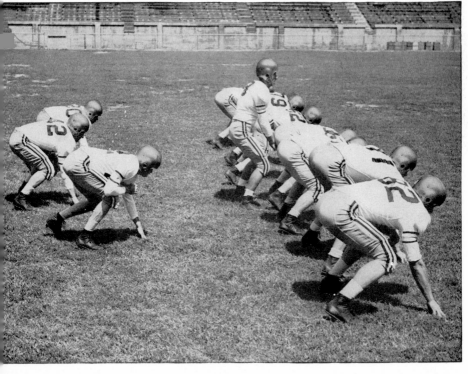

Throw-back pass vs. Auburn, Darrell Crawford to Buck Martin

Buckle play
ith Hardeman

lay away from
(see pages 100–

Goal line belly play *(see pages 123–124)*.

Covering the kickoff, Georgia-Georgia Tech *(see pages 277–278)*.

The huddle

Efficiency in forming the huddle, getting the play called, and lining up at the line of scrimmage is an important phase of the offense. The quarterback is in complete charge and no information should be offered by other players while they are in the huddle.

The huddle should be formed about eight to ten yards behind the ball. The center selects this spot after each preceding play. He should raise his arms above his head and holler to help players see his position so they can form around him quickly.

The open huddle is the most popular used (Figure 29). It has two definite advantages: (1) It makes it more difficult for the players to talk to the quarterback, and (2) Immediately after the quarterback calls the play, the players can look at the defense and be thinking about their assignment.

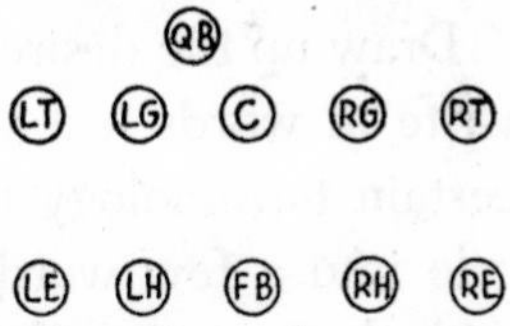

Fig. 29. The open huddle.

Immediately after the quarterback calls the play, the center and any flankers should leave the huddle. The center needs more time to get set than other linemen, and, of course, the flankers should leave earlier because they have much further to go to line up. After these players leave, the quarterback has a little time, and he can repeat the play. After repeating the play he calls "Break" and everyone breaks the huddle and advances to the line of scrimmage.

Rule blocking for offensive linemen

Blocking assignments for linemen should be simple and concise. The individual play book for each lineman should not consist of over one page.   With simplified rule blocking, there is no excuse for "busted assignments."   Certainly, if the player wants to play he is willing to learn one page of assignments so that he can execute them properly.

Rule blocking is nothing but telling the linemen what to do in words.

One big advantage of rule blocking is that the linemen do not have to recognize particular defenses; instead, each man has a zone or area that he is responsible for.   It makes no difference to him whether it is a 4-man or a 9-man line, he is only responsible for one particular area.

Another advantage is that the lineman knows his assignment the moment the play is called in the huddle.   He does not have to wait until he gets to line of scrimmage where the tackle or quarterback might call 5, 6, or 7, to give him his assignment.

How to set up rules

Draw up the desired blocking against basic defenses.   Then, write in words just what the linemen are doing.   There is a certain terminology that must be learned that can simplify a rule into a few words.   Also, this terminology may do away with the majority of the gap rules.

Terminology

OVER.   A defensive lineman is considered "over" the offensive lineman when in charging straight ahead he would make contact with a part of the defensive man.

GAP.   "Gap" is the term used when the defensive man is between two offensive men, but not "over" either one.

INSIDE.   "Inside" is the term for the gap directly to the lineman's inside or towards the center.   If a player's rule contains the word "inside," this means he will block anyone lined up in this inside gap.   (For example, the right tackle's rule could read *over, inside*.)   (See Figure 30.)

OUTSIDE. The gap directly to the lineman's outside or away from the center.

Over   Inside

Fig. 30. Positions of defensive linemen.

INSIDE, OUTSIDE. The tackle, on a quick play over him, will have both gaps listed in his assignment. Inside is listed first and takes preference.

LINEBACKER YOUR SIDE. See Figure 31.

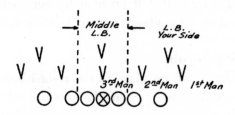

Fig. 31. Blocking terminology (shown here with 5-man line).

OFF LINEBACKER. The linebacker on the opposite side of the center.

LINEBACKER AS WIDE AS YOU. Only the end will have this among his rules. This means that the end will block any linebacker over him or to his outside.

SECOND MAN. The second man on the line of scrimmage, numbering from outside in. The second man will be anywhere from the end's outside shoulder on a 7-man line to nose-on to the tackle on a 5-man line. (See Figure 35.) *(Coaching point—any man "over" the end is always considered the second man.)*

THIRD MAN.   The third man from the outside will be lined up anywhere from nose-on tackle on 7-man line to nose-on center on 5-man line.   (See Figure 31.)

FAN.   A lineman going downfield and blocking back toward the line of scrimmage is said to "fan."

WEAK SIDE.   This term will be found only in a center's playbook to designate his block *away* from the direction of play.

STRONG SIDE.   Term used only in center's playbook to designate his block *toward* the direction of play.

FOUR MAN.   The defensive halfback on the side the play is going.

FIVE MAN.   The safety man.

SIX MAN.   The halfback away from the direction of play.

FILL.   The term "fill" applies to the guard or center on pass protection.   It means that if no man is over them they drop back and clean up on anybody that may break through.

Guards basic gap rule

For the right guard: on plays to the *right* inside, the gap is considered over the guard.   On plays to the *left* there is no gap rule.

For the left guard: on plays to the *left* inside, the gap is considered over the guard.   On plays to the *right* there is no gap rule.

See Figure 32.

Fig. 32.   Guards' basic gap rule.   Left formation and right formation.

Centers basic gap rule

On plays to the right, the *left* gap is considered over the center.

On plays to the left, the *right* gap is considered over the center.

5-man line

The following is an example of how to write up the blocking rules.

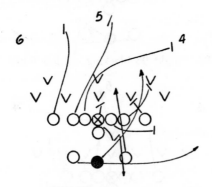

Fig. 33. Right 96 blocking, against 5-man line.

Right 96: Draw up the desired blocking against a 5-, 6-, or 7-man line (see Figures 33, 34, and 35).

RE [*right end*]: 2nd man.

RT [*right tackle*]: LB [*linebacker*] your side, unless 3rd man over or inside.

RG [*right guard*]: pull right 1st man to show.

C [*center*]: over, 4 man.

LG [*left guard*]: over, 4 man.

LT [*left tackle*]: 5 man.

LE [*left end*]: 6 man.

When the rules are made up they should be checked against a gap 8-man line. If the rule holds up, it will usually work on any defense. (See Figure 36.)

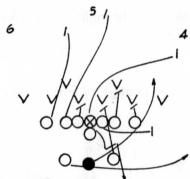

Fig. 34. Right 96 blocking, against 6-man line.

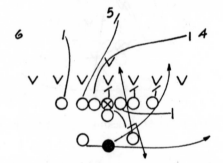

Fig. 35. Right 96 blocking, against 7-man line.

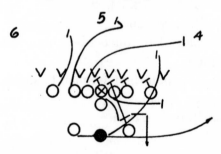

Fig. 36. Right 96 blocking, against 8-man line.

PLAYS IN SERIES

For a good over-all offense there are four basic series and a few special plays. The series are designated the 90-, 80-, 60-, and 50-series, and we will now consider them in that order.

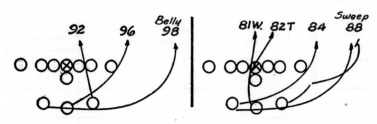

Fig. 37 (*left*). The 90-series.
Fig. 38 (*right*). The 80-series.

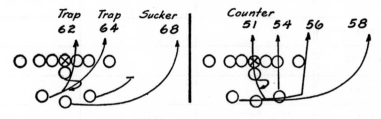

Fig. 39 (*left*). The 60-series
Fig. 40 (*right*). The 50-series.

90-SERIES

The 90-series of plays is a quick hitting series that is designed for straight blocking and that is effective against almost any defense. Very good deception can be obtained by incorporating the "belly fake" into the off-tackle and end-run plays.

NOTE: For all play rules, see the coaches' play book, Figure 41, pages 96–97.

PLAY	WEAK END	WEAK TACKLE	WEAK GUARD
92	5-man, unless LB is as wide	Over, Inside, Outside LB his side	Over, Inside, None, Wedge on center
96	6-man	5-man	Over, 4-man
98-BELLY	"	"	Over, Fan
81-WEDGE	Over, Inside, LB your side	Over, Inside, LB your side	Wedge on center
82-TRAP	6-man	Over, Inside, LB your side	Pull, Trap 1st. man Over beyond our guard
86	6-man	5-man	Pull thru 6-hole for LB
88-SWEEP	"	"	Pull around end
62-TRAP	"	Over, Inside, LB your side	Pull, Trap 1st. man over or beyond our guard
64-TRAP	Over, Inside, LB your side	"	Pull, Trap 1st. man beyond guard
68-SUCKER	5-man	"	"
54-QUICK	6-man	5-man	Over, LB your side
56	"	"	"
58	"	"	Over, Fan
QUICK SWEEP	"	"	"
SALLY RAND	"	"	"
GOAL LINE BELLY	"	"	"
DRAW-1	Release for Quick Pass and Fan for safety	LB your side	1st. man to Left
POWER-96	6-man	5-man	Over, 4-man
51-COUNTER	2nd. man, unless LB is as wide as you	Man on center, Fan right for MLB, None, Over, Inside, Outside	Post, Over, Inside None, 1st. man to Outside
PASSES			
"0" PROTECTION		2nd. man	3rd. man, unless Over center, then Fill
"3" PROTECTION		"	"
"7" PROTECTION		Over, Inside, None, 1st. man to Outside	Over, Inside, None, Pull side for 1st. man to show

Fig. 41.   The Coaches' Play Book.

CENTER	STRONG GUARD	STRONG TACKLE	STRONG END
Over, 1st. man to weak side	Over, Inside, Wedge on center	Over, Inside, Outside LB his side	2nd. man, unless LB as wide
Over, 4-man	Pull, Fake 1st. man to show	LB your side, unless 3rd. man Over, or Inside	2nd. man
Over, Fan	Pull, Fake end, Release for HB	"	"
Over, Wedge is on you	Wedge on center	Over, Inside, LB your side	Over, Inside, LB your side
Over, 1st. man to weak side	Man on center None, Pull right	MLB, None, LB your side	5-man, unless LB is as wide as you
Over, 1st. man to weak side	Pull, 1st. man to show	3rd. man, unless Over center, then MLB	2nd. man
Over, Fan	Pull around end	Over, Outside, LB your side	Over, widest LB
Over, 1st. man to weak side	Man on center None, Pull right	MLB, None, LB your side	5-man, unless LB is as wide as you
"	Over, 1st. man to left	Man Over guard None, MLB	LB your side
"	Over, MLB	LB his side	4-man
Over, Off LB	Over, MLB, None, LB your side	Over, Inside, Outside LB your side	2nd. man, unless LB s as wide
"	"	"	"
Over, Fan	"	"	Fan for floating end, None, Turn for HB
"	Over, Outside, None, MLB	Over, Outside, LB your side	Over, widest LB
"	Over, Fan	Over, Inside, None, Fan	Fan back for end
"	Over, MLB, None, LB your side	Over, Inside, Outside LB your side	2nd. man, unless LB is as wide as you
Over, 1st. man to left	Over, Outside, MLB	Over, 1st. man to Outside	Release, as for Quick Pass and Fan for LB
Over, 4-man	Pull, Block 1st. man to show	2nd. man, unless 3rd. Over	2nd. man
Over, 1st. man to weak side	Over, Inside, None, Post man on center	Over, Inside, off LB	5-man
Over, Fill	3rd. man, unless Over center, then Fill	2nd. man	
"	"	"	
Over, None, Pull to weak side	3-man	2nd. man	

Fig. 41 (*cont.*). The Coaches' Play Book.

Backfield starts

The following starts are used by backs for the 90-series:

1. *Right halfback*—Straight ahead start.

2. *Fullback*—Direct start by stepping up with the right foot at an angle toward the offensive right end.

3. *Left halfback*—Cross-over start.

Play No. 92 (See Figure 42)

Quarterback maneuver

1. The quarterback comes back at an angle to hand off to the halfback.

2. He continues and fakes to the fullback with both hands and "rides" with the fullback a few steps.

3. He pulls the hands out and fakes a lateral to the left halfback.

4. He drops back as if to pass.

Coaching points for fullback

The fullback pulls both arms in as if he has the ball.   He runs with his weight leaning forward and takes short digging steps.

Coaching points for right guard

On an even defense, the guard should block the man over him in the direction of his (the defensive lineman's) rush.

If it is an odd set, the three middle men try to drive the defensive man over the center and into the middle linebacker. Sometimes it is possible for one of the guards to slide off the wedge and fake the middle linebacker.   (See Figure 43.)

Coaching points for right halfback

The right halfback runs over his guard and breaks behind the optional block of the guard.

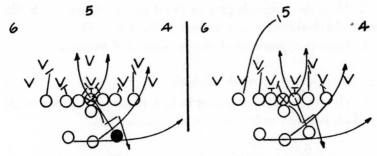

Fig. 42.   Play No. 92, against 5-man line (*left*), and
against 6-man line (*right*).

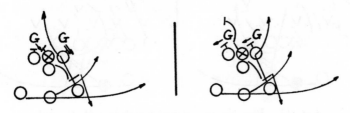

Fig. 43.   Guard sliding off wedge.

If it is an odd set where wedge blocking occurs, he must keep
his head up and break wherever the hole might show itself.

Summary

The 92-play is most effective against angling 6-man lines.   It
gives the linemen good position blocks for any type of defense
"stunt."

Play No. 96 (See Figure 44)

Quarterback maneuver

1. The quarterback comes back at an angle and hands off
the ball at the crossing point of the halfback and the fullback.

2. After handing the ball off, the quarterback tries to ride
with the fullback a few steps.

3. After the fullback gets in front of the quarterback, the quarterback should fake a lateral to the left halfback.

4. Then the quarterback drops back as if to pass.

Coaching points for right halfback

1. The right halfback comes in low, placing his hands in the hand-off position as he goes by the quarterback.

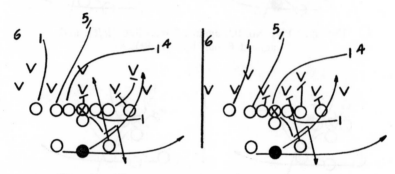

Fig. 44.   Play No. 96, against 5-man line (*left*), and against 6-man line (*right*).

2. The right half must block the man over the guard on an even defense, and the middle linebacker on an odd defense.

Summary

The 96-play is very effective against penetrating defenses. Also, it should be used when short yardage is needed for a first down or for scoring from inside the 5-yard line.

Play No. 98-belly (See Figure 45)

Quarterback maneuver

1. The quarterback comes back at an angle to fake to the fullback.

2. He makes a *distinct* fake movement of handing the ball

off to the fullback with both hands on the ball. (To help make the fake *distinct* the quarterback should have to reach and must keep at arm's length from the fullback. See Figure 45.)

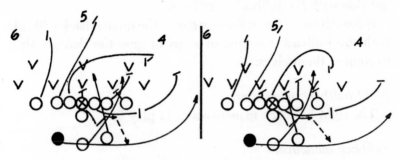

Fig. 45. The 98-belly play, against a 5-man line (*left*), and against a 6-man line (*right*).

3. In "riding" a few steps with the fullback, the quarterback should be a little behind the fullback—and he should remember to stay arm's length away. This is important to the quarterback because if the fullback gets tackled the quarterback will be in a clear position to lateral the ball to the left halfback.

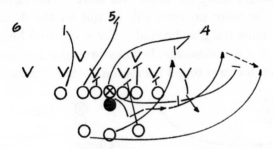

Fig. 46. The 98-belly play, quarterback inside end.

4. When he pulls the ball away from the fullback, the quarterback never stops his feet but continues running and tosses a short two-handed lateral to the left halfback.

5. If the defensive end does not take the fake but plays wide

for the lateral, the quarterback can keep the ball and run inside the end, then lateral to the left halfback.   (See Figure 46.)

If the defense is a penetrating defense, the quarterback does not ride with the fullback very long.

If the defense plays a floating game, the quarterback will ride with the fullback a couple of steps to give the defense time to commit themselves.

Right halfback maneuver

The right halfback maneuvers as in play 96.

Fullback maneuver

1. The fullback runs with his weight falling forward and takes short digging steps.

2. He must make a distinct movement of closing his arms over the ball when it is put into his stomach.

Left halfback maneuver

The left halfback should sprint directly parallel to the line of scrimmage, using the cross-over start.   The farther out he can get, the more pressure will be put on the defense.   The halfback must not give ground.   For every step he goes away from the line of scrimmage, he loses two steps, because he must take a step forward to get back even.   (See Figure 47.)

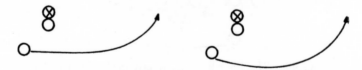

Fig. 47.   Left halfback maneuver, 98-belly play.
Left, the correct way; *right,* the wrong way.

In giving ground the halfback allows the defense more time to catch up with him before he turns downfield.

Right guard maneuver

1. The guard must hug the line of scrimmage so that he can pass inside the defensive end.

2. After passing the end, the guard should not go downfield at all, except to find the halfback coming up and his block to take place about on the line of scrimmage. (See Figure 48.)

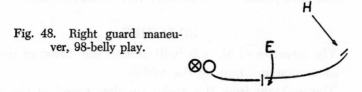

Fig. 48. Right guard maneuver, 98-belly play.

Right end maneuver

If the defensive halfback is coming up too fast for the guard, the blocking should be changed and the end releases immediately for the halfback. The guard can fan back for the clean up. Call this play "98-belly, E blocking," meaning that the end releases for the halfback. The defensive tackle will nearly always tackle the fullback on this play. (See Figure 49.)

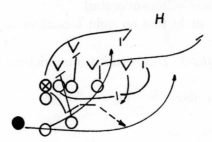

Fig. 49. Right end maneuver, 98-belly play.

Summary

The 98-belly play is very effective because the defensive end thinks that it must be an inside play since the right half and the fullback are faking to his side.   Also, the fact that the end sees the fullback with the ball in his stomach makes him commit to the inside.

It is important that the quarterback be slightly behind and at arm's length away from the fullback to insure that he is not seen by the defensive end.

Remember in coaching this series (or any series) that the backs must follow the same maneuver on all the plays.

80-SERIES

The 80-series of plays is built around the threat of the fullback wedge and trap up the middle.

The end run from this series requires speed at the guard spots.   If, unfortunately, the guards are not speedy, eliminate the end run—but keep the series because the fullback play up the middle will keep the defensive guards "honest" and because this series is very effective to pass from.

Backfield starts

The following starts are used by backs for the 80-series:

1. *Left halfback*—Cross-over start.

2. *Fullback*—Right foot on right formation, and left foot on left formation.

3. *Right halfback*—Direct start toward defensive end.

Play No. 81-wedge (See Figure 50)

Quarterback maneuver

1. As he receives the ball from center, the quarterback takes a short backward step with his right foot, turning his toes to the inside.

2. He brings his left leg around, and turns back to the line of scrimmage.

NOTE: Steps 1 and 2 are the same on all 80-series plays.

3. He hands the ball off with his right hand to the fullback.

4. He steps with his right foot, fakes both hands to the half-back, and turns his shoulders and head in the direction of the left halfback.

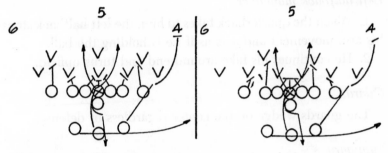

Fig. 50. The 81-wedge play. *Left,* against a 5-man line; *right,* against a 6-man line.

5. He takes an additional step, hopping into a passing position. He makes a slight delay before turning around to prevent the defense from knowing whether or not he still has the ball.

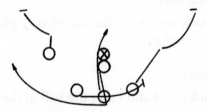

Fig. 51. Quarterback bootleg, 81-wedge play.

6. The quarterback should "fake bootleg" on this series occasionally. This will keep the defense from pursuing the ball carrier as quickly. Then, if the defense begins neglecting him, the quarterback should bootleg with the ball. (See Figure 51.)

Fullback maneuver

1. The fullback receives the ball on his second step.
2. He breaks left or right, wherever the hole shows itself.

Left halfback maneuver

1. When the quarterback fakes to him, the left halfback stops his arm movement and acts as if he is holding the ball.
2. He continues his fake around end and turns upfield.

Guards

The guards wedge on the center regardless of defense.

Summary

The 81-wedge is a good consistent short-yardage play. If the opposing team is using a floating or stunting defense, take good splits and run on early downs.

Play No. 82-trap (See Figure 52)

Quarterback maneuver

The quarterback maneuver for the 82-trap play is the same as that for the 81-wedge.

Fullback maneuver

1. The fullback starts and takes the ball in the same manner as the 81-wedge.
2. He must break to the right directly behind the trapping guard.

Left halfback maneuver

The left halfback maneuvers in the same manner as for the 81-wedge.

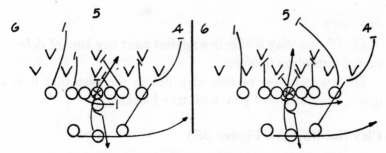

Fig. 52. The 82-trap play. *Left*, against 5-man line; *right*, against 6-man line.

Guards

In each guard's individual play book, at the top of the page, will be a gap rule: *"Know center's gap rule"*; that is, both gaps are over center.

This gap rule tells the guard that if there is a man in either gap he should consider him over the center. The guard's rule on the 82-trap is: "Man on center, none; pull right as in 88." (See Figure 53.)

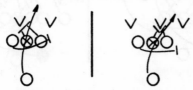

Fig. 53. Guards and center, 82-trap play.

If there are men in both gaps, the center takes one to the weak side. It should be expected, of course, that much more yardage will be gained running over the middle with two defensive men that close to center. (See Figure 54.)

Fig. 54. Men in both gaps, 82-trap play.

Summary

The 82-trap play is effective against most any kind of defense except a stunting defense.

The effectiveness of this play lies in the fact that it is a quick, straight ahead play with trap blocking.

Play No. 86 (See Figure 55)

Quarterback maneuver

1. The quarterback uses the same footwork as on all 80-series plays.

2. He fakes the ball with both hands to the fullback, then hands off to the left halfback with his left hand.

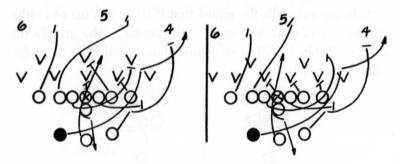

Fig. 55. Play No. 86. *Left*, against 5-man line, and *right*, against 6-man line.

Left halfback maneuver

The left halfback should cut for the hole immediately after passing the quarterback. After clearing the hole at the line of scrimmage he should break for the sideline to pick up the block made by the right halfback.

If the right halfback is set as a flanker away from the play, "B set"; the left halfback, after clearing the hole, should break

over toward the safety man to pick up the weak-side linemen.
(See Figure 56.)

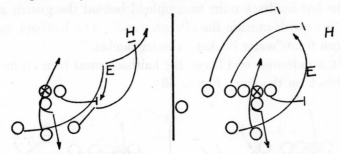

Fig. 56.   Left halfback maneuvers, 86-play.

Right halfback maneuver

1. The right halfback goes directly at the defensive end,
fakes a block, and turns downfield.

2. He gets an outside position on the defensive halfback and
throws a roll block.

Play No. 88-sweep (See Figure 57)

Quarterback maneuver

The quarterback follows his maneuver for the 86-play.

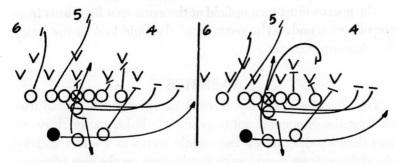

Fig. 57.   The 88-sweep play.   *Left,* against 5-man line;
right, against 6-man line.

Left halfback maneuver

The left halfback must turn upfield behind the guards at a spot five yards outside the offensive end. The halfback must not run from "water bucket to water bucket."

If the defensive end floats, the halfback must turn up inside the block on the end (Figure 58).

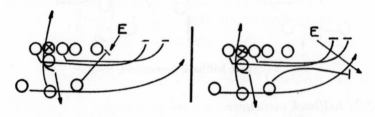

Fig. 58. Left halfback maneuver, 88-sweep play. If the defensive end floats (*right*), the halfback turns up inside the block.

Right halfback maneuver

1. The right halfback roll blocks the defensive end.
2. If the defensive end floats out, the halfback must block him out.

Guard

The guards must turn upfield at the same spot five yards from the offensive end. The second guard should look to the inside for clean-up purposes.

60-SERIES

The 60-series is a delayed series in which the first fake tries to draw the opponents out of position. Faking a quick sweep and then handing off up the middle serves as a check to keep the defense from pursuing or floating out on the line of scrimmage with the flow of the backfield.

Backfield starts

The following starts are used by the backfield for the 60-series:

1. *Left halfback*—Direct start with foot placed at an oblique angle toward the line of scrimmage.

2. *Fullback*—Direct start with foot being placed back in order to give ground slightly if necessary.

3. *Right halfback*—Direct start toward defensive end.

Play No. 62-trap (See Figure 59)

NOTE: The same blocking is used for this play as for the 82-trap.

Quarterback maneuver

1. The quarterback reverses his pivot and makes a distinct fake of a two-handed lateral to the fullback.

2. He brings the ball back through his stomach and hands off with his right hand to the left halfback.

3. He drops back as if to pass.

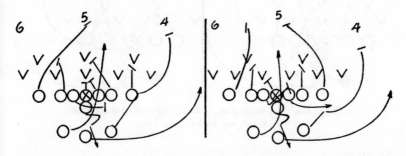

Fig. 59. Play No. 62-trap. Note that blocking is the same as on an 82-trap (*see* Figure 52).

Summary

The 62-trap play is most effective when the halfbacks are good slant runners. It is also effective when the defense is keying off the fullback.

Play No. 64-trap (See Figure 60)

Quarterback maneuver

The quarterback should step with his right foot down the line of scrimmage before reverse-pivoting. This puts him wider so that the ball carrier can run the correct hole.

Left halfback maneuver

The left halfback makes the same start as on a 62-trap, but angles in at a slightly deeper angle.

Right end maneuver

If the tackle is directly over the end, he must release for the linebacker on all-fours.

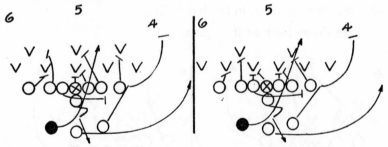

Fig. 60. 64-trap play. *Left,* against 5-man line; *right,* against 6-man line.

Summary

The 64-trap is definitely a power play. A long run cannot be expected because no one is assigned for downfield blocking.

The double block on the guard makes it effective against stunting defenses.

Play No. 68-sucker (See Figure 61)

Quarterback maneuver

1. The quarterback uses the same fake as on a 64-trap.

2. After faking with both hands to the left halfback, he pulls the ball back to his stomach and makes a one-handed lateral to the fullback. (NOTE: On a left formation, the quarterback should make a two-handed lateral.)

Fullback maneuver

The fullback takes two fast steps, then slows up and looks nonchalantly out the line of scrimmage as if making a "poor" fake. Just as the quarterback begins to make the lateral, the fullback turns on the speed again.

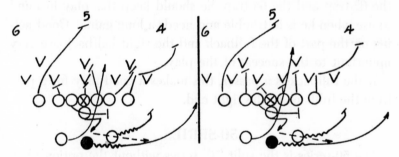

Fig. 61. The 68-sucker play. *Left*, against 5-man line; *right*, against 6-man line.

Right halfback maneuver

The right halfback makes a "poor" fake by just loafing toward the sideline. He keeps his eyes on the defensive end. Should the end crash, the halfback must roll block him quickly or he will penetrate too deep into the backfield.

Most ends will play a "waiting" end, and the halfback should time the faking so that he is just outside the end when the quarterback begins to make the lateral.   As the halfback sees the end recognize the play he should turn and reverse roll block him.

Right end maneuver

The right end should go out on the line of scrimmage and be ready for the halfback to come up fast when he recognizes the play.

Left guard maneuver

The left guard goes ahead and traps the first man to show.

Summary

The 68-sucker play has a good chance of developing into a long run.   After the quarterback has set this play up by running the 62-trap and the 64-trap, he should keep this play in mind to use when he is in trouble and needs a long gain.   Good acting on the part of the fullback and the right halfback are very important to the success of the play.

If the fullback is a passer, this makes a good play for a pass from the fullback to the right end.

50-SERIES

The 50-series is the split "T" series without the option play. Many teams have incorporated the ideas of the split "T" and the regular "T."   The best plays of these two formations (with passes coming from fakes of these plays) will present many problems to the defense.

A quarterback must be rugged and have the ability to run well to make the optional play a success.   Some coaches do not want to risk their quarterback being injured, and, therefore, do not run the play. The optional play requires a great deal of practice and some coaches would rather spend this time to develop a more varied offense and to develop a more flexible pass offense. With the threat of a wide play, it is wise to develop this series with the many innovations the split "T" coaches have originated.

Backfield starts

1. Right halfback—Straight ahead start over the 4-hole.

2. Fullback—Cross-over start.

3. Left halfback—Direct start with halfback getting depth of five yards from line of scrimmage.

Play No. 54-quick (See Figure 62)

Quarterback maneuver

1. The quarterback takes a short direction step as he receives the ball from center. This step must be at least parallel to the line of scrimmage, and it is better for it to be slightly forward.

2. He takes a long cross-over step and stretches out to put the ball on the halfback's far hip.

3. He takes additional steps and fakes to the fullback; after fullback he fakes a lateral to the left halfback.

4. He drops back as if to pass.

Right halfback maneuver

The right halfback must run straight ahead until he receives the ball from the left halfback. Since the tackle has an optional block on the man over him, the right halfback must be looking straight ahead so that he can cut to the proper side of the block. The cut of the halfback should not be over one step before turning directly goalward.

Fullback maneuver

The fullback cuts off his right foot over the 6-hole.

Right tackle maneuver

The right tackle has the option of blocking the man over him in the direction of his charge.

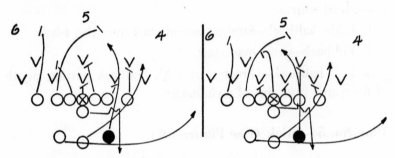

Fig. 62.   The 54-quick play.   *Left,* against 5-man line; *right,* against 6-man line.

Summary

The 54-quick is the fundamental play of a "T" formation offense.   For a successful offense this play must make consistent yardage.   With speed at the halfbacks, this play can go for long touchdown runs many times during the season.

Success on this play will force the defense to adjust, and over-all offense will be much more effective.   If the scout returns with the idea that the quick-opening play is not much of a threat, the other players in the offense are in for a rough time.

Play No. 56 (See Figure 63)

Quarterback maneuver

1. The quarterback drives out with a front pivot coming back at slight angle *away* from the line of scrimmage.   Since the

end is not being blocked, this has the tendency to draw him across the line of scrimmage.

2. After passing behind the right halfback, the quarterback takes a deep step back with his right foot and at the same time fakes a two-handed lateral to the left halfback.

3. The quarterback steps forward and hands the ball to the fullback fairly close to the line of scrimmage.

4. He fakes a lateral again, then drops back as if to pass.

Right halfback maneuver

The right halfback fakes into the 4-hole and helps block the same player the tackle is blocking.

Fullback maneuver

In starting, the fullback should look directly to the sideline. After cutting off on his right foot toward the 6-hole, he must quickly see the block being made by the right end. The end has the option of blocking the man over him either way, and, since there is a wide fake many times, the end will block the tackle over him to the outside.

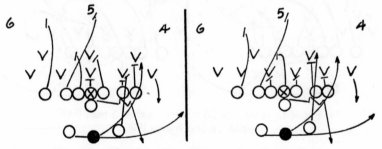

Fig. 63. Play No. 56. *Left,* against 5-man line; *right,* against 6-man line.

Summary

The 56-play has had the best average per try for many of the top split "T" teams in the country. For this play to be successful the series must have the threat of a wide play to force the defensive end to protect his responsibility.

The fake tries to draw the end across to protect his flank and then the ball is handed *forward* to the fullback who goes directly toward the line. This makes it nearly impossible for the end to make the tackle.

The pass to the right halfback in flat from this fake has been very successful.

Play No. 58 (See Figure 64)

Quarterback maneuver

1. The quarterback executes the 56-play.

2. In faking to fullback, the quarterback puts the ball into the fullback's stomach and leaves it there momentarily, letting his (the quarterback's) arms ride with the fullback.

3. He pulls the ball from the fullback and tosses a two-handed lateral to the left halfback.

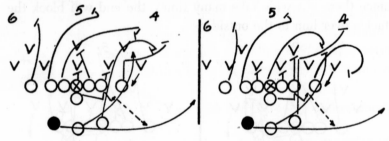

Fig. 64. Play No. 58. *Left,* against 5-man line; *right,* against 6-man line.

Right halfback maneuver

The right half should fake through the 4-hole, then turn down the line of scrimmage and try to get in position for a block on the defensive halfback. If he cannot get there in time, he should turn back and clean up on any pursuer.

Right end maneuver

If the defense plays basically a penetrating defense, let the end release for the halfback. If the defense is basically a floating defense, they will nearly always have a tackle "*over*" the offensive end, forcing the end to fan back and block the defensive end.

Summary

Because the right end fan blocks on the defensive end, the 58-play should consistently put the left halfback on an open field with only the defensive halfback in position to prevent a long run. Many times the right halfback or center gets position to make a fair block on the defensive halfback.

SPECIAL PLAYS

There are some plays that are needed in the attack that do not have comparable plays that enable you to form a series. These are special plays and should be given a name instead of a number. There are also plays developed from the original series that only require the change of assignment of one or two men. These are special plays within the series.

Quick-sweep (See Figure 65)

Quarterback maneuver

1. The quarterback makes a reverse pivot and either hands off or laterals to the left halfback immediately.
2. The quarterback fakes a bootleg away from the play.

Right halfback maneuver

The right half roll blocks the end. If the end should retreat out, the halfback blocks him out, ending up in a roll block.

Fullback maneuver

The fullback leads the play and blocks the defensive half-back. He must cut inside the floating end.

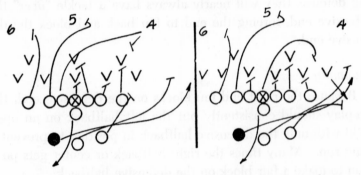

Fig. 65.   The quick-sweep play. *Left*, against 5-man line; *right*, against 6-man line.

Left halfback maneuver

The left half makes a cross-over start. After getting the ball from the quarterback he should see if the defensive end is floating out. If the end is floating, the left half should run directly at the end. If the end continues floating, the ball carrier can cut inside quickly. If the end should come back to the inside, the halfback can break back slightly and get around him for a long gain.   (See Figure 66.)

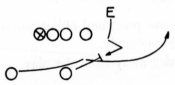

Fig. 66.   Left halfback maneu-ver, quick sweep. Floating end cutting back to the inside.

Figure 67 illustrates the right and wrong way. It is easy to visualize the number of steps saved by the ball carrier running directly at end.

Linemen

Linemen should use cut-off blocks, since there is no fake to help their block.

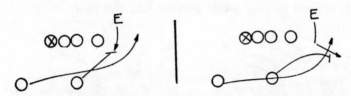

Fig. 67. Left halfback maneuver, quick-sweep. *Left,* end charging; *right,* end floating, halfback cutting inside.

Summary

The quick-sweep play is needed against penetrating defenses, where no inside fake is needed to run wide. There is a good chance for a long run when this play is used on short yardage. The quarterback is going to the weak side in case the defense is keying on him. Also, he is setting up the Sally Rand.

Sally Rand (See Figure 68)

Quarterback maneuver

The quarterback's maneuver is the same as on the quick-sweep. The quarterback will block the end if he penetrates very deep.

Right halfback maneuver

The right half comes across like the quick-sweep, but running at three-quarter speed. After receiving the ball from the quarterback, he places both hands on the ball for the hand off to the left halfback.

Left halfback maneuver

The left half takes a direct step, then crosses over with his right leg and pivots around and starts running the other way. He must be looking at the defensive end, so as to know how much ground to give while getting into the clear.

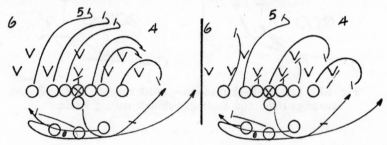

Fig. 68.   Sally Rand play.   *Left,* against 5-man line; *right,* against 6-man line.

Right end maneuver

The right end performs a fan block on the end.   If the end sees the quarterback block the end, because of the deep penetration, he should then block the defensive halfback.   (All offensive linemen going downfield should be taught to set up a wall similar to a punt return.)

Summary

The Sally Rand should be run at least twice each ball game. This forces the defense away from the direction of the play and to stay put a little longer, thus increasing the possibility of a longer run on any play to the strong side.

As the quarterback runs the quick sweep, he should be alert and watch the defense.   By doing this he will know the most opportune time to run the Sally Rand.   This play can be run very effectively with left halfback set to the left ("D set"). (See Figure 69.)

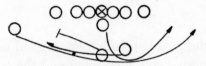

Fig. 69. Left halfback in "D set," Sally Rand play.

Goal line belly (See Figure 70)

The goal line belly is a variation of the belly play that is very effective on the goal line. The blocking in the line is straight away on the side of the play.

If a fake occurs in the backfield it is very dangerous to pull linemen on the goal line, because of the possibility of a defensive man coming clean and causing a fumble.

Quarterback maneuver

The quarterback, fullback, and left halfback perform the same as on the 98-belly, except that the quarterback reverses his turn to give the play a little deception.

Right halfback maneuver

The right half starts directly for the inside shoulder of the defensive end, as if he is going to block him out. When the end takes the fake of the fullback with the ball, the right halfback dips around him and blocks the defensive halfback.

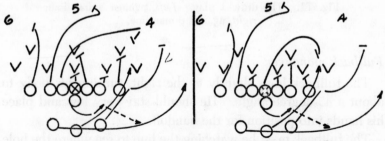

Fig. 70. Goal line belly play. *Left*, against 5-man line; *right*, against 6-man line.

Summary

The reason the goal line belly play is good on the goal line is that the defensive end is crashing and the halfback is very close to the line of scrimmage. It is impossible for the right end to block defensive halfback; the only man who can is a player leading the play such as the right halfback.

Draw 1 (See Figure 71)

Quarterback maneuver

1. The quarterback comes straight back as if to pass.

2. As he passes the fullback, the quarterback slides the ball into fullback's stomach with his left hand.

3. He continues dropping back as if to throw a deep pass.

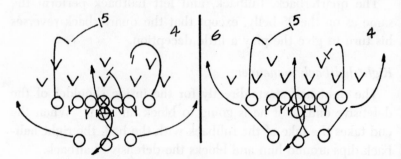

Fig. 71. The draw 1 play. *Left,* against 5-man line; *right,* against 6-man line.

Fullback maneuver

The fullback hops slightly to the right, turning his body to about a 45-degree angle. He should stay very low and place his hands into position for the handoff.

The fullback must be watching the line to see where the hole is going to open up. The fullback must delay until the hole shows itself. It is a mistake for the fullback to start forward looking for a hole.

A good coaching point for the fullback is: *Make the hole come to you.*

Linemen maneuvers

All linemen drop back as they do on passive pass protection. Then they should drive the defensive man in the direction of his rush.

Right end maneuver

The right end must keep his eyes on the linebacker as he releases for a pass, so that he can get proper position for a block.

Power-96 (See Figure 72)

The power-96 is a special play within the 90-series. "Power" called before "96" means:

1. A double block by the tackle and end.
2. The fullback will lead the play over the 6-hole.
3. The left halfback will carry the ball through the 6-hole.
4. The quarterback will fake to the right halfback and then turn and hand off to the left halfback. (This is slightly different than on the regular 90-series.)

Quarterback maneuver

1. The quarterback makes a front pivot and makes a two-handed fake to the right halfback.
2. He pivots off his left foot, turning back to the line of scrimmage, and hands off to the left halfback.

Fullback maneuver

Drives directly over 6-hole looking for linebacker at hole.

Left halfback maneuver

Uses crossover start, slanting into hole.

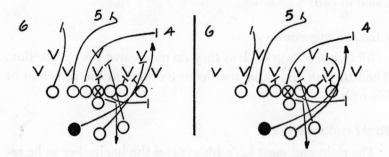

Fig. 72. The power-96 play. *Left,* against 5-man line;
right, against 6-man line.

Summary

The power-96 is, of course, a power play. It can be used against any type of defense. Should the defense be over-shifting to the wide side of the field, this is the best play to hit the short side with.

51-counter (See Figure 73)

The 51-counter is a "special" play within the 50-series. "Counter" means that it is a delayed play away from the original fake.

Quarterback maneuver

1. The quarterback front pivots and crosses over with his left leg, keeping the ball in his stomach with his right hand.

2. He fakes to the right halfback with his left hand.

3. He steps back toward the line of scrimmage with his right foot and hands off to the fullback.

Right halfback maneuver

Slants in slightly for fake with quarterback and continues through line and blocks linebacker his side.

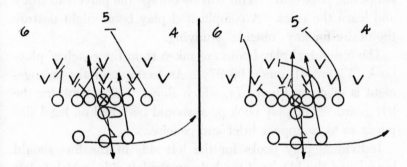

Fig. 73. The 51-counter play. *Left,* against 5-man line; *right,* against 6-man line.

Fullback maneuver

1. The fullback takes a direct step to his right and looks to the side line.

2. He drives off his right foot in direction of the left leg of the center.

3. He receives the ball from the quarterback close to the line of scrimmage.

Right guard maneuver

On odd defense the right guard should crab-block the man on the center to get his attention, and the center can drive him to the right—where the original fake occurs.

When there is a man over him, the right guard should make the same block as on play 54, ending up, if possible, in a reverse body block.

TEACHING RULE BLOCKING

The method the coach uses of organizing and teaching the rules is very important. The individual play book should consist of one page only. This will encourage the players to study and learn the rules. A complicated play book might destroy the desire for any "outside" studying.

The individual play books are taken from the coaches' playbook (Figure 41, pages 96–97). An example of the arrangement is given in Figure 74, which shows a play book for the left guard. The play book page should be typed on legal size paper so as to appear brief and concise.

Individual play books for the left side of the line should have listed the blocks at the hole on the left side, which is left formation.

After distributing the play books, the coach should explain the terminology to be used. Follow this by taking a work sheet and apply the rule for one position against every defense listed (Figure 75). Repeat the rule orally each time before marking in the assignment. It should not take over a minute or two to complete the sheet. The work sheet should contain any defense that may be encountered during the season.

The players should then fill out the work sheets for the first series to be entered. Each time he should repeat the rule to himself before marking down his assignment. This will help him to learn the rule and become accustomed to where to look for his blocking assignment.

The coach should take up the work sheets and grade them for mistakes. By doing this, the coach will learn what the players failed to grasp from the lecture, and he can correct these mistakes on the field that afternoon.

After practice, inform the linemen they will have a written test the next day on the rules they have been practicing. This will encourage them to study their play books at home.

LEFT GUARD

Gap Rule: 1. On traps and wedges, know center rule (both gaps over center)
           2. On 4, 6, and 8 hole plays, inside gap over you
           3. . Plays away, no gap rule

Left Formation	Play	Right Formation
Over, Inside, None, Wedge on Center	92	Over, Inside, None, Wedge on Center
Pull Left for 1st man to show	96	Over, 4-Man
Pull Left, Fake End, Release for HB	98-Belly	Over, Fan
Wedge on Center	81-Wedge	Wedge on Center
Man on Center, None, Pull Left	82-Trap	Pull, Trap 1st man Over or Beyond our Guard
Pull Left, 1st man to show	86	Pull Right Thru 6-hole for LB
Pull Left around End	88-Sweep	Pull Right around End
Man on Center, None, Pull Left	62-Trap	Pull, Trap 1st man Over or Beyond our Guard
Over, None, 1st man to Right	64-Trap	Pull, Trap 1st man Beyond our Guard
Over MLB	68-Sucker	" " " " " " "
Over MLB, None, LB your side	54-Quick	Over LB your side
" " " " " "	56	" " " "
" " " " " "	58	" " " "
Over, Outside, None, MLB	Quick Sweep	Over, Fan
Over, Fan	Sally Rand	" "
Over, MLB, None, LB your side	Goal-Line Belly	" "
Over, Outside, None, MLB	Draw 1	1st man to Left
Pull Left 1st man to show	Power-96	Over, 4-Man
Over, Inside, None, Post man on Center	51-Counter	Post Over, Inside, None, 1st man to Outside
	Passes	
3rd man, unless over Center, then Fill	"O" Protection	3rd man, unless over Center, then Fill
" " " " " "	"3" Protection	" " " " " "
3-Man	"7" Protection	Over, Inside, None, Pull Left, 1st man to show

Fig. 74. Example of an individual play book.

129

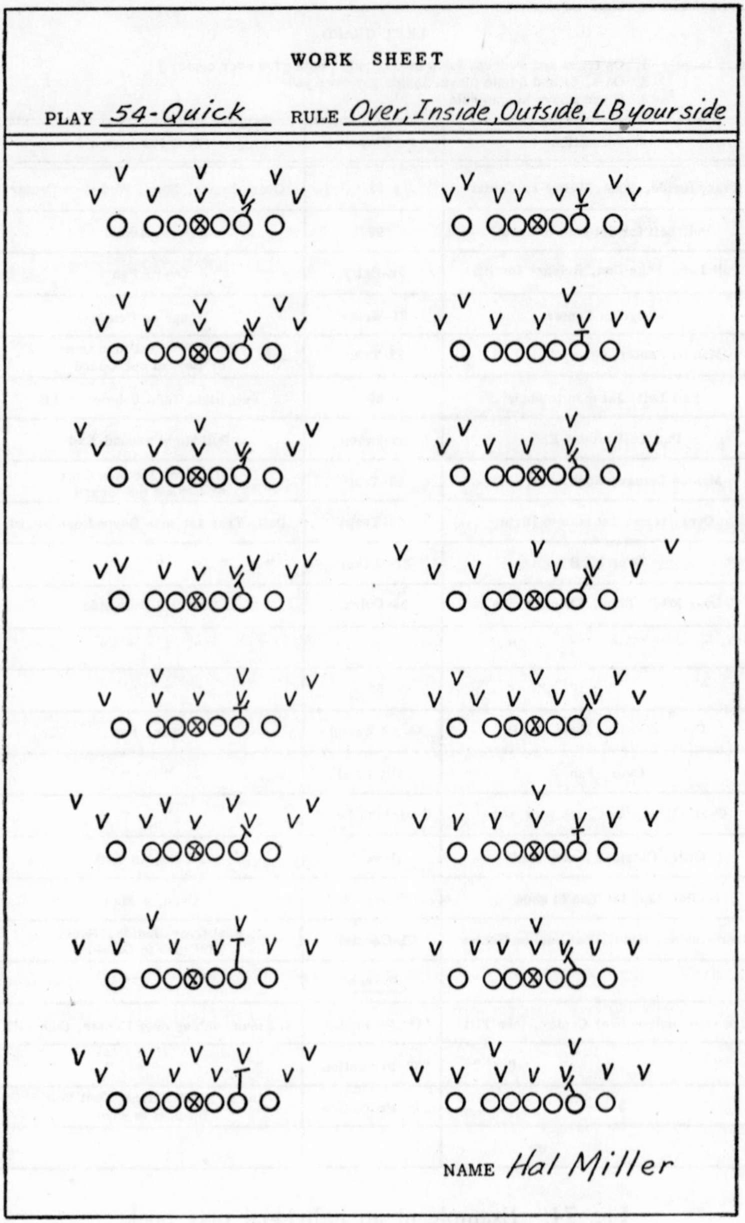

Fig. 75. Players' work sheet.

130

The next day, in the lecture, hand out quiz sheets for each player. The coach lists on the board the plays he wants them to write the rules for. The test sheet should have the same structure as the individual play books, but with the rules omitted. (A mimeograph stencil should be made for both the work sheet and test sheet.) The test should be completed in about three minutes. (See Figure 76.)

So the players can learn to apply the rules, the defense should remain 5-, 6-, or 7-man lines for the first few days. After this, do not limit the defenses in any way.

The players should be given a test about twice a week throughout the season. This will allow the coach to keep a close check on the players. And, it keeps the players from becoming careless about their rules.

As the coach adds new plays to the offense, he also adds them to each test. After the first few tests, the players should always turn in a perfect paper, and, in case of mistakes, the player should have to take additional tests until he can turn in a perfect paper. The players will soon be able to complete the tests in about five minutes.

On the Monday before each game, the coach should prepare a new work sheet consisting of the defenses expected from the opponent that week.

After the coaches have decided on the offense to be stressed against the opponent's defenses, allow the players to fill out work sheets for each play. This prepares them for what to expect in the game. And again the coach has the opportunity to check his players and be sure they are prepared for the game.

The work sheet should be given on Monday, and the test sheet on Wednesday and at the pre-game meal on the day of the game.

Name: *Hal Miller*   **Position:** *Right Tackle*

QUIZ SHEET

Left Formation	Play	Right Formation
	92	
	96	
	98-Belly	
	81-Wedge	
	82-Trap	
	86	
	88-Sweep	
	62-Trap	
	64-Trap	
	56	
	58	
	Quick Sweep	
	Sally Rand	
	Passes	
	Draw 1	
	51-Counter	
To be filled in by Player at least twice a week.		

Fig. 76.   Quiz sheet.

Summary

Rule blocking is a very simple way to teach assignments. As coaches, we all know that we cannot expect to win games if our players make "mental mistakes." Don't let the players become worried because of the various terms used. Insist that they learn the meaning of this terminology first. The rest of the learning will be simple.

THE PASSING GAME

As a part of a team's offense, the passing attack may be its (1) basic weapon, (2) a supplemental weapon to the running game, or (3) a complement to running game.

Some teams use the passing game as their "basic weapon." These teams usually put the ball in play by threatening a pass even if the play ends up in a running play.

Other teams use the pass as a surprise in conjunction with the running attack. These teams usually put the ball in play by threatening a running play that sometimes ends up in a pass.

The ideal offense should be a balance between the running game and the passing game. This will force the defense to be ready for everything. The result will usually be that they are not entirely ready for anything.

It is not possible for every team to have a perfectly balanced attack. The coach must study his personnel and determine which phase of the game will establish the basic weapon of his attack.

There are two basic types of pass plays: (1) passes after faking a running play, and (2) straight passes that have no threat of a running play. These two types should be incorporated into every pass offense.

The majority of passes should develop after a running play fake, but there are times, such as third down and ten, when it becomes useless to fake a running play.

A balanced pass attack should include:

1. Passes that show immediately (70-series).
2. Running play passes—toward fake and away from fake.
3. Running passes.
4. Screens.
5. Fake pass and run.

Base the passing attack on how good a passer you have, and the kind of receivers available. Study the passer and know his every qualification. If he is short and a good runner, stress the optional running pass by having many various routes. If he is tall and not a good runner, he should throw the majority of his passes from his pocket, and let the halfbacks throw the running passes.

Learn the receivers' qualifications. The patterns should vary according to the ability of the receivers. If the ends are tall and do not have break-away speed, concentrate on throwing "stop" passes to the ends, and throw the deep passes to the faster backs.

It would be wasting a pass to try and have a big, rather slow end try and outmaneuver a defensive halfback. If the ends have speed and quickness, concentrate on them on faking, so they can outmaneuver the defensive backs. (Pass receiving technique has been discussed under offensive end play, page 70.)

The passer—passing technique

There is much truth to the famous statement that great passers are born, not made. Since there are but a few great passers playing football today, the majority of coaches have as their passers boys that have a great deal of room for improvement. Great passers may be born, but good passers can be developed only by hard work by the coach and the player.

1. *The grip.* There are many ways to grip the ball to pass

successfully, because the proper grip for each individual should come naturally. Some players prefer to place their fingers on the laces, while others choose to use their thumb. The size of the boy's hand is a big asset and will help determine the most natural grip for him. Sometimes, in trying to develop or improve a young passer, changing his grip will have good results.

The most popular grip today is placing the first joint of the two middle fingers over the lace of the ball and slightly to the rear. The index finger is behind the laces and points slightly toward the rear of the ball. The little finger is below the laces and points slightly toward the "front" of the ball. The thumb is below the ball with a good firm grip. The two middle fingers and the thumb are the principal grip fingers.

If the passer's hand is not large enough to place both middle fingers over the lace of the ball, he can move his hand forward until just the third finger is over the laces.

2. *Releasing the pass.* The following procedure applies:

(a) Shift the weight to the right leg.

(b) Always step with the forward foot in the direction of the throw and allow the left hand to come forward.

(c) Release the ball as if it were a dart, and keep the wrist turned inward.

(d) *Arm action should be fast and snappy,* with a good follow-through motion.

(e) As he releases ball, the passer should holler "ball" to tell the linemen to release blocks and "cover" the pass in case of interception, and, at the same time, he should "cover" the pass also.

3. *When to throw.* The greatest error made by most passers is not knowing *when* to throw the ball. Too many passers try to wait until the receiver gets open, instead of having the ball hanging there just as he breaks away from the defensive man. If the passer waits until the receiver is in the open, the defensive

man has usually had time to recover by the time the ball arrives and either intercepts or knocks down the pass.

Types of ball to throw

The most important phase of successful passing is the ability of the passer always to throw the ball *away* from the defensive man. To do this properly he must be able to throw: (1) bullet passes, (2) soft, floating passes, and (3) arch passes with good carry.

It may be that a receiver is open on the spot and the passer must throw a hard, bullet pass to get the ball there quickly. It may be that a receiver, going deep, has gotten even with the defensive halfback, so the passer should throw a soft floating pass and let the receiver run under it.

Many times receivers have been open for touchdowns and the passer has thrown the ball with a flat trajectory, allowing the defensive man a chance to intercept or knock down the pass. An arched pass with good carry is needed on many passes where the ball must be thrown over a defensive linebacker's or end's head, but the ball must arrive quickly to the spot before the defensive halfback or safety, who have been decoyed back, can react and come up.

What to do when receivers are covered

The passer should be drilled thoroughly on what to do when his receivers are covered, so he won't throw the ball up for "scrambles" or take a big loss. The passer should have two options: (1) To overthrow the receiver, completely out of reach of everyone, and (2) To run straight up the middle.

The passer should be able to do either of these. If the passer is a good runner, he can stress running the ball when the receivers are covered. Should the passer not be a good runner, he can stress the option of overthrowing everyone. If the passer is drilled on these fundamentals he will save himself the embarrassment of taking big losses.

Set to pass

The "T" formation quarterback is handicapped slightly because on most of his passes he must retreat five or six yards before throwing the ball. This is a slight handicap as compared to the single wing tailback who is in a passing position when he receives the ball from center.

The quarterback may be required to throw the ball: (1) From directly behind the line on quick passes, (2) From five to seven yards behind the line, and (3) On the run.

The quick pass over the line is usually called by the quarterback when he gets to the line of scrimmage and sees the defensive alignment has left one of his ends uncovered. "Uncovered" means there is no linebacker in front or close enough to the end to interfere with the pass.

To throw the quick pass the quarterback:

1. Steps back with his right foot (for a right handed passer) and raises the ball to a passing position as high as possible.

2. Steps with his left foot in the direction of the pass, releasing the ball from a high position.

On the quick pass the quarterback must remember not to over-throw the receiver, since it will result in an interception most of the time.

Sometimes the defense will shift and cover at the last minute. Instruct the quarterback never to retreat because, usually, this results in a big loss of yardage, or, if he finally throws, an interception. The linemen should be blocking aggressively, similar to a quarterback sneak.

After the quarterback has received the ball from center and

sees that neither end is uncovered, he can tuck the ball under-arm and run a quarterback sneak. This will result in a two- or three-yard gain, instead of a five-yard loss or interception.

Throwing from five to seven yards back

In a straight "comeback" pass the most essential part is for the quarterback to "set up" as fast as possible. With continu-ous work on driving back and getting set, it is possible for the quarterback to get set to throw from five yards in one second. It is good to use the stop watch to give the quarterback some concrete facts on the time he takes getting set to throw. The watch can be used also as an incentive for him to improve his time.

On maneuver passes thrown deep, it is necessary for the quarterback to "set up" slightly deeper. Seven yards should be the maximum depth the quarterback ever "sets up" to pass. On the deep pass he should first fake the ball by hitting his empty hand. It is necessary to set up a pocket for protection and the passer must stay in the pocket.

To "set up" at five yards the quarterback:

1. Drives away from center by stepping back with his right foot and turning his body perpendicular to the line of scrim-mage.

2. Crosses his left foot in front of his right and hops off his left foot, and lands on both feet in position to pass. (If quar-terback is short in height he may have to take an extra step before he can set up at five yards.)

In setting up at seven yards, the quarterback takes an extra two steps, still hopping to position off the left foot.

Where the quarterback is looking should depend on the par-ticular pass called:

1. *Optional passes.* With two or more receivers in one zone,

the passer comes back to throw and looks at the defensive man who is covering the particular zone.

2. *Pattern passes.* The quarterback comes back looking straight downfield on a pattern pass.

3. *Maneuver passes.* When an offensive man is trying to outmaneuver a particular halfback or safety, the quarterback comes back looking away from the receiver and makes a fake with the ball away from the receiver.

It is very important that the passer does not get in the habit of looking at his receivers all the time he is setting up to pass. The defense can certainly take advantage of this and the pass offense will suffer accordingly.

If there is a running-play fake, the quarterback, after faking to back, sets up in a similar way as fast as possible.

4. *Running pass.* A running pass should always be an optional run or pass. Always tell the passer that the *first* option is the run, and that he should keep this in mind until the defense is in position to stop the run. If the defense has reacted to stop the run, then the pass receiver should be open for the pass.

To throw the ball, the passer plants his right foot and throws, or sometimes leaps into the air off the right foot to throw. In running to the left, if he throws deep he should use the crossover method by planting his left foot and pivoting around, throwing off his right foot. If he is to throw short he can continue running and throw off the right foot.

Position of passer

When he throws, the passer should remember the following:

1. His body should be perpendicular to the line of scrimmage and his feet fairly close together.

2. His weight should be evenly distributed on the balls of

both feet.   He must always have balance.   (Throwing off balance causes 75 per cent of interceptions.)

3. He should stand as tall as possible.

4. He should hold the ball high and in both hands.

5. He must stay in the pocket.

Helpful tips for passers

The passer should be checked continuously on the following common errors:

1. Throwing off balance.

2. Not stepping in the direction of the pass.

3. Throwing side-arm.

4. Telegraphing his passes by watching the receiver all the way.

5. Dividing his attention—looking at rushers, rather than receivers.

6. Retreating too deep before throwing.

7. Waiting until his receivers are open before throwing. (If he waits the ball will get there late and give the defense more time to react and spoil the pass.)

8. Covering the pass and warning the blockers so they can cover.

Pass numbering system

The numbering system for passes should be co-ordinated with the running game, and it should be flexible enough so that the quarterback can take advantage of any defensive weakness.

For the passing attack the ends are lettered the same: "X" and "Y."   The halfbacks, when used as receivers, are given odd numbers to differ from the even numbers used for running plays.   (See Figure 77.)

The ends' letters do not change with the formation because

their routes will have no bearing on whether the formation is right or left.

The backs change numbers because their routes will depend on the formation called.

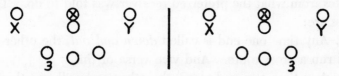

Fig. 77. Numbering of halfbacks used as receivers. The ends are lettered the same: "X" and "Y."

The first digit in the number explains:

1. The series to be used.

2. If the series is from the running game, aggressive blocking on assignments.

3. If it is the 70-series (straight comeback), passive protection on assignments.

The second digit should signify which receivers are to release for the pass and give blocking assignments to be used by the remaining players. (See coaches' play book, Figure 41.)

After the number the signal caller will tell the receivers which particular pass cut to run.

The key for receivers to release is as follows:

When the second digit is 0 or 7, both ends and the extra back not assigned to block the end release.

When the second digit is 3, the strong side end and the halfback on that side release.

Every receiver should not only know his route, but the route of the other receivers forming the pattern. No receiver should be called a "decoy." Receivers should be listed as *preferred, second,* or *third* choice. In practice the passer should throw the ball sometimes to the second or third choices. This will encourage them to put 100 per cent effort into their part of the pattern.

The receivers, other than the preferred, will know their routes from what the preferred receiver was told to do. Their rules are:

1. Any time one end is called *down and out*, the other end will run a cross route. And vice versa of this.

2. Any time one end *stops*, the other end will run through the safety.

3. Any time a halfback is called *"flat,"* the strong-side end will run through the defensive halfback.

4. Any time the halfback is called deep, the strong-side end runs deep spot.

5. Any time one end is called on quick route, the other end will run through safety.

The quarterback should be able to throw the basic routes from any of the series fakes, and also from the 70-series, which shows a pass immediately (Figure 78). If one particular series is working effectively during the game, the quarterback will want to throw his passes with that particular fake in the back-field.

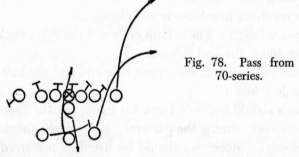

Fig. 78. Pass from 70-series.

For example, if the quarterback wants to throw to "X" down and out and away from the fake of the play, and the

80-series has been effective, he calls, "Right 80 X down and out." (See Figure 79.)

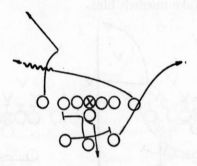

Fig. 79. Pass to "X" down and out, 80-series.

Passes from running game

A pass developed from the running game accomplishes two purposes: (1) It forces the defense to remain in position until they are sure that it is not a running play, and (2) It will release some of the pressure of rushing, which a team may be applying to your passer.

There are five basic pass routes that can be adopted to most running series: (1) Flood toward fake, (2) Flood away from fake, (3) Stopping passes, (4) Running pass, (5) Screen passes.

These passes should be taught against both the two-deep and three-deep defenses.

Each series will be used to illustrate the above-mentioned passes.

Flood toward the fake

The flood toward the fake pass can be used from nearly any series. It is necessary as a weapon to keep the defensive secondary toward the fake from coming up fast. The 50-series will be used to illustrate this (Figure 80).

Some teams on a 3 deep defense have the end trying to cover the flat. This pass will prevent the end from dropping off because of the fake towards him.

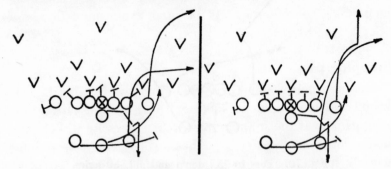

Fig. 80.   Flood toward the fake, 50-series.

This pass should be successful against the 2 deep, also. The outside linebacker should be pulled upfield because of the threat of the wide play. The offensive end changes his route so as to keep the deep man to the inside. When the pass is thrown to the halfback, it is much deeper pass on this defense than on a three deep.

Flood away from the fake

The flood away from the fake pattern should be thrown from all of the series. It is used effectively against a pursuing

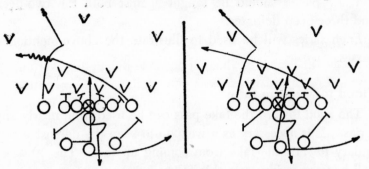

Fig. 81.   Flood away from the fake, 60-series.

defense. One or two completions on this pass will force the defense stationed away from the fake to hold their position a little longer, thus allowing your running a better chance for long run. The 60-series will be used to illustrate this pass. (See Figure 81.)

Stopping pass

Stopping passes should be used from the running fake to keep the defensive linebackers from concentrating on the running game. If the stopping passes are successful it will eliminate a lot of stunting defenses, thus, again, giving your running game a better chance to get started. The 80-series will be used to illustrate this pass. (See Figure 82.)

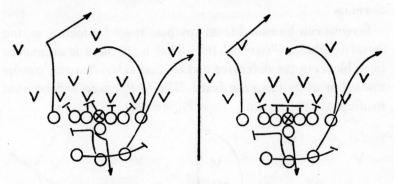

Fig. 82.   Stopping pass, 80-series.

Running pass

All the time spent on the practice field practicing the running pass will be of great benefit to the offense. It is very difficult to set a defense for an optional running pass. The passer should be taught that it is a *run* until the defense *forces* the pass. By doing this he is most likely to make a good fake of the run. The 90-series is used to illustrate this pass. Because the quarterback does not throw the pass, the number is given the same as the play followed by the word pass. (See Figure 83.)

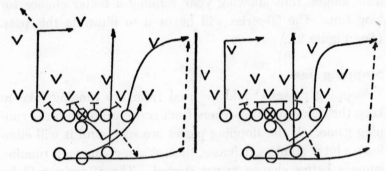

Fig. 83. Running pass, 90-series.

Screens

Screens can be called from any pass route by merely saying "screen right" or "screen left." That is, if there is an end or back blocking the defensive end on that side. Screens can be toward or away from the fake. The 53-flat pass will be used to illustrate the screen. (See Figure 84.)

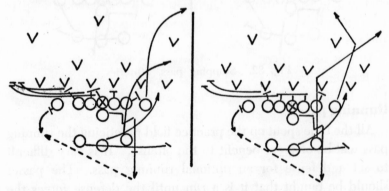

Fig. 84. Screen pass, 53-flat.

Should the situation be such that the passer is small but a good runner, it is advisable to throw the majority of the passes from the roll out. There are enough alternate routes from this series to keep the defense confused. (See Figure 85.)

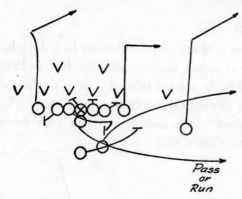

Fig. 85. Pass from the roll out.

Straight comeback series

In using the straight comeback series, the offense should be deployed in a spread to force the defense to cover the width of the field quickly. This should take some of the defensive men out of the rushing. The passer will not have as long to pass from this series, as there is no running-play fake to delay the rushing.

In this series there should always be a flanker set, and most of the time an end spread either toward the flanker or away from the flanker. There are any number of pass routes available from this series. In preparing this series, study the scouting report, pick out the weakest defender among the opponents, then set your flankers and spread so as to put your best receivers in his territory.

There are many crossing routes, delayed routes, and "stop and go" routes that are good from this series, but always keep in mind that these require excellent pass protection.

There are five basic ideas that should be included in this

series: (1) Sideline cuts, (2) Stops, (3) Flooding zone, (4) Screen, and (5) Draw (fake pass run).

Sideline cuts

The sideline cuts are usually thrown to a detached receiver, so the passer does not have to hold the ball as long. The receiver should make a good fake of a deep down and out, then he should cut toward the boundary and come back slightly toward the passes. It is best to use this pass away from the flanker. (See Figure 86.)

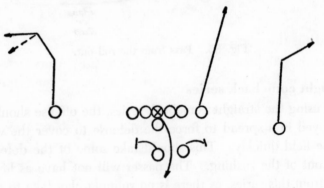

Fig. 86.   Sideline cuts.

Should the passer want to throw to the halfback breaking toward the sideline, he would call: "Right 70 flanker flat." On the right, also, a good pattern is to send the halfback deep and to break the end toward the sideline. This would be called "Right 70 'Y' flat."

Stops

The stopping routes can be called with both ends stopping on just one end. It is preferable to have both ends stop to give the passer an option. (See Figure 87.)

The right end will stop either to the inside or outside, according to where the defense is.

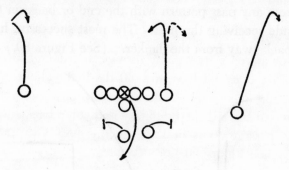

Fig. 87. Stops.

Flooding the zone

The passer should have a choice of receivers in a specified area. The flood pattern is successful against a zone style defense. (See Figure 88.)

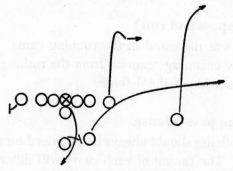

Fig. 88. Flooding the zone.

Screens

A team that can use screens successfully will discourage opponents from concentrating on rushing. This is the most underrated play in the offense. Statistically, this play usually averages more than any other play or pass.

Screen blocking is the same as in the running game, except with "passive" protection. Screen-right or screen-left can be called from any pass pattern with the end or back on the particular side receiving the pass. The most successful has been the fullback away from the flanker. (See Figure 89.)

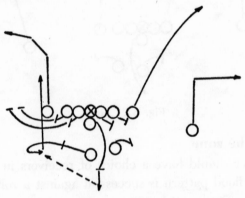

Fig. 89.   Screen.

Draw (fake pass and run)

This play was discussed in the running game. The screen and the draw encourage caution from the rushing of both the middle and outside of the defense.

Coaching the pass offense

The pass offense should always be practiced on a lined regulation field. The timing of each route will differ slightly according to the position on the field. The passer and receivers must know this and can only obtain this proficiency with continual practice. Also, work as much as possible against defensive personnel trying to break up the passes. Have someone in front of the ends trying to delay them, so the timing of the pass will be the same as in a game.

Put special time each week on passes from the 20-yard line goalward. The routes of the receivers will change the closer the ball is to the goal line. The passer and receivers should practice here, because this is where games are won or lost.

7

Quarterback Generalship

FOOTBALL authorities agree that of all the factors that produce success in games, the proper selection of plays is by far the most important. A poor choice of plays will nullify the finest teamwork and will eventually break down the highest morale. One the other hand, even a mediocre eleven can rise to unthought-of heights when it is directed by a brilliant quarterback.

The quarterback should be the first player to be considered by the coaches in making their plans for a successful team, as he is obviously of prime importance. (*Note:* Selection of a quarterback has been discussed in Chapter 4, pages 25–26.)

Principles

There are certain basic principles upon which all generalship must rest. First, *an advance by rushing of more than forty*

152

yards is rarely successful. Something happens—a fumble or a penalty, a "busted" assignment—and the advance is stopped. Therefore, the quarterback should not plan to use his rushing attack over stretches more than forty yards.

The second rule for successful generalship is *never lose the ball on downs.* Always kick the ball forward when stopped; surrender the ball for thirty-five yards of valuable territory. Of course, this rule will not apply in scoring zone.

The third rule is *"Make and play for the breaks."* The problem of defeating a weak team is simple to solve, but the problem of beating an equal or better team generally turns on the application of this rule. It means taking advantage of opponents' weaknesses, and these weaknesses may be in pass defense, a proneness to fumble punts, allowing punts to be blocked, or perhaps in having a particularly poor player.

Remember, a fumble lost, a blocked punt, or an intercepted pass may mean a loss of thirty-five yards. Usually, the team that makes the fewest mistakes wins.

Make and play for the breaks. When one comes your way, score.

Training the quarterback

In order to develop and "polish up" a first-class quarterback, a coach must spend a great deal of time with him. Often, when a close game has been lost, a coach may be prone to put the blame on the quarterback. Instead of doing this, he should think back and see if he did his part in the job of preparing the boy.

It is the coach's responsibility to see that the quarterback (1) knows the offense thoroughly, (2) knows the capabilities of his teammates, and (3) masters certain general rules for play selection.

The quarterback must be made to realize that signal-calling

is no "grab-bag" procedure. The quarterback may think the correct procedure is to mix up his plays to keep the defense guessing. This is incorrect. The quarterback should be taught to throw his strength against opponents' weaknesses. To do this he must be willing to learn the assignments of every man on every play.

The quarterback must know the capabilities of his teammates so that he can use them to the best advantage. He must know which boys will come through when the chips are down and which are apt to fold up.

To master certain general rules for play selection, he must learn the principles of defense as well as offense. He must understand and be able to predict the shifting of defensive strength to meet his most successful plays.

He must understand how the defense is apt to use the position of the ball in relation to the field in setting up their defensive strategy.

It is not good for the coach to hold the quarterback to any rigid rules regarding the calling of certain plays on certain downs. When the quarterback becomes too consistent in his choice of plays in certain situations, he is making it easier for the defense, because they, knowing what is apt to be called, can set themselves up to meet the offense to better advantage.

It is not healthy to give a quarterback a long list of *do's* and *don'ts*. Far too many situations arise during a game for a boy to be able to memorize what to do on each one. He will do a lot better if given only a few general rules.

Before each play, or series of plays, the quarterback must consider the following: (1) the down and distance to go, (2) the position on the field, (3) the score, (4) the time remaining to play, (5) the opponent's probable defense, (6) the personnel of his team, and (7) the weather.

He will have been told before the game when to kick, when

to pass, when not to pass, what to do in scoring territory, what to do deep in his own territory, and so on.   A coach must not take too much for granted.   He has gone over the plays and situations that may arise over and over, and, consequently, all these things appear rather simple to him.   The coach must realize that inexperienced quarterbacks do not see the picture quite so clearly.

One of the most important rules is that the quarterback is responsible only to the coach.   He is the coach's personal representative on the field.   The team must have complete confidence in the quarterback, and he must be the master of the huddle.   The coach should make it understood that talking to the quarterback in the huddle will not be tolerated.

Generalship

In addition to lectures, private conversations with the coach, and practice on the field using hypothetical situations, the quarterback should have available for study other material prepared by the coach.   This material should be prepared under normal conditions with the principles used being sound and practical.

General instructions to the quarterback

1. Know your offense thoroughly.
2. Learn the capabilities of your fellow players.
3. Learn all you can about your opponent's team from the coach and from scouting reports.
4. At the beginning of the game, check to see if your opponents are using the strategy given in the scouting report. If not, use basic plays until the coach is able to give you new information.
5. Learn when to expect certain defenses.
6. Know how to attack these defenses with your offense.

7. Have a reason for each play.

8. Always present a voice of confidence when calling the play in the huddle.

9. Know the proper selection of plays and passes for:

(a) 1st down

(b) 2nd down, short yardage (less than four yards to go for a first down)

(c) 2nd down, long yardage (more than four)

(d) 3rd down, short yardage (less than three)

(e) 3rd down, long yardage (more than three)

(f) 4th down, short yardage, deep in opponent's territory

(g) 4th down, long yardage, deep in opponent's territory

10. Learn how the sideline effects play and passes.

11. Know beforehand the plays to use when you are deep in your own territory.

12. Learn thoroughly the goal-line plays and passes.

13. Consider weather conditions.

14. Know when *not* to pass.

15. Know that when in doubt, you should punt.

16. Know the value of using flankers in strategy.

17. Know when to take a chance.

Plays to opponent's weaknesses

Plays to your opponent's weaknesses may be of several kinds, but we can divide them into (1) those that have been reported by scouts, and (2) those directed against weaknesses found during the game. The big thing is to be able to recognize the latter immediately, or at least before it is too late. Examples of such weaknesses are:

1. Line shifting too far, leaving short side vulnerable.

2. Leaving gaps in the line.

3. Tendency to fumble punts.

4. Forward pass defense weak.

5. A "one-man" weakness, such as an end, tackle, or back who can't defend against passes.

The quarterback must learn that he should call a kick on early downs to a team with a good defense and a weak offense; and that he should kick later to a team with a strong offense and a weak defense.

How to take advantage of defensive tactics

1. Against a penetrating or crashing defense, the following tactics apply. (A crashing defense strategy will stop a lot of plays for no gain or for losses. But when a play is successful, it will usually result in more than enough yardage for a first down.)

(a) Run quick pitchouts around end.

(b) Trap or cross block the inner lineman.

(c) Use screens and the fake pass and run to slow down the defense's rushing of the passer.

(d) When throwing deep, use a running-play fake to allow your receivers to get deep downfield. Do not try to throw deep without a fake of a running play.

2. Against a waiting defense:

(a) To run wide there must be a good inside fake.

(b) Run power plays over inner linemen and punch out first downs.

(c) Use reverses to draw waiting linemen out of position.

(d) Do not use many screens or fake-pass and runs.

(e) Throw optional passes with three or four receivers out. You should be able to hold ball long enough for passer to pick out open receiver.

3. Against a stunting defense:

(a) The wide play should be set up so the back can run

inside or outside the defensive end depending upon how the end plays.

(b) Use power plays when running inside tackle. Traps and cross-blocking plays may result either in a loss or a fumble.

(c) The majority of the stunting defensive teams have their linebackers running through to stop the running game. *Therefore, throw a great many short passes over the line after faking a quick running play.*

(d) Setting flankers and splitting ends will do away with most of the stunts used by the defense.

(e) Most of the stunts will favor the wide side of the field. Run your plays back toward the boundary.

4. Use "check" or "companion" plays:

"Check" plays are plays devised to catch opponents who are concentrating on stopping your strong plays, and consequently are leaving themselves open to effective use of check plays.

"Companion" plays are those that start exactly alike but end up quite differently. Such plays taken separately may have no great strength in themselves, but, when used in combinations, they get opponents off balance and may achieve great success.

5. Use flankers to deploy the defense.

(a) If a team will shift its defense with a flanker, set the flanker and run your plays *away.*

(b) If the team does not shift its defense with the flanker, set the flanker and run your plays *toward* the flanker.

6. If your opponents are injured:

(a) If an opposing lineman is slightly injured, shoot a play at him.

(b) If a back is limping, throw a pass in his territory. Many a game has been "won" and then lost because the coach was unable to recognize from the bench the injured condition of one of his men that the opposing quarterback was playing upon.

Generalship of the downs

1. First and ten:

Plays on first down should be selected that will yield five yards, or more, if successful. This usually means off-tackle plays or end runs. Quick traps through the middle can belong in the same class. If you are in passing territory, throw *behind* the linebackers from a running-play fake. On first down most teams will use linebackers close to the line to help stop the running game.

2. Second and short yardage:

(a) This is long gainer situation. A fake inside and a run wide may result in a long gain.

(b) Do not trap or cross block in this situation.

(c) A pass from the running game may result in a touchdown. *Caution:* Never take a loss in this situation. *Always overthrow the receiver should he be covered.*

(d) If going for first down, run off tackle with power play.

3. Second and long yardage:

(a) First, spread the defense by setting flankers and possibly by splitting the end out. If a running play is called, you further your chances, because the defense has been forced to loosen up to cover the width of the field.

(b) Traps, a fake pass and run, and screen passes are logical choices for this situation.

(c) Stopping passes from straight comeback series fit into this class also.

4. Third and short yardage:

(a) As a general rule, try for a first down with a slant

off tackle or with a quick hitting play with your best ball carrier.

(b) Here, again, do no trapping or cross blocking.

(c) Occasionally *fake inside* and go *wide* for a long gainer. Your opponents must respect your quarterbacking in this case to keep them from overloading the inside.

5. Third and long yardage:

(a) *Be cautious;* the defense is prepared to take advantage of any mistake made trying to gamble for long yardage.

(b) Spread the defense by setting flankers.

(c) If you are in passing territory, use screens or sideline cuts that can be overthrown easily if the receivers are covered. *Do not throw in the middle.*

(d) Use a fake pass and run if you are in your own territory.

(e) Kick the ball if in doubt.

How the score affects the choice of plays

1. *Do not punt on early downs when you are behind.* (This is a general rule.)

2. *Do not save your passing game until you are behind;* it will not work then.

3. When six or more points behind, you want a touchdown. *Gamble for it with pass, double reverse, and special plays.*

4. When three or less points behind, you want a touchdown, but *keep in mind the field goal.*

5. When you are ahead, *expect the defense to move up strong to stop your running game,* gambling that you won't throw.

6. When you are behind, *expect the defense to loosen up to stop long gainers.*

7. If you are ahead six points, *consider the score even and work for an additional touchdown.*

8. If you are ahead in the last minutes of the game, *play all kicks absolutely safe.*

The element of surprise

The element of surprise is as important in football as in warfare. Catching the enemy in a state of unpreparedness prevents him from taking effective counter measures, and often compensates for lack of strength.

However, *the quarterback must not get the impression that he should select every play with the idea of fooling his opponents.* It is not by radical violation of every rule that surprise is obtained, but by adhering in large part to conservative methods of play, carefully planning and building for a situation where a radical departure from such tactics will yield a rich harvest of yards. In other words, *you must set the trap before you spring it.*

General rules for the quarterback

1. *When to speed play.* Speed up the play in the scoring zone, and when the wind is to your back. Slow the tempo when wind is facing you, when playing for time when your team is ahead, near the end of the half, etc.

2. *When to take a chance.* When you are behind, open up with tricks and passes, and so forth. You have nothing to lose and everything to gain. If you fail to score the first time in scoring territory, gamble for a score the next time with your best pass or trick play.

3. *Special weather conditions.*

(a) In wet weather, with a muddy field, it is best to kick a lot and let your opponents do the fumbling.

(b) Wide runs, and plays in which backs have to cut in sharply, may be out of the question in wet weather.

(c) Quarterbacks must encourage his backs to hold onto the ball with *both* hands.

(d) Kick, almost invariably, on third down, or sooner.

(e) If you have a man who can pass a wet ball, passes are very effective on wet days.

(f) In very windy, or very cold weather, much the same tactics should be followed, being sure always to speed play and use the kicking game *WITH* the wind, and to slow down play and try to punch out first downs when *AGAINST* the wind.

(g) Try to avoid bad spots on the field.

4. *Special plays.* In the scoring zone use special scoring plays given to you.   Use plays that are not likely to lose ground.

5. *When to pass.*

(a) Any time outside your thirty-yard line, whenever you think it will go.   This usually means when your opponents are not expecting a pass.

(b) Some examples of characteristic surprise pass situations are: (1) First down, on your forty-five-yard line, just following a twenty-yard run by one of your backs. (2) First down, at the middle of the field; you have just recovered opponent's fumble. (3) First down, on your opponent's thirty-five-yard line, following two first downs by line plunging. (4) First down, opponent's twenty-five-yard line, you have the ball by recovering a fumble, or by blocking a kick. (5) Second down, one yard to go, on your forty-yard line. (6) One of their good pass defenders injured and left game.

6. *Use psychological plays early in the game.* It is well to use special plays early in the game, against opponents known to be high-strung and nervous.   Also, against any opponents, it is well to use early those plays devised to prevent

opponents from taking up defensive distributions designed to nullify your strongest plays. The early use of short-side plays and special check plays is bound to have (if successful) a strong psychological effect upon your opponents who think they have your attack diagnosed and stopped by special defensive distribution.

7. *Find out what defensive player is stopping your play.* This may suggest another play to you. For example, a tackle playing wide can stop a play *outside* his position, but may be helpless on one to his *inside*.

8. *Think ahead.* This is in line with the previous paragraph. It consists of laying the trap for your companion plays, and also comprises the visualization of probable plays, should the ones fail that you are in the act of trying.

9. *When in doubt, punt.* This is a safe rule to follow in kicking territory. *Do not try to make first down when you have fourth down, one foot to go, at any point outside the opponent's forty-yard line.* Kick the ball forward. This rule may be modified when you are behind in the latter part of the game, or at any time when playing an opponent who is strong offensively and weak defensively.

10. *Break any rule of generalship in order to win.* Rules are not made to hamper quarterbacks, but to help them. If necessary to break one, do so, and none will question the success you so achieve. But a word of caution is in order here: The rules of generalship are not often broken with impunity, so you must take care that you are not the sufferer thereby.

Position on the field

Figure 90 shows a map of the field, giving zones of play. The zones must be regarded as very elastic, susceptible to change in order to meet any particular opponent or situation. The zones are:

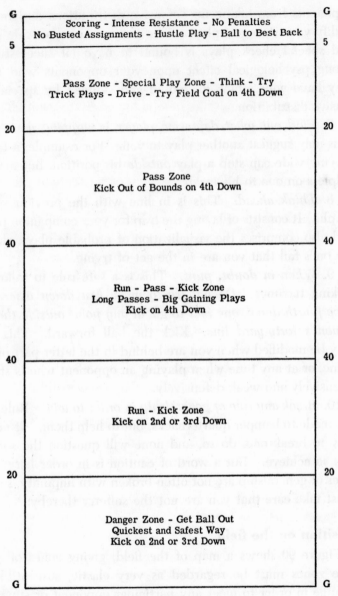

Fig. 90. Zones of play.

164

1. *Danger zone.* (From the goal line to your own twenty-yard line.)

(a) Think of getting the ball out the quickest and safest way possible.

(b) Kick on first or second down if you are inside the ten-yard line. A mistake here is too costly to gamble.

(c) Try to punch out a first down before having to kick.

(d) Avoid laterals, cross bucks, etc.

(e) Give the ball to your best back.

2. *Run and kick zone.* (From your own twenty to your own forty-yard line.)

(a) Continue safe hand-off plays.

(b) Try to break out a runner for a long gain.

(c) Use a fake pass and run on long yardage.

(d) Don't expect to march for a touchdown. One or two first downs before kicking will put you out of the hole.

(e) Do not throw in the middle or flats. Use screens and sideline cuts.

(f) Ideal quick kick zone.

3. *Run, pass, and kick zone.*

(a) Use long-gainer plays here, or a successful pass play, to put you into scoring territory.

(b) Here is where the defense must be ready for anything. Do not kick until the fourth down.

4. *Pass zone.* (Your opponent's forty to your opponent's twenty.)

(a) Defense will be moving to stop running game.

(b) Trick plays may result in a long gainer.

(c) Any type of pass from a running game.

(d) Try to get the ball close enough for a field goal.

5. *Special play zone.* (Your opponent's twenty to five-yard line.)

(a) Run wide with an inside fake.

(b) Give the ball to your best ball carrier.

(c) Do not fumble or get a penalty.

(d) If you throw on third down, overthrow the receiver if he is covered, and try for a field goal. A passer should never be tackled for a loss.

(e) If you have no field goal kicker, always throw the ball to your best receiver *over* the goal line, hoping that he may be able to take it away from the defensive man, or that interference may be called. The cardinal sin is not to throw the ball and take a loss.

6. *Scoring zone.* (From your opponent's five-yard line goalward.)

(a) Use a "hustle" play.

(b) Give the ball to your best back.

(c) Make sure you get no penalties.

(d) Don't use traps or cross-blocking plays.

(e) Off-tackle slants are your best plays.

(f) On fourth down, the ball should be squarely between goalposts.

(g) Passing on third and fourth down; same principles govern here as in special play zone.

7. *Sidelines.*

(a) Since the ball will be moved in slightly over seventeen yards, all plays (except wide laterals) are feasible.

(b) Quick sweeps are occasionally successful if run to the short side.

(c) Use the trap to the wide side of the field.

(d) Run off tackle to the short side.

Conclusion

When a quarterback disregards entirely the basic principles of generalship, he will make critical errors of which his opponents will hasten to take immediate advantage. He destroys the morale and spirit of his team, and the game usually ends in a disgraceful defeat, of which he is the chief cause.

If, on the other hand, the quarterback sticks to "commonsense" rules, tending always to the conservative, if he makes no critical mistakes, and, even if he is not a brilliant strategist, he is at least dependable, such generalship is bound to win in the long run.

The "brilliant" strategist prefers yet another course. In the main he follows a coolly conservative plan, sounding out his opponent's weak spots, verifying the reports of the scouts, getting the full value of his kicking game, and striving to shake a runner free. But he does not show his full hand until he gets an opportunity to score.

Like a master boxer, the good quarterback spars coolly for the opening, feinting here, thrusting there, saving his best punches for the proper moment. While he is following this methodical plan, he and his team are watching hawk-like for a break. If one comes their way, they snap into it hammer-and-tongs for a score. If they don't get an unexpected break early in the game, they will make one before long, but meanwhile the quarterback is laying the basis for his surprise plays. The opponents are being brought to the point where they think they have the quarterback "figured." The trap is now set, and when he switches sharply at the decisive moment, every condition is favorable to success.

Thus, brilliant strategy, though depending upon the element of surprise as its essential feature, must rest upon and rise above the broad base of a generalship that makes no critical mistakes.

Helpful hints for the quarterback

1. *Know and study your attack.*
2. *Learn everything you can about your opponents.*
3. *Know your personnel.*

4. *Prepare beforehand what is to be your strategy on: short yardage situations, long yardage situations, scoring plays, special plays, etc.*

5. *It is essential that you present to the team, at all times, a confident attitude.*

6. *Allow no talking in the huddle.*   Get the team together in timeout periods and discuss your opponent's weaknesses.

7. During the game always know: (a) *the position of the ball on the field,* (b) *the down and distance to gain,* (c) *the number of minutes left to play,* (d) *the score,* and (e) *the defensive scheme of your opponents.*

8. *Determine why a pass has failed.*   Even though a pass is incomplete, it serves to keep the defensive backs in position.

9. *In a pinch, use your best play or call on your best back.*

10. *Get that second touchdown.*

11. *Play a minor opponent with the same intensity as one of major opposition.*

12. *Do not insist upon using plays that do not work.*

13. *Do not call for a line plunge on third down with fifteen yards to go.*

14. *Organize against an opponent who is continually breaking through.*

8

Individual Defensive Play

THERE cannot be any better way to start on individual defensive play than with a discussion of the correct "angle of pursuit." A man may be blocked but he never *stays* blocked. He will recover and begin his "angle of pursuit." There is some angle that every man on the team can take on the ball carrier. If the man starts his pursuit at the wrong angle he immediately eliminates himself and winds up running the inside arc of the ball carrier.

DEFENSIVE LINE PLAY

Angle of pursuit

Figure 91 shows an example of the correct angle of pursuit by an end who has been partially blocked on a sweep.

In taking his angle, the defensive man must always consider

his speed in relationship to the ball carrier to make sure he has the correct angle.   One of the most pathetic sights in football is to see a defensive man running the inside arc in pursuit.

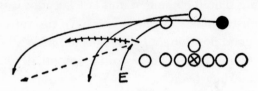

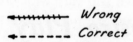

Fig. 91.   End's angle of pursuit.   The correct and incorrect ways are shown.

The general angle of pursuit of an entire team against an end run is shown in Figure 92.

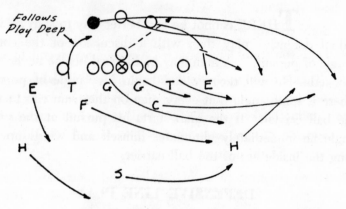

Fig. 92.   Team angle of pursuit.

Always coach the correct angle of pursuit on every defensive play.   This will be the only way you will get correct and satisfactory execution.

Tackling

The first thought in relation to defense is probably tackling. Tackling should come first and last because it is the "ultimate" in defensive play. A player can have the correct angle of pursuit, a good position, but if he fails to tackle all is in vain. The highest tribute that can be paid to a football team is, "They are a fine tackling team."

Tackling consists of two basic factors: First, *DESIRE*, which is by far the most important and is probably 75 per cent of tackling, and, second, *FORM*, which will vary with defensive positions. You cannot improve desire but *form* can be taught.

Important elements of tackling

Some important things for a tackler to remember are:

1. Keep the eyes always on the target. Head should be up, the back straight.

2. Body control with speed.

3. Time the shoulder contact. Always have recoil in your legs. Tackle *through* the ball carrier; make full shoulder contact and drive through. Tackle small, shifty backs *high* and hard-running backs *low*. Do not look at the ball carrier's foot —concentrate on his midsection. The tackler should never leave his feet until contact.

4. There are four types of tackles, and most can be categorized into one of the four:

    (a) Head-on (usually in close line play).
    (b) Angle tackle.
    (c) Open field tackle.
    (d) Tackle of a passer.

Head-on tackle

A head-on tackle is not as common in football as might be expected.   When this type of tackle presents itself it is usually in close quarters with the possibility of quick help from other defensive men.

Contact should be made with the head aimed at the ball carrier's waist to allow for any fake he may use to elude the tackle.

On contact, the tackler should broaden his base, and, with a slight dip, he will go "under" and at the same time put more spring in his legs.

There should never be any arch in the tackler's back.   If the head is up it will usually control the position.

Simultaneously with contact, the tackler's arms should encircle the ball carrier and he should seek to lock his hands and wrist and snap the ball carrier's legs to his body to break the drive of the ball carrier.   The tackler must remember to *follow through*.

The tackler seeks to lift the ball carrier and drives through with continuous leg drive with whatever part of the ball carrier he has grasped.   The follow through is important since it may save a first down or set the ball carrier up for the second man to carry him backwards.

The **angle tackle** is one of the most common on the line of scrimmage.   The angle tackle is the only way a lineman can break the rush of an offensive back from a weak lateral position.

Approach.   With head up and eyes open, drive head and shoulder past the ball carrier.   This will help to eliminate arm tackling.

On contact, simultaneously lock the hand and wrist and drop the outside shoulder, at the same time bringing the ball carrier into the body with a quick snap.

Follow through. From the contact position, the tackler should seek to roll in the direction in which the tackle started. This will enable the tackler to use some of the ball carrier's drive to help take him to the ground.

Open field tackling

The open field tackle could easily be construed as the most important tackle of all because when it is missed it results in more damage. This tackle doesn't want to be "pretty." The approach should be under controlled speed if the defensive man has the angle on the runner. The tackler should pull up and broaden his base and from a slight crouch make the ball carrier show his direction. This will help to protect the tackler from taking the ball carrier's fakes. The tackler can also keep his feet and will have a better chance to recover should he fail in his initial effort. With such an approach he should be able to slow the ball carrier down to enable the pursuit to catch up.

Contact in open field tackling is the same as for other forms of tackling, only it should be higher. The tackler should grasp the ball carrier around the chest, and, from this position, throw him to the ground. This is the safest, surest way to stop the runner. The runner may make a few extra yards because of this type of tackle, but it is not important in open field tackling. It *is* important to stop the runner.

Follow through is of minor importance. The main objective is to put the ball carrier on the ground anywhere.

Tackling the passer

Tackling the passer certainly deserves note because a different tackle is used from any of the others.

Approach.   The approach for tackling a passer is more reck-less and high.   Keep your eyes on the passer's eyes and he will "tell" you what he is going to do.   When within two or three yards of the passer the hands should be raised as high as possible to go for the ball.   *Tackle the ball.*   Many fumbles will result from this type of tackle.

Contact.   Contact should be high and around the shoulders, pinning the passer's arm to his side.   This will stop the passer from making any "desperate" pass or from a legal grounding of the ball.

Follow through.   Follow through here is not too important, but the tackler should always be alert for any fumble and be mentally ready to recover it.

There are other factors involved in tackling.   The second man up should always go for the ball.   He can be more reck-less and make an effort to separate ball and ball carrier.   It will pay dividends sometimes to work on this second man.   This sometimes may be the only way you can gain possession of the ball.

Drills for tackling

The coach should never let a day go by in which the team does not have some form of tackling practice, either live or dummy.

A good drill for teaching tackling form is to have the men make two lines ten yards apart.   One line should be on offense and one line on defense.   (See Figure 93.)

The coach can back up in the middle and observe each tackle more closely.   Alternate each side from offense to defense. From this drill you can coach angle and head-on tackling.

The tackling dummy is still a good way to coach form.   The coach can get next to the tackling dummy and observe the form —eyes open, head up, and follow through.

Keeping the eyes open is probably the hardest to coach because it is a natural reflex in tackling to close the eyes.

A final reminder is that tackling is 75 per cent *DESIRE* and 25 per cent *FORM*.

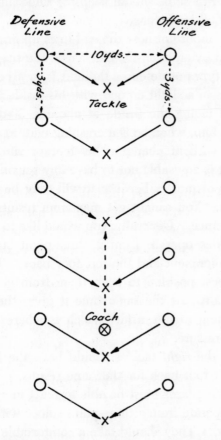

Fig. 93.   Tackling drill.   Rotate the lines from offense to defense.

Stress pursuit and gang tackling.   Never let one man make a tackle.   Tackling will usually take care of itself if the defense is being given its proper place in your organization.

Individual defensive stance of the line

Ends. The end is asked to play differently on various defenses. He may be a *crashing end,* a *waiting end,* or a *drifting end.* On all of these he should keep the same initial stance so he will not tip off his defensive play.

It is not too important how the end lines up because he cannot be reached by an offensive blocker on the snap of the ball.

To play all types of defenses the end is in a better position to start if he is in a slight crouch with his inside foot forward. He should be facing the inside at about a 30-degree angle. This will help him, when he is a crashing end, to carry out his responsibility without changing his feet or running an arc.

Tackles. It is advisable not to have any set rule for the defensive stance of tackles because it will only be necessary to break the rule. You cannot get maximum results by sticking to a uniform stance. Generally, you would like to have the left defensive tackles operate from a three-point stance with a heel-and-toe alignment and the left foot back. This will put them in the best position to keep them from getting cut off from the outside. At the same time it gives the tackles the strongest position to the inside, which is where they usually get the most pressure.

Conversely, the *right* tackles should have the left foot forward and right foot back for the same results.

Guards. The guards must be able to react in any direction. They should operate from a three-point stance with little or no weight forward. They should take a comfortable stance, then lean forward and touch the ground. It will help if they have their outside foot back to give them a strong position to pursue outside on their side of the line. This insures strength to the inside and lateral speed to the outside.

Linebackers. A linebacker should operate out of a slight crouch with his feet parallel and in a comfortable position so that he will be able to react immediately in any direction.

Individual responsibility of linemen

The over-all discussion of the various responsibilities of the line is covered in the following paragraphs.

Ends. The ends have more responsibilities than anyone on the line. They are asked primarily to protect their outside against any running play. To enable them to do so they should cross the line of scrimmage on the snap as quickly as possible and meet the first potential blocker as deep in the backfield as they can. Then, by use of their hands they must ward off blockers and turn the play to the inside or string it out into the sideline. With this responsibility, if a pass develops the end must rush the passer hard from the outside.

The ends may also have a primary responsibility to cover the flat zone on passes. To accomplish this they should line up a yard and a half to two yards wider on the line of scrimmage, or drop off the line of scrimmage a yard and a half to two yards. When assigned this responsibility the end usually plays a waiting game so that he will not be across the line of scrimmage. Any penetration will make his job of covering the flat zone much more difficult. When covering this flat zone the ends must get back; two yards of penetration will cut down four yards of depth.

The third responsibility the ends have is to become hard rushers to the inside or crashing ends. In this case they have no outside responsibility and are usually protected by the linebacker. When they are crashing ends they must have good body lean and be prepared to meet force with force.

The end's responsibility is the off-tackle play if it is a run. If a sweep develops the end's way he merely tries to force the play as deep as possible and to strip it of all encircling interference. If a pass shows he is in good position to put quick pressure from the outside on the passer.

Tackles. The tackles are responsible first for the off-tackle and inside-tackle hole. They have various ways to protect this hole. They may be loose on the line and have the job of stopping the "quickie" play for a two and a half yard gain on a first down and ten situation; a five-yard gain might be a satisfactory job on a *third* down and fifteen to go situation.

On short yardage the tackle must be aggressive and he is asked to stop the play on the line of scrimmage for *no* gain.

The tackle, like every defensive man, is affected by down and distance, but tackles and guards are more directly influenced because they can put pressure on the offense quicker than the rest of the defensive personnel.

On passes, the tackle has one or two responsibilities. He must be required to keep the passer "in the pocket." (*Definition:* It is the responsibility of a defensive man to rush the passer at a spot one yard behind the passer to make sure that the pass is thrown on rhythm to the intended receiver.)

When the tackle's responsibility is to keep the passer "in the pocket," the end is usually "dropped off" to defend the flat zone.

If the receivers are covered and the passer elects to try to run out of the pocket, the tackle must take a new angle aimed to keep the passer to his inside. (See Figure 94.)

It is very important for the tackle to keep the passer to his inside because if the passer once gets out of the pocket it forces the defensive end and halfback to release and come up and leave a zone undefended.

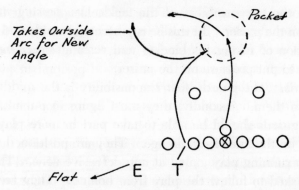

Fig. 94. "In the pocket" angle for tackle. The end is dropped off to defend the flat.

Drill to keep the passer "in the pocket"

A good drill can be worked out to help teach this "in-the-pocket" phase of defensive play. Have a quarterback (or another lineman) take the ball from a center, then let him go back and get set to throw or fake a throw and then run out either way. This will give the tackles work on keeping the passer "in the pocket" and let them practice taking a correct angle if he swings out of the pocket. (See Figure 95.)

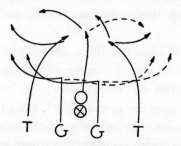

Fig. 95. "In the pocket" drill for guards and tackles.

Guards may also be used in this drill and the coach can check their responsibility for the middle in addition to their angle when the passer runs out of the pocket.

The other responsibility of the tackle in a passing situation is to rush the passer. In this he is protected outside and he has the option of faking his blocker and rushing either inside or outside to put pressure on the passer.

Guards. The guards' first responsibility is the middle zone between them. Secondly, they must figure in pursuit.

The guards should be able to take part in more plays than anyone on the line of scrimmage. They are positioned to pursue *any* running play aimed at *any* defensive zone. They are never asked to follow the play from behind. They are never asked to keep the passer "in the pocket." They *are* asked to penetrate less than anyone on the line of scrimmage, and this helps them to be protected from trap plays.

Guards should be somewhere close to the ball carrier on all plays. On passes, guards may use any maneuver or fake to rid themselves of the offensive block, but they must always be conscious of the zone between the tackles and should try to keep some relative distance to each other. In case of a fake pass or delayed pass, they should back up the middle.

Linebackers. Linebackers have different responsibilities. They are sometimes called on to be ends, tackles, guards, or simply linebackers, depending on the defensive set that has been called.

In a passing situation the linebackers' first responsibility is a *pass*, and, second, a *run*. In a running situation their first responsibility is a *run* and then a *pass*. In "normal" situations ("first and ten"), they are responsible for both equally.

The linebackers are the key to the defensive team. There has never been a "great" defensive team without great linebackers. They can cover up for more defensive line mistakes than is ever realized.

Linebackers must be smart and not susceptible to backfield fakes. They are sometimes asked to key on offensive personnel, while at other times they must ignore the offensive personnel.

All-in-all, linebackers are the key to your defense. Select them with all of these responsibilities in mind.

When linebackers are asked to "fire," they should conceal this assignment as long as possible. (*Definition:* When a linebacker "fires" it means he is taking the responsibility of a guard or tackle by going through the line of scrimmage when the ball is snapped.)

Once committed, linebackers must continue on and rush the passer or play the running play. A common error is for a linebacker to penetrate and *then* try to drop back and cover on passes. As a result, he winds up in the middle doing nothing.

If a pass develops the linebacker is in a good position to break clean and rush the passer without drawing an offensive block. When the linebacker is protecting an end outside, he has assumed the end's responsibility. He conceals this position as long as possible, but must protect this responsibility until he is sure there is no threat of a play in his zone. If he should delay in going to his responsibility he will allow the offense to get position on him and, as a result, he will make it impossible for him to protect his assignment. (This responsibility is usually referred to as a "tight stunt.")

Individual defensive maneuvers

The basic defensive maneuver for men on the line of scrimmage is the "forearm shiver."

The only advantage defense men have is the use of the hands. They must learn to take advantage of this. The hands can be moved faster than the offensive man can move his whole body, *if* the defensive man is prepared. A "forearm shiver" is the best known way to keep the offensive blockers from getting to the defense.

Some coaches believe in the "forearm shield" or "lift," but to make contact with the forearm you necessarily have to take your body in closer to the offensive blocker, which affords him better blocking position.   Do not give up on the "forearm shiver"—it is a basic maneuver.

Using the "forearm shiver" you can figure on 30 per cent more pursuit.   Remember you are not trying to *stop* a team for no gain in a first down and ten yards to go situation.   You *want* them to *make* two and a half to three yards and try to run again, hoping that finally they will wind up with a fourth down and about two yards to go for a first down.

Your defensive theory is important and you must stick to this theory through all phases of defensive play.   You cannot have a sound defensive theory if you are trying to stop a team for no gain on every play.

Remember: *minimum penetration, maximum pursuit; maximum penetration, minimum pursuit.*

To sell the players on the importance of quick contact with the hands use a simple demonstration.   Put one hand lightly on an offensive blocker's head and tell him to block you.   You will find that by applying pressure you can direct his charge in any direction you desire.   He is helpless because he cannot gain momentum and must go into the direction in which his head is led.

The "forearm shiver"

The "forearm shiver" correctly executed consists of three parts:

1. *Step and hit simultaneously.*   Shoot the heel of the hands for the offensive blocker's shoulder pads.   This initial move must be from down to up under the offensive blocker.   He should try to straighten him up.

The most common error in this part of the "forearm shiver"

is that the defensive men will hit and *then* step, or step, *then* hit. *The two must be co-ordinated.* It doesn't make too much difference which foot is brought forward, but, preferably, move the front foot slightly forward and move the back foot slightly backward to gain the same position.

2. *At contact, lock the wrist and elbow.* This is the only way to deliver a blow with strength. Once the elbow is locked you have as much strength as you would with shoulder contact. If the elbow is not locked the offensive blocker can collapse the arms back into the defensive man.

3. *Follow through with short driving steps until the ball or the pressure is located.*

Drills for the "forearm shiver"

You must have drills to coach such an important part of the defensive play. Players can build up strong wrists by continued work on the "buck-board."

Line the defense up in three lines and have them, on the snap of the ball, take three quick "forearm shivers." The procedure is for the coach to snap the ball after a set signal. The three defensive men up at that time, "forearm-shiver" the board, and, as quickly as possible, return to their defensive position ready for another snap of the ball.

Repeat this maneuver three times. Make the defense watch the ball. Make them always conscious that they start their play on the snap of the ball. (You will find also that this drill serves as an excellent conditioning drill.)

Another drill for the "forearm shiver" takes in a little more reaction. This drill is also operated on the "buck-board."

Defensive men form two lines in the center of the board with two men operating at a time. On a set signal and with the snap of the ball, they "forearm-shiver" the board and work laterally to the end with short forearm jabs. Upon reaching the end they "roll out" and land in a four point stance and recover to tackle a dummy. This drill develops lateral speed and reaction, the "forearm shiver," and a bit of tackling form. (See Figure 96.)

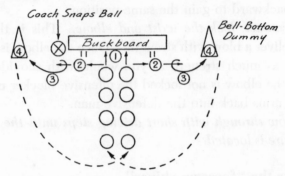

Fig. 96. "Forearm shiver" drill. (*1*) Forearm shiver; (*2*) walk the board; (*3*) roll out; and (*4*) tackle dummy.

The men should be reminded to switch lines after each time they are up. There is one way that most men react laterally. If you do not stress changing lines they will always line up in the same line.

The natural way to coach the "forearm shiver" is to put two lines facing each other. One line, on defense, employs the "forearm shiver"; the other, on offense, blocks straight ahead with a drive block. After the execution of the forearm shiver, give the defense a signal to "roll left" or "roll right."

The coach should always be seeking to add a maneuver to any drill that may increase speed and reaction. Two and three yard bursts of speed are the most important. Never miss a chance to try and improve it.

One-on-one drill

A similar drill may be employed to see how slow or fast the offense or defense are reacting. This drill is called "one-on-

one." The coach stands behind the defense and gives the offense the signal, indicating in which direction to try to contain the defense. On the snap of the ball, the defense "forearm-shivers" and fights the lateral pressure. (See Figure 97a.)

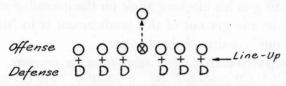

Fig. 97a. One-on-one drill.

Carrying this drill further, use a center and ball carrier and work on the angle of pursuit. Let the center snap the ball and have the ball carrier run a sweep either way or a play straight up the middle. (See Figure 97b.)

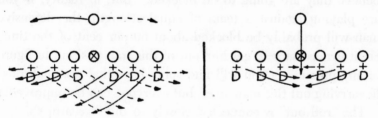

Fig. 97b. One-on-one drill, with angle of pursuit.

In this drill you can check very easily the correct angle of pursuit of interior linemen.

Forearm shield or forearm lift

The forearm shield should be used only on short yardage by the guards and tackles. It is the best way to penetrate and meet force with force. The shoulder and forearm should be co-ordinated with the forward foot, which will give the strongest possible position. This maneuver should always be executed from as low a position as possible.

The "roll out"

The "roll out" defensive maneuver has slowly evolved into an important part of individual defensive play. When an offensive man gets his blocking angle on the defensive man, the only way he can get out of this predicament is to "roll out." The "roll out" consists of three steps:

1. *A drop step with the foot away from the pressure.*
2. *A quick roll using leverage, if possible, from the offensive man.*
3. *Recovery and continuance of pursuit.*

Some coaches still feel it is a mistake to coach the "roll out." They say it is teaching a boy to do something *after* he has been blocked. They think it is bad psychology to allow players to believe they are going to be blocked. But, in reality, if you are playing against a team of equal strength, the defensive man will probably be blocked about 50 per cent of the time. So, it is necessary to get him out of this trap position to figure in any pursuit. (You will find some boys that are "naturals" in carrying out this maneuver, but everyone can be improved.)

The "roll out" is connected closely to the "forearm shiver." The "forearm shiver" keeps the defensive man away from the offensive blocker far enough to make the power or "stagger-step" block very awkward—the offensive man can never get the angle of position he needs. As soon as the pressure is located, usually a shallow roll will put the defensive man in the middle of the offensive hole. *Any time there is a double-team block, the play has been called in the next offensive hole or just past the double block.*

Drill for the "roll out"

A good beginning drill for the roll out is to split the players into groups of four, three for offense and one for defense. The

coach should stand behind the defensive personnel and give
the signal to use a double-team block, either right or left. The
offensive men get down on a four-point stance.

On the snap of the ball, the middle man, who is always the
"post blocker," moves quickly into the defensive man and allows himself to be "forearm-shivered." At the same time the
power blocker hops quickly to his lateral position but does not
try to move the defensive man. This should, from the snap,
put the defensive man in a pocket, which will force him to
"roll out" toward the pressure. The man who is not involved
in the block turns quickly to the outside.

This has some of the elements of full speed work but is actually "dummy" work. It will help to give the defense confidence in the "roll out" and at the same time, develop form.
(See Figure 98.)

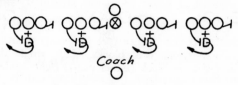

Fig. 98. "Roll-out" drill.

Three-on-one drill

The best drill to develop defensive football players is a three-
on-one drill: three men on offense against one defensive man.
(See Figure 99a.)

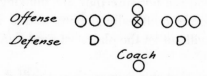

Fig. 99a. Three-on-one drill line up.

Use a center and a ball, with never more than two groups
operating at a given time, no matter how many men you have.

(You will get better performance out of everyone if all the personnel is not working at the same time. It is advisable to have some players watching since the boys have as much pride working in front of their own teammates as they do in front of their coach.)

If possible, the coach should have someone working with the offensive group. They can coach, correct, and comment on this group's performance and make it a much tougher drill. Someone will invariably look good or bad on each play.

If it is impossible to have the coach with the offensive group, the coach should stay behind the defensive personnel and give the signal for four different blocks. These blocks approximate nearly all game conditions: (1) the single drive block, (2) the double-team block in both directions, (3) the wedge block, and (4) pass protection blocks. (See Figure 99b.)

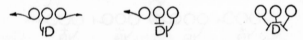

Fig. 99b. Three-on-one drill blocks. *Left,* single drive block; *center,* double-team block (either way); *right,* wedge block.

This gives the coach a wonderful opportunity to do a lot of individual instructing and to pick out his best personnel.

One thing to do always in this drill is to call the down and distance. You do this because it changes the play of the defense. You can get them to thinking in terms of down and distance. If you are not sure they are thinking of down and distance, purposely omit calling them, and if they are well-schooled they will not let the play start until they get the down and distance.

It can be seen that this is more than a drill if the coach will take advantage of the many things that can be taught and practiced. If there was only *one* drill I could have for developing individual defensive linemen, this would be it.

Additional line stunts

There are many additional line stunts commonly employed. The best time to exploit these is when you find a player who has the natural ability to use the stunt.

Dip charge. The dip charge can be used when a lineman is playing the gap or shoulder. His initial charge is a quick dip under the offensive men's shoulders, splitting them with the initial force. Then he comes up, recovers, and broadens his base.

Double co-ordination. This stunt is very effective when the defensive man is positioned in the gap between two offensive blockers. He plays one blocker quickly with his hand, then steps and drives with a low shoulder into the other blocker. (This is particularly a good stunt for a tackle playing an end and a wingback in the single-wing formation.)

Limp leg. On this stunt the defensive man quickly drives either foot into the gap between the offensive blockers, and shifts all his weight to this foot. As the offensive blocker gives the opposite leg pressure, the defensive man swings it up and allows the blocker to slide off the limp leg.

Reaction drills

A reaction drill such as the following will do more to develop fast reaction than any drill I have ever seen. I have seen marked progress in the reaction of every player who was willing to concentrate on this drill. I have proven this by comparing a group of linemen who had been working on the drill for a period against backfield men who had not. It was astounding to see how much more clever the linemen were than the backs. The drill had developed them in this respect. The drill also has good conditioning results and is a relatively simple drill.

Line up the men in three lines about five yards apart (Figure 100). This will give three men operating as a group. The coach stands ten yards in front of them and gives *oral* commands—do not give a hand or foot signal in this drill. Sharp, oral comands will get better results—it makes the players think before reacting. They will move much quicker and sharper from oral command.

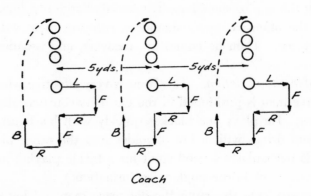

Fig. 100. Reaction drill. The coach gives the commands: left, right, front, back.

The group that is up automatically starts running in place. Then, give them one of the 5 commands: (1) Front, (2) Back, (3) Left, (4) Right, or (5) Down (on this signal they hit the ground and come up running as quickly as possible).

All movements must be at right angles. Do not let the players run in an arc. Tell them to use a cross-over step to change lateral position. Every man should seek to cover as much ground as possible between given commands. Each group should be given twelve to fifteen commands, then they swing back into the end of their line. Four to six rounds for each group is a good work-out each day.

Circle drill

The circle drill is a good drill for developing defensive linemen. Work your men in two or three groups, depending on the number you are working with at a given time, with a group of seven or eight being ideal.

We simply have seven or eight men form a circle with a radius of approximately six feet. Then, one man takes his defensive position in the center as in Figure 101.

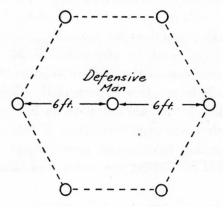

Fig. 101. Circle drill. Line off circle for accurate position.

While working his feet and maintaining his position, the center man plays off would-be blockers with his hands and elbows. The blockers approach him from any direction at half speed but only one at a time, with a slight delay between each man. To avoid being knocked down, the center man, of course, will have to shift his feet, weight, and change direction, which will help him develop agility and balance. Never leave a man in the center more than twenty or twenty-five seconds; otherwise, it would cease to be fun.

Rushing the passer

Trying to rush the passer wastes more effort than any phase of line play. Too many boys try to rush the passer *through* offensive blockers. This cannot be done unless the rushers are physically much stronger than their opponents.

In order to reach the passer the defensive man must completely rid himself of the offensive blocker. If the defensive man has outside responsibility he must keep the passer in the pocket. With this responsibility he should fake inside and drive outside. Or he may use a double fake; driving outside hard, and then fake inside and come back out. He should always use his hands to try to rid himself of the block.

If the defensive man does not have outside responsibility, he has the option of going on either side of the blocker. He should take advantage of this and try to go *inside* the blocker with an outside fake. This is particularly applicable to the ends and tackles if they are not given an inside rush too frequently. If they will avail themselves of this opportunity it will help when they have outside responsibility.

The best drill for rushing the passer is to have the men do just that.

Pass-rushing drill

For the pass-rushing drill, have a man take the ball from center and go back to the passing spot, or have a direct snap of the ball to the passing spot. Give a signal to designate each player's responsibility on each play. (See Figure 102.)

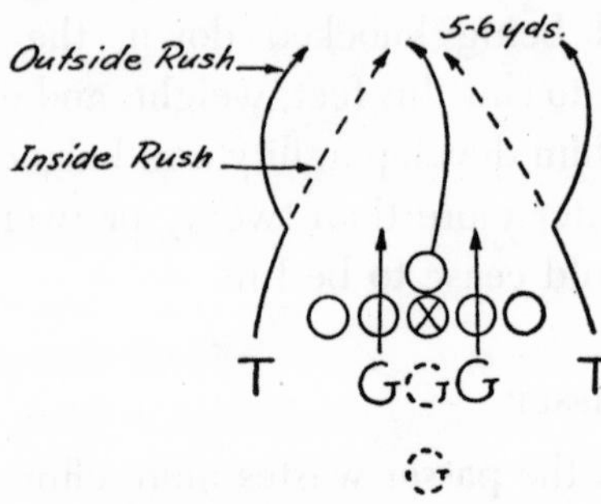

Fig. 102.   Pass-rushing drill for guards and tackles.

To create a little interest in this drill, use a stop watch to see who can reach the passer the quickest.

The drill usually works best with the tackles and guards operating as a unit and the ends and backfield working as a unit. The ends and backs can organize their drill at the same time they are working on pass protection.

Down and distance

The down and the distance to go for a first down or a score affect *every* man on *every* play. To get players to realize the importance of down and distance the coach must first educate the boys to realize how and why his play should be varied. The simplest way is to put the various play situations into three broad categories:

1. *Long gain situations,* which are with over five yards per try left for each remaining down ("excluding the kicking down if the ball is in the kicking zone").

2. *Short gain situations* are with less than two yards to go, with only *one* down remaining to make the yardage necessary for the first down. This is very important because we make an exception with second down and one or two yards to go for a first down. Concede that the offense will make the first down running, but do not give them the opportunity for a long gain in this situation.

3. *Normal gain situations* prevail if the remaining yardage approximates three yards. "Out in the field of play eliminate the kicking [fourth] down."

These are all broad categories and will change with the score, time remaining, or weather conditions. With this background the men should be aware of the difference in situations in terms of down and distance.

FORWARD PASS DEFENSE

The first thing that we tell our backs and safety men is, "Every play is a pass." From this phrase we work toward setting up an adequate pass defense.

The four things that are a big factor in the success of any pass defense, whether it is a zone or man-to-man, are: (1) having good aggressive linebackers and tackles to delay the ends getting out, (2) having good aggressive linemen to rush the passer, (3) having good defensive halfbacks to cover receivers after they once clear the line of scrimmage, and (4) interception of the pass.

At Georgia Tech we are firm believers in a zone defense, but in order to have a good pass defense you must sell your players on what *you* believe to be the best, whether it be man-to-man or zone.

Defensive halfback stance

On defense it is as important for a defensive halfback to have a good stance as it is for an offensive halfback on offense. First of all, he must have a good wide base. His body must be turned to the outside and his hands must be on his knees. His head is turned at a 45-degree angle so that he can see both the quarterback, or tailback, and offensive end with split vision. The reason that a halfback, or safety man, should have a wide base is that it gives him better balance, which enables him to react faster.

The halfback should line up eight to ten yards deep. The first thing for him to remember, and always the most important thing, is that a halfback, or safety man, should never let a receiver get behind him at any time. The first movement after the ball is snapped for the halfback will always be a step back because the responsibility of the halfback is any receiver that is *outside* or *deep*.

Safety man's stance

The safety man's stance is similar to the halfback's. The only change is that in the middle of the field he should always *face the quarterback*. He should turn slightly, about half-face, always to the wide side of the field, if the ball is not in the middle of the field. The safety man should play ten to twelve yards deep.

In playing a zone defense the halfbacks and safety man have a responsibility to play one-third of the field at all times. It is always important to any halfback that, if there is no receiver in his zone, he continue to get his depth. This is done to guard against the possibility that a receiver will cross out of one man's zone into another man's zone.

Halfbacks should practice taking proper angles from "hash mark to hash mark" to cover their one-third of the field.

Halfbacks and safety men should keep in position so that they can at all times overlap each other. That is, if a ball is thrown *between* the left halfback and safety man either one should be in position to catch it.

We use a drill, which we call the "overlap drill," for halfbacks and safety men. This drill is shown in Figure 103.

The safety man is given the responsibility of being the "quarterback" on defense as far as telling, or reminding, the halfbacks of the down and distance on every play. Down and distance are very important for any halfback or safety man to know, since the situation will determine how close he should play a receiver coming downfield. As soon as the ball is thrown the defensive backs must ignore the receiver and play the ball.

It is very important also that when the ball is thrown the halfbacks and safety man play the ball as "high" in the air as they can.   This is done in order to prevent a receiver coming

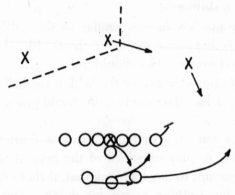

Fig. 103.   The off halfback ready for the throw-back.   He must cover two-thirds of the field.

downfield and taking the ball from a halfback or safety man.

Always try to intercept *all* passes thrown—except when it is fourth down and you may lose yardage.   (This is another reason why it is important for halfbacks and the safety man to know down and distance.)

Much practice is necessary to perfect a good pass defense because there is no such thing as a "perfect" pass defense.   Do not neglect to let halfbacks and safety men have the opportunity to catch passes on defense, as shown in the various drills. It is quite different for a back to catch a pass on defense.

To cover flankers, tell the halfbacks always to be in position so that the flankers cannot run a straight down-and-out on them.   Always keep the defensive halfback to the *outside* unless the flanker moves to the sideline; then he should take a position *inside* the flanker.   If a flanker is set to the left (standing on defense), the halfback will move out.   The safety will move over slightly, always in position to cover his third of the field.   All these "deep" men still have to be in position to cover one third of field.

Speed is a good thing to have to play a good zone defense, but *not* the most important.   Look for a smart boy who can react quickly and intelligently to passes.

Helpful hints on pass defense

Some hints on pass defense that will always be helpful are:

1. *Never let a receiver get deep or in behind the deep backs.*
2. *Always be alert for a pass because "every play is a pass."*
3. *Be ready to block if the pass is intercepted.*
4. *Pressure on the passer is the best pass defense.*
5. *Let your opponents complete the short ones, but never the deep pass.*
6. *Keep both the passer and the receiver in view.*
7. *Always intercept a pass; never give them another chance to get the touchdown.*
8. *Go for the ball when it is thrown.*
9. *Always know down and distance.*
10. *The closer the offense gets to your goal line, the closer you play the receivers.*

Pass defense drills

Drills that we use for pass defense are as follows:

DRILL 1.   This drill is done by halfbacks, safety men, linebackers, and ends.   (1) Start the defensive man back by using a cross step (by this we mean *right* foot over *left;* this enables him to move faster).   (2) The passer throws the ball rather hard over the defensive man's head.   (3) Keep the defensive man with a wide base, and not moving too erectly. (4) The defensive man should always catch the ball at its height.   (Note: In all drills we make the defensive man run with the ball.)

Fig. 104.   Pass defense, Drill 1.

DRILL 2.   This drill is done by having the passer take a position twenty yards from the defensive back or linebacker. (1) Start the defensive man forward at full speed.   (2) The passer throws the ball *over* the defensive man's head (this drill will get him used to catching a ball thrown at him).   (3) It is all right for the defensive back to break his stride to catch the ball.   (4) The defensive man should judge the ball so as to catch it at its height.

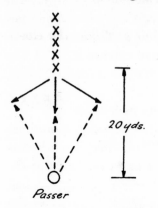

Fig. 105.   Pass defense, Drill 2.

DRILL 3.   This drill is used mostly for linebackers and ends. (1) Take two defensive men and put them about five yards apart.   (2) On the snap, they use a cross step and back up. (3) The passer throws the ball between them, and they fight for ball (we always have head gear and pads on when we do this drill).   (4) Have them fight for the ball, and catch it at its height.

We also use Drill 3 and let the defensive linebackers and ends come forward.

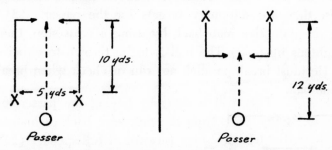

Fig. 106.   Pass defense, Drill 3.   *Left,* defense going away; *right,* defense coming forward.

DRILL 4—THE "TIP DRILL."   The "tip drill" has been one of our most successful drills in teaching a defensive man to re-act quick.   (1) Take a passer and put him about twenty yards from two defensive men.   (2) The two defensive men start running forward, one behind the other.   (3) The first man goes up and tips the ball and the second man catches it.   (4) The ball should be thrown good and firm; it's like a catcher, catch-

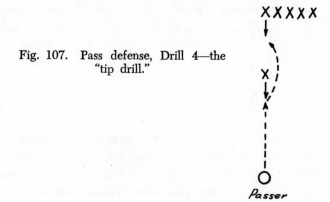

Fig. 107.   Pass defense, Drill 4—the "tip drill."

ing a foul tip. (At least six times a season we make pass interceptions on deflected balls.)

DRILL 5. For linebackers and ends, this drill, along with
the "tip drill," has been the best. (1) We take two offensive
ends and put them downfield between fifteen and twenty
yards; they are stationary targets for the passer. (2) We
start the defensive man back by using a cross step, then he
straightens up. (3) The ball is to be thrown to either end.
(4) He must break parallel, not run or check when breaking
for the ball.

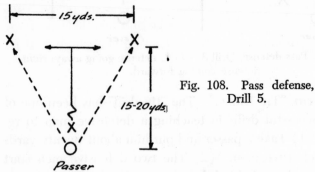

Fig. 108. Pass defense,
Drill 5.

DRILL 6. (1) Take your offensive ends (usually four) and
put them downfield about ten or twelve yards deep. (2) Al-

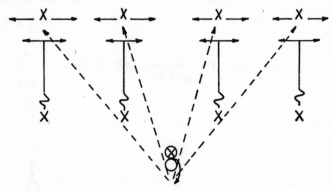

Fig. 109. Pass defense, Drill 6.

low them freedom to move parallel and forward, not back;
they move on snap of the ball. This drill gives the offensive
ends experience in taking the ball from the linebackers, and
gives the quarterback experience in picking his targets. This
drill you can work both for offense and defense; it also gives the
ends and linebackers their responsibility in covering in their
zones.

Drill 7. This drill we call "quick start for halfbacks."
(1) Send an offensive end downfield, and have him run down-
and-out pattern. (2) Don't let the halfback move until the end
gets about one or two steps on him. (3) Have the passer hang
the ball outside so the halfback can go and take it away from
end. (This will also teach the halfback to play the ball at its
height.)

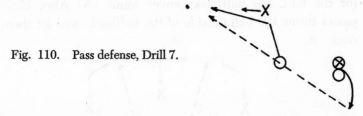

Fig. 110.   Pass defense, Drill 7.

Drill 8.   (1) Take halfbacks and safety men downfield
about fifty yards. (2) Let the passer throw the ball about
thirty yards and let halfbacks and safety men come forward fast
and judge the ball for a catch at its height. (This drill is done
to let deep men get the feel of the ball as they are coming forward at full speed. This drill should be done every day for the
deep men.)

Drill 9.   As has been stated before, our halfbacks are responsible for one-third of the field, and should be in position
at all times so they can over-lap each other. (1) Take the
passer and center; on the snap, the halfbacks and safety men
start back. (2) The ball is thrown between them. (3) If

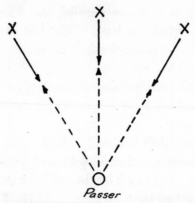

Fig. 111. Pass defense, Drill 8.

the left half calls for the ball, the safety is always covering him up—that is, he gets behind him. (4) If the safety calls for the ball, the halfbacks cover him. (5) Also, have the passer throw the ball outside of the halfbacks and let them run under it.

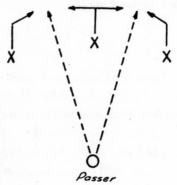

Fig. 112. Pass defense, Drill 9.

DRILL 10. (1) Take the offensive ends and line them up on hash marks. (2) Let them run about fifteen to twenty-five yards downfield. (3) Have the passer throw to either one and let the safety play them both.

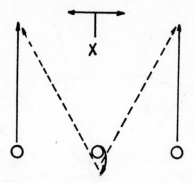

Fig. 113. Pass defense, Drill 10.

DRILL 11. In this drill (1) Take end and halfback and send them in the halfback's zone. (2) The halfback keeps the deep man, the end, so as to cover him first, and then he comes up fast if the ball is thrown to the short man. (3) The more width the halfback keeps, the better position he is in to cover both receivers.

Fig. 114. Pass defense, Drill 11.

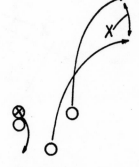

DRILL 12. This drill is used as a team drill for ends, line-backers, halfbacks, and safety men. Throw the ball in each zone to get linebackers and ends to react in their zones and get them to work as a team.

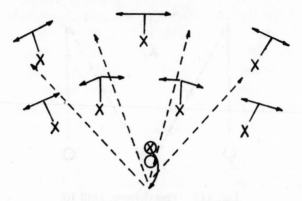

Fig. 115.   Pass defense, Drill 12.

DRILL 13—RUNNING PASS DRILL. If the quarterback runs out of the pocket it becomes a running pass. We make a running pass by having the quarterback run out to the right or left, outside of the offensive tackle. (Arrows show the way linebackers, halfbacks, safety cover. See Figure 116.)

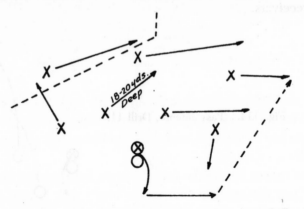

Fig. 116.   Pass defense, Drill 13—running pass drill.

Defensive halfbacks

Defensive halfbacks have a tough job, but a most important one. Against runs, if the offensive end comes downfield, he must be sure that the safety man has come over (on sweeps), before he can go up to tackle.

We tell halfbacks always to take two steps back; this will slow them down and stop them coming up too fast.

As far as our halfbacks are concerned, we play them as if they were safety men. If the runner "turns the corner" (gets around the defensive end), halfbacks should work outside-in. The safety should follow the play and be ready to tackle when the halfback turns the play in. The "off" halfback then becomes the safety man. (See Figure 117.)

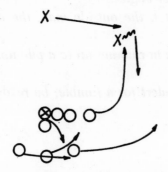

Fig. 117. Safety man following the play.

The defensive halfback and safety job will be easier if the offensive ends block on the line of scrimmage. Then the halfback can key on the end, and come up faster, but always under control.

If the runner has gotten into the open field, we tell the halfback, "Let the twelfth man tackle him"; that is, run him to the side line.

(Note: The linebacker's and end's responsibilities on all defenses are covered in team defense, pages 207–245. Linebackers and ends must step to their responsibility first before they are ready for a pass.)

Some helpful hints for halfbacks and safety men

1. *Protect your own territory first.*
2. *Know the position on the field, the down, and the distance.*
3. *Be ready for tip offs.*
4. *Don't let anyone get behind you.*
5. *Use your eyes to follow the play.*
6. *Always be alert; talk to each other.*
7. *Always go for the ball, after the play has developed; be sure to take proper angles.*
8. *Always watch the outside man, the end; on a flanker, man-in-motion.*
9. *Be cautious in running up to a pile up, a back may spin out.*
10. *Always be alert for a fumble; be ready to get that ball.*

9

Defensive Team Play

IN RECENT YEARS there has been a steady de-
emphasis of the over-all value of defensive football. And I am
sure there are times that too much stress is put merely on out-
scoring the opposition.

There is truth still in the old game axiom that "the best offense is a good defense." There are times that all coaches
will not have good offensive personnel, no matter where they
are coaching—and then the coach will realize he can't win without a sound defense. Good defense will always keep you in
ball games, even sometimes when you have no reason to be in
the game.

One of the primary reasons for upsets in football is that the
favorite team fails to score when they have the opportunity
and the underdog team capitalizes on a break and wins the
game.

The defensive game should be given the same importance as the offense.   Much time and coaching must be spent on defense.   The coach should sell his team on the idea that there is as much glory in stopping a team from scoring as there is in scoring themselves.

The coach should remember that you can develop a good defense quicker than an offense.   And pride is one of the first essentials in developing a good defense.   Many times a team will find it is easier to stop the opposition than to score themselves.

DEFENSIVE AXIOMS

There are several basic principles involved in the defensive game that must be kept in mind at all times.

1. *Every defense should be a co-ordinated defense.*   Every man must know his responsibility.   Remember: a team cannot get beat on defensive mistakes.   Each man on the team must know that he must play his position first, *then* react.

2. *Follow the ball.*   This will provide the winning edge in football—if eleven men follow with relentless pursuit after they have protected their initial responsibility.

3. *Angle of pursuit.*   Taking the correct "angle of pursuit" sounds like a simple axiom to follow, but it is probably broken more than any game fundamental.   There is some correct angle that *every* man can take to pursue the ball carrier.   Angle of pursuit is something that every coach must work on—he can't just *talk* about it.   The coach can never take for granted that his players will take the right angle—it must be coached.

4. *Gang tackle.*   The gang tackle is the most demoralizing maneuver in football.   With gang tackling a team will soon kill some of the incentive of the opposing ball carrier.   The ball carriers will soon realize that they have little chance of

making a long run, and gang tackling can demoralize the offensive team to the point where it will cut down on their downfield blocking. Until the whistle blows on a play, every defensive man must figure he is going to tackle the ball carrier.

5. *Interception of the forward pass.* Every time the offense throws a forward pass the defense must react to the ball—not after it has been completed or intercepted but *while the ball is in flight.* As soon as the ball leaves the passer's hands everyone on defense should go for the ball. The personnel in the immediate vicinity of the receivers should try to intercept or make the tackle if the pass is completed. Everyone else should be moving to a position to block if the pass is intercepted or to a tackling position if the pass is completed.

These remarks may sound elementary and logical and easy to sell to players, but they are the hardest things to coach. The natural reaction of defensive players is to wait and see what happens, *then* react. A coach will find that if he is successful in getting his team to react first, with the ball in flight, he will find they can react five to ten yards while the ball is in the air, depending on the type of pass thrown.

To coach this successfully a coach must have some sort of a signal to give as soon as the ball has left the passer's hand to alert the entire team so that they can react to the ball. The signal can be almost any kind, but it should be something short and impressive. Have everyone on the team give this signal as soon as the passer turns the ball loose. Every time a pass is thrown you must coach this. And the coach will find that it pays off—"a player's value to his team varies inversely with the distance he is from the ball."

6. *Make them go the hard way.* This axiom is a composite of the previous ones: Every player should first "play his position," follow the ball, gang tackle, and react immediately when

a forward pass is in the air. Every defensive player should know that he must not give the opposition the "easy touchdown"—they must earn it.

It takes a very good team to move the ball in a sustained drive if every man on defense is carrying out the game axioms. Every time the offense runs a play the chances for a mistake increase. The defense must be sold on these principles and then must be coached in them every day they are on the field.

There are many ways to carry out this axiom effectively. The coach should not make the mistake of letting his team go into a ball game with only one defense—there is no reason for a team to be caught in such a situation if the defensive game is receiving the proper amount of time in practice. The coach should start in spring practice working on defenses to be used against every type of offense that his team will encounter the following season. If this is done, the team will start fall practice with knowledge of two or more defenses.

There are two elementary ways to vary these basic defenses:

(1) Shift the defenses and angle the defenses. If properly executed the shift can be one of the most demoralizing things used against the offense. A shift will usually force the offense to change their starting signal or it will make them use some other counter maneuver with which they are not too familiar. This is bound to impair the efficiency of any offense to some degree. In the first half of a game, for instance, a team can use the shift occasionally, then in the second half they can come out and shift repeatedly. Invariably the offensive team's half-time report will try to adjust the offense to the defense used in the first half of the game. It will upset a team to re-adjust to something they were told specifically the defense was not doing. In any phase of the game it is wise to vary your offensive and defensive attack in the first and second half.

There is one important thing in the use of the shift: The coach must sell his team on the idea that if the offense runs a play while the defense is shifting *the defense has the advantage.* But the *offense* will have the advantage if the defensive team is not mentally prepared for a play being run every time during the shift. If the defense is prepared for this situation it is a fine chance to break defensive men clean and to stop the offense for no gain or for a loss.

(2) Angle or looping. This is another way to vary the basic defenses. The team will line up in one defense and on the snap of the ball they will "angle" to another defense. This maneuver must be co-ordinated, with every man angling to another responsibility. This type of maneuver is sound if it is coached correctly. The coach should make sure the team keeps one important thing in mind: *No one can be cut off* in the defensive line who is angling. The line men may have to retreat to get to their responsibility, but they cannot be cut off. They must never be forced to release inside an offensive man.

PENETRATION

Penetration cuts down on pursuit: Every step of penetration cuts down two steps of pursuit. It is basically more logical to play on the line of scrimmage, and to penetrate just enough to give you a change of pace. You will have to come in with penetration on certain situations where the down and distance require it. If you are to carry through with the axiom of pursuit you must keep penetration to a minimum. You do not want to play for the "fourth and ten"—you are playing for the fourth with two or three yards to go for a first down. A team that tries to stop the offense for no gain each time is leaving themselves open for the long gain.

DEFENSING THE NORMAL "T"

There are four basic defenses against the normal "T" formation. They are all sound and with stunts will give you the necessary needed variations. The more defenses you can learn and still not make defensive mistakes the tougher you can make it on the offense. Some teams play most of their games against normal "T" teams. If this is true you will be able to have all four of these defenses in your attack. (See Figure 118.)

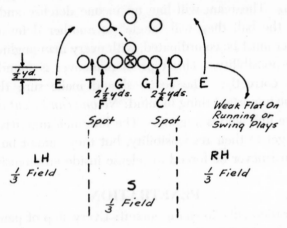

Fig. 118.   Loose 6-man line vs. straight "T" formation.

Figure 118 shows what is commonly referred to as *even defense*. From this alignment you can get good stunts, good pursuit, and adjust the splits and spreads with a minimum of adjustment.

Defensive responsibility by positions

Ends. The ends, tackles, guards, and linebackers have the same responsibilities on both sides so this will let us consider the responsibility at the same time. Ends line up two and a half to three yards outside of their defensive tackle. If a run develops their way they are responsible for the end run. To play this responsibility they should meet the first potential blocker as quickly and deeply as possible, then by use of their hands stay on their feet and turn the play inside or string the play out the sideline to allow the pursuit to catch up. If a pass develops they are responsible for rushing the passer hard from the outside.

Tackles. Tackles should line up about one-half yard off the line of scrimmage on the inside shoulder of the offensive end. The tackle's first responsibility is to step with his outside foot and protect himself with a "forearm shiver" from any pressure that he might get from the offensive end. This position gives him a good chance to follow the development of the play; with no penetration he should be able to help out on plays inside and outside his original position.

The tackle's initial responsibility on running plays is the off-tackle play. He is not required to stop this play for no gain. A two or three yard gain on an off-tackle play is considered a satisfactory job. It is important that he always take eighteen inches off the line of scrimmage—this position will give him a slight advantage over the offense since it will force the offense to come to him. If a pass develops the tackles can rush the passer either inside or outside the offensive block.

Guards. The guards' position is also eighteen inches off the line of scrimmage. They line up head-on to the offensive guards. On the snap of the ball their reaction is to "forearm shiver" the offensive guard from this position. The guards should first protect the territory between each other, and at the same time be ready to be prepared to figure in pursuit. Guards playing in this manner should be able to recover quickly and often figure in pursuit of sweeps on their side. If a pass develops they rush the passer hard going on either side of the blockers.

Linebackers. Linebackers line up on the outside shoulder of the offensive tackles with a normal position of about two and a half yards off the line of scrimmage. This position will naturally vary with the down and distance. The responsibility on a run is the "quickie." They should key on the halfback on their side through the offensive tackle. After protecting their initial responsibility linebackers must figure in pursuit of any type of running play. If a pass develops they are responsible for the spot zone on their respective side.

Three deep men. The two halfbacks and a safety man are responsible for their respective zones. Their responsibility remains constant through the loose six defensive alignment so I will not refer to their responsibility after this.

Offensive splits. The above responsibilities in original position are all given with a normal "T" formation split. Many teams will vary their line splits when running from the normal "T," so it is necessary to include some discussion of an adjustment to these splits.

The end will keep his normal position as long as the offensive end remains on his side. Should the offensive end take a greater split than the original position, the defensive end should "loosen up" and stay nose-on to the offensive end until he goes five yards from the offensive tackle. If the end goes further than five yards, the defensive end can come back in and play his normal position without giving the end blocking angle.

The tackles should line up on the defensive guards and never should vary their original position. If tackles will always be conscious of lining up on the defense they will always be in the right position. Being off the ball one-half yard has helped tackles in playing splits because the offense must show them the pressure.

Guards must always be alert for more than the maximum split of the offensive guard. They never vary their original position because this is the widest position they can take and still protect the quarterback sneak. Should the guards take *more* than the normal split the coach might give the guard the option of dropping straight back a foot. This will help him in recognizing the play and locating the ball. Linebackers are always playing their zone and should never be deployed out of position as they will play the halfback through the tackle.

Adjustment to flankers

The end will play a *normal* or a *counter* flanker very similar to a split offensive end. With a close flanker up to three yards outside the offensive end, he will play his original position. With a wide flanker the end should loosen up. How far he should go should depend on his position on the field. The ends are always responsible for the outside on this defense and should remember that they are positioning themselves in the best position to play this responsibility. (See Figure 119a.)

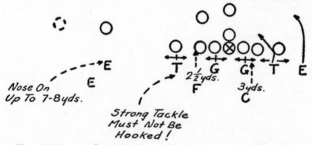

Fig. 119a. Adjustment to flankers: normal flanker.

Tackles toward a flanker have one slight adjustment—they should move nose-on to the offensive end and must never be "hooked." A linebacker toward a flanker should loosen up to four yards and move back three to four yards if the halfback is still in on his side. If it is a counter flanker and the halfback is removed, then the linebacker should move outside to about nose-on to the offensive end.

The short side linebacker away from the flanker has similar responsibilities. If the halfback is still there he must protect the "quickie" first. If the halfback is removed then he should loosen up and move over behind his offensive guard. The guards still have to play their same responsibilities because there is always the threat of the fullback or quarterback up the middle. Any other unusual spread should be met with an automatic defense—usually some type of an overshift.

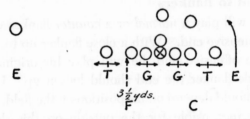

Fig. 119b. Adjustment to flankers: counter flanker.

Stunts from the loose-6

Split stunt (see Figure 120). On the split side the end still has the same outside responsibilities as on the loose-6 defense. The tackle, stepping with his outside foot, angles to a position over the outside shoulder of the offensive end. He must not be cut off by the offensive end. Pass responsibilities are the same as on the loose-6 for the guards and tackles. The guard angles to a similar position over the offensive tackle.

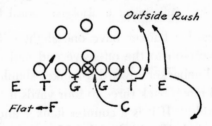

Fig. 120. Split stunt (loose 6-man line). The end does not rush on a pass; he has flat responsibility.

The linebacker should key on the fullback and step to his inside position over the offensive guard. If the fullback comes his way he should hold his position and take his angle of pursuit as soon as he diagnoses the play. If the fullback shows it is a pass on the snap then the linebacker will be responsible for covering the spot. If there is a fake of a run and a pass develops the linebacker should go ahead and rush the passer.

Tight stunt (see Figure 121.) The end converges as quickly as possible and is ready to meet force with force. He is responsible for the off-tackle hole and if he receives inside pressure he must close from the outside. His charge is at a 45-degree angle—the same as the tackle. The tackle converges head-over the face of the offensive tackle; he is also responsible for his inside. Linebackers should conceal as long as possible, then on the snap of the ball go quickly to the outside to protect their responsibility. The linebacker has now assumed the end's responsibility for sweeps and should a pass develop he will be responsible for the flat zone. The end and tackle should be in good position to put pressure on the passer from this stunt.

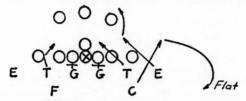

Fig. 121. Tight stunt (loose 6-man line). The tackle and end converge in the same plane at about a 45-degree angle.

Tackle-linebacker stunt. The end and guard have the same responsibilities as on the loose-6. The tackle angles over the face, and converges over the offensive tackle; the linebacker keys on the offensive end. If the offensive end blocks *in* on the tackle, the linebacker comes on through. If the end *releases,* the linebacker holds and covers the spot on passes or takes his angle of pursuit on a running play. (See Figure 122a.)

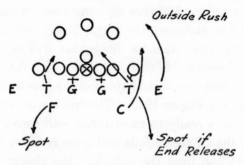

Fig. 122a.   Tackle-linebacker stunt (loose 6-man line).

There is one change which should always be kept in mind in this loose-6 defense.   There are only two men involved in the variation and it is very important against certain types of passes.   By a signal the end tells the tackle that if a pass develops he is going to drop off and cover the flat—in turn this tells the tackle that he must be responsible for keeping the passer in the pocket.   (See Figure 122b.)

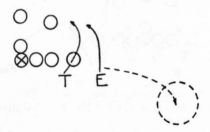

Fig. 122b.   End-tackle variation of pass defense responsibility.
The tackle must keep the passer in the pocket.

To play this responsibility the end can line up a yard and a half wider than his original position.   He takes no initial step on the snap of the ball but waits to see the play develop.   If a *pass* develops, he is in a much better position to get width and depth quicker. If a *run* develops, he can meet the first blocker at the same relative spot that he could have in his original position.

5-3-2-1 DEFENSIVE ALIGNMENT

Figure 123 shows most desirable 5-3-2-1 defense because it is so flexible. It can vary from a 3- or 5-man line to an 8-man line. It is easy to adjust to flankers and spreads and can be used as an automatic defense.

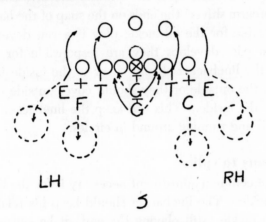

Fig. 123.   5-3-2-1 defense.

Individual responsibilities by positions

The *ends* line up two yards outside the defensive tackles. If a run develops their way they are responsible for the outside and should get depth as quickly as possible. If a pass develops they are responsible for the flat zone.

Tackles line up on the outside shoulder of the offensive tackles on the line of scrimmage. Their first step should be with the outside foot and at the same time they "forearm shiver" the tackle. The tackle must not be hooked. From this position he plays the running game. If a pass develops he is responsible for keeping the passer in the pocket.

Guards. One guard will be lined up on the center's nose, about eighteen inches off the line of scrimmage. From this position he will be able to angle over either guard without being cut off. The other guard is lined up directly behind, and, by a signal, directs the front guard either right or left, then adjusts in the opposite direction. Both guards should take the angle over the outside shoulder of the offensive guards.

The *linebackers* line up nose-on to the offensive ends. They should "forearm shiver" the ends on the snap of the ball. They are responsible for the off-tackle play if a run develops their way. If a pass develops they are responsible for the spot. Normally the linebacker should cover to the inside if the end releases to the outside or they should cover outside if the end releases to the inside. This will keep the linebacker from losing the end and running around in circles.

Adjustments to splits

The most common adjustment necessary is for the linebacker and the tackle. The linebacker should keep his relative position to the tackle (still playing the end) if he can reach him with his first step. If the end is taking a split greater than this the linebacker should loosen up and go straight back two or three yards. Tackle should maintain his initial position. If the tackle takes a maximum split, the tackle will be in about a nose-on position and will still have the responsibility of not being hooked. This defense cannot be played if the tackle tries to keep the outside shoulder with a tackle split. The guards will have more territory than they can possibly cover.

Adjustments to flankers

This is one of the merits of this defense and its adjustments to flankers. (See Figures 124a and 124b.)

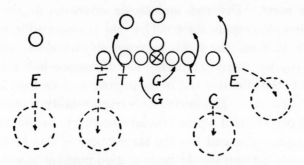

Fig. 124a. 5-3-2-1 adjustment to flankers.

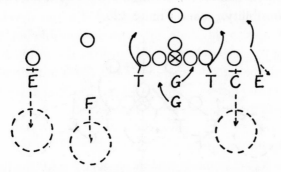

Fig. 124b. 5-3-2-1 adjustment to end flanker.

With an end split or as a flanker, the defensive end always takes the first man and will be nose-on to him up to a width of seven yards.   If the end flanker goes further the defensive end should loosen up to gain width or depth.   With an end split the linebacker drops straight back to about two yards depth. With an end-and-flanker split the end takes the first man and the linebacker plays the second.   Since this rule is constant, it is a simple adjustment to most common spreads and flankers.

Stunts

(NOTE: Since the guards operate as a separate unit they will not be figured in any stunts for this defense.)

Tight stunt. The end and tackle converge in the same plane at a 45-degree angle. The end is responsible for the off-tackle play and the tackle is responsible for inside pressure. The linebacker should be off the line about one-half yard and nose-on to the offensive end to try to draw a block from him on his initial charge. The linebacker's responsibility is outside on running plays, and if a pass develops he covers the flat zone.

"X" stunt. The end has the same responsibility he had on the six tight set and should be in a good position to put quick pressure on the passer. The linebacker also has the same responsibility he had on the six tight set. The tackles have normal responsibility. (See Figure 125.)

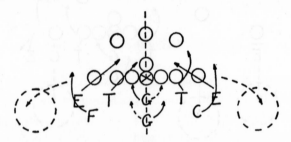

Fig. 125.   Off 5-3-2-1.   *Left,* tight stunt; *right,* "X" stunt.

Overshifted 6-man line

Any time there is a normal flanker or an unusual spread an overshift may become the soundest possible defense. It is always wise to have this overshift available among your defenses if it is at all possible.

The overshift is also very valuable in playing certain teams to the wide side of the field.   (See Figure 126.)

The strong end is responsible always for the outside. If the flanker goes seven yards, the end stays nose-on; if the flanker goes eight or ten yards, the end drops off a yard and a half. If he goes twelve or fifteen, the end drops three or four yards.

The tackle should never be hooked. His first responsibility is step with his outside foot and not give ground and he must control the end.

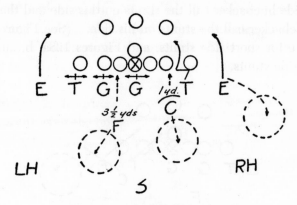

Fig. 126. Overshifted left defense.

The guards are fighting lateral pressure. This gives you the strong tackle and both guards operating in the same plane. They should never penetrate until they find out where the ball is. This is one of the key coaching points in the defense. If one man penetrates, you give a gap for the offense to play, whereas if they all operate on the same plane, they can cover twice the territory.

On a normal set on the short side, the tackle should play on the inside shoulder, and should play the end. He feels the outside pressure and sees the inside pressure. If the play develops away from him, he follows the play *deep;* that puts the short end in the flat on passes.

The center lines up on the inside foot of the defensive tackle and faces the backfield at an angle. Also, he is in a better position to close the big hole by converging from the outside.

The coach must tell his players the weakness of the defense and sell them that they must all react to the short side of the overshift defense.   Many times this has looked like the strength of the defense by reaction of the team.

Stunts on the short side and on the strong side.   Let the weak side linebacker call the stunts on this side and the strong side linebacker call the stunts on his side.   (See Figures 127a, b, and c for short side stunts, and Figures 128a, b, and c for strong side stunts.)

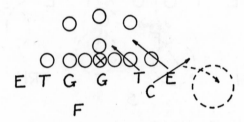

Fig. 127a.   Short side stunts, off overshifted defense: tight stunt.

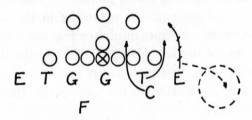

Fig. 127b.   Short side stunts: center "fire."

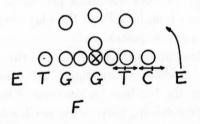

Fig. 127c.   Short side stunts: 7-man line set.

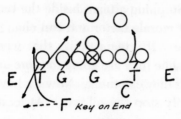

Fig. 128a.   Strong side stunts, off overshifted line: tight stunt.

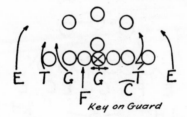

Fig. 128b.   Strong side stunts: split.

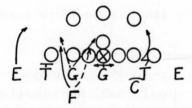

Fig. 128c.   Strong side stunts: fullback and strong guard stunt.

GOAL LINE DEFENSE

Certainly a team must have a good goal line defense.   The psychology used in coaching this defense in this zone is most important.   The coach must sell his team that when they hit the ten-yard line the defense has the advantage because they have cut down the territory to defend on passes and runs and eleven men are in position to tackle on the line of scrimmage without worrying about eligible receivers getting behind them.

Be sure to work your defense in this zone a lot when you are scrimmaging. Stopping a team inside the ten-yard line is also a very important morale factor and can change the complexion of any ball game. If a team thinks that when the opposition hits the ten-yard line they are going to score anyway they probably will. But if they can think, "Now *we* have the advantage," they will probably stop the offense. At least this is certainly the psychology a coach must go on if he is going to have a decent goal line defense. (See Figure 129.)

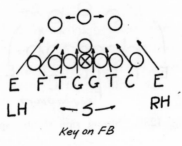

Fig. 129. Goal line defense, gap 8.

Individual responsibilities

Ends come in sharp at 45-degree angles sealing the inside. Linebackers line up on the inside shoulder of the offensive ends. The linebacker's first step is in to the end as low as possible and is not moved from this initial step; then he converges in the same plane as the end. This protects the linebacker from being completely "collapsed" by the offensive end and times his charge with the defensive end. Tackles line up on the inside shoulder of the offensive tackles and converge hard and low for penetration.

Guards line up on the inside shoulder of the offensive guards and drive hard and low for penetration.

Halfbacks are lined up outside the offensive ends and are linebackers. They should tackle for no gain on sweeps their way. The safety man keys on the offensive fullback; he will take him to the point of attack.

DEFENSING THE SINGLE WING

The single wing has lost some of its following in recent years but is still one of the soundest offensive formations in football. If you are not careful you will be defensing the other formations you see more frequently and allow a team using this formation to run over you.

There are more double blocks and more power available from this formation than any of the various "T" formations. You can use the same basic defenses against the single wing that are used against the normal "T" by making a few adjustments. In defensing the single wing you can take the loose-6 and overshifted-6 and adjust to the single wing formation. (See Figure 130.)

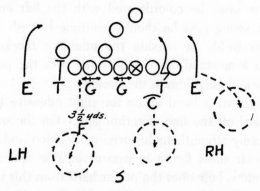

Fig. 130. Overshifted line vs. single wing.

The overshifted-6 is the most logical defense that can meet the strength of the formation. I will give the individual responsibilities from an unbalanced right single wing formation.

Individual defensing responsibilities

The *left end* should line up two and one-half yards outside the left defensive tackle. If a run develops he is responsible for the outside and should get his depth as quickly as possible. He should key on the fullback as he is the first potential blocker. He must not be knocked off his feet and can give ground laterally to turn the play inside or string it out to the sideline. On any type of a running or swing pass he must come across and rush the passer hard from the outside. On a stand-up pass or straight back pass he drops off in the flat and is responsible for any receiver in this zone.

The *left tackle* lines up nose-on to the wingback and on the snap of the ball plays the wingback as quickly as possible. In going for the wingback he should "forearm shiver" the end to help him get to his responsibility. He is responsible for the off-tackle zone and should not be blocked in or out of this zone. He is not primarily responsible for tackling in this zone but mainly he is required to keep it "congested." If a pass develops he must be co-ordinated with the left end. On a running or swing pass he should continue to rush the passer from either inside or outside the offensive blocker. On a straight back or stand-up pass he must rush the passer from the outside and keep him in the pocket.

The *left guard* is lined up on the right offensive tackle and one-half yard off the line of scrimmage. On the snap of the ball he merely strengthens his original position and diagnoses the play. He must figure in pursuit outside and inside. If a pass develops he rushes the passer hard from this position.

The *right guard* lines up on the right offensive guard on the line of scrimmage. On the snap of the ball he penetrates through the guard and fights pressure. If a pass develops he also has the option of rushing the passer either way.

The *right tackle* lines up on the inside shoulder of the left offensive end on the line of scrimmage. On the snap of the ball his first step is a low "jab" step with his outside foot, with a "forearm shiver" to protect himself from a block from the end. He feels the pressure from the outside without turning his head. If he feels pressure from the end he retreats or rolls out and pursues laterally along the line. If the end disappears and he sees pressure coming from the tackle, he comes down the line of scrimmage to meet this pressure. Should both disappear and the play develops away from him, he follows the play from behind. If a pass develops he is responsible for keeping the passer in the pocket. The only exception would be a reverse pass.

The *right end* lines up two and one-half yards outside of the right defensive tackle. If the play develops away from him (either a run or a pass), he drops off into the weak flat zone. If the play develops his way he must come across the line of scrimmage and is responsible for the outside, the same as the left end.

The *fullback* lines up three and one-half yards behind the left defensive guard. From this position he has an angle to hit any running play along the line. He can play a sweep his way from inside out and should be careful not to over-run the play. If a pass develops he is responsible for the strong spot. If no one comes in this zone he may be able to help out in the delayed flat.

The *center* lines up just inside the right defensive tackle. He turns at a slight angle and works through the center and offensive fullback. From this position he has a better view to diagnose the play. If a pass develops he is responsible for the weak spot. The two halfbacks and safety men still play their zone responsibility of one third of the field.

Stunts from the overshifted-6

Short side stunts

1. *Tight stunt* is with the end and tackle converging at a 45 degree angle and both responsible for the inside. The linebacker protecting the end outside.

2. *Tackle-linebacker stunt.* From his original position the tackle angles around the offensive end. To help him get to this responsibility he might loosen up a foot and a half from the line of scrimmage. The linebacker watches the offensive tackle, masks his fire and lets the offensive tackle commit himself, then "fires" over his original position.

3. *Seven-man line variation.* The linebacker moves in head-on to the offensive end and from a crouched position plays him on the snap of the ball with a "forearm shiver." Tackle lines up head-on to the offensive tackle and on the snap "forearm shivers" the tackle and fights lateral pressure. The end play is normal.

Another variation which may sometimes be needed from the 7 set to bring the end in just outside the linebacker, hold up the offensive end. This may be a very valuable defensive weapon in certain situations. (See Figure 131.)

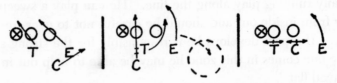

Fig. 131. Short side variations of overshifted defense vs. single wing. *Left,* tight; *center,* tackle-linebacker stunt; *right,* 7-man line set.

Strong side stunts

1. *Split.* The tackle should step around the wingback on the snap of the ball and from this position he fights pressure. Guard angles around the offensive end. The fullback conceals his position as long as possible, moves up within a yard and a half of the line of scrimmage, and from that position fires over the inside shoulder of the outside offensive tackle. On passes he now is responsible for rushing and should not try to drop back. End has normal responsibility.

2. *Tackle-linebacker stunt.*   The tackle converges hard over
the outside shoulder of the offensive end and should get penetration.   The linebacker moves up within a yard and a half of
the line of scrimmage in front of the offensive end, then as
the tackle converges he fires over the wingback.   The end has
normal responsibility.   (See Figure 132.)

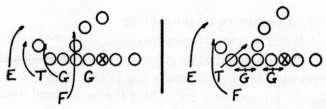

Fig. 132.   Strong side variations of overshifted defense vs. single
wing.   *Left,* split; *right,* tackle-linebacker stunt.

ANGLE TO THE OVERSHIFT

Lining up in a loose-6 or undershifted-6 you can vary this
defense by angling to overshift responsibilities.   The two
guards and strong tackles should be off the line of scrimmage
a foot and a half, which will give them better position to go
to their responsibilities.   From the angle to the overshift you
could still have your short side stunts but you would eliminate
your strong side stunts.   (See Figure 133.)

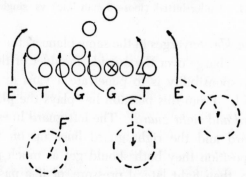

Fig. 133.   Angle to the overshifted defense.

Loose-6 vs. single wing formation

In playing the loose-6 against the single wing it is commonly referred to as an *undershifted-6* with the line shifted away from the offensive strength and the linebackers overshifted to compensate. (See Figure 134.)

Individual defensive responsibility

The *left end* on a snap comes hard over the outside shoulder of the wingback and must meet force with force and penetrate and strip outside plays of encircling interference. If a pass develops he is responsible for rushing the passer hard from the outside. (See Figure 134.)

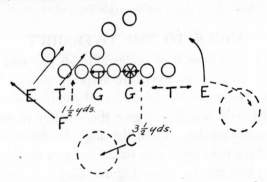

Fig. 134.   Undershifted (loose 6-man line) vs. single wing.

The *left tackle* converges in the same plane as the end, which will make his charge over the *outside* shoulder of the offensive end. His responsibility is to penetrate a yard and a half in the backfield. From this position he "plays the play."

Left guard and right guard. The left guard lines up on the outside guard and the right guard lines up on the center. From this position they both should get as much penetration on the snap, then fight lateral pressure, or if a pass develops, rush from either side of their blockers.

The *right tackle* is lined up head-on to the offensive end. On the snap he "forearm shivers" the end and fights lateral pressure. If the play goes away from him he follows the play deep. If a pass develops he should keep the passer in the pocket and rush from the outside.

The *right end* is lined up two yards from the defensive tackle. If a run develops away from him he revolves behind the line of scrimmage and becomes a second safety man. If a pass develops he drops off into the weak flat.

The *center* lines up three and one-half yards deep and in line with the offensive center and tailback. If a run develops he can hit any offensive hole along the line of scrimmage. If a pass develops he is responsible for the strong spot.

The *fullback* lines up a yard and a half behind his defensive tackle, and, on the snap of the ball, goes quickly to the outside and assumes outside responsibility on any run. He is responsible for the flat on passes.

Short side "X" stunt

The *end* and *tackle* swap responsibilities. The tackle on the snap steps quickly to the outside and assumes the end's responsibility. The end converges a sharp angle almost down the line of scrimmage. If a pass develops he must take angle to keep the passer in the pocket. (See Figure 135.)

Strong side stunt

The tackle angles to a position over the outside shoulder of the wingback and must not be cut off by the wingback. (See Figure 135.)

The *left guard* angles over the tackle's position. The fullback, on the snap, "fires" over the left guard's original position. (See Figure 135.)

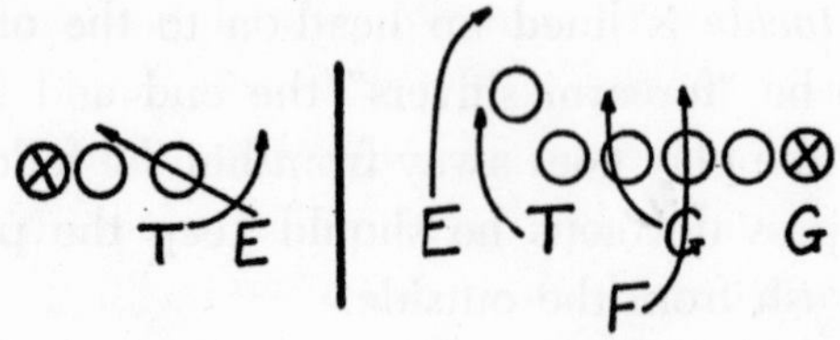

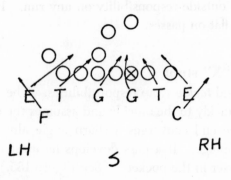

Fig. 135. *Left*, weak side "X" stunt on undershifted 6-man line vs. single wing. *Right*, strong side stunt on undershifted 6-man line vs. single wing.

GOAL LINE DEFENSE VS. SINGLE WING

The best short-yardage defense against the single wing is a tight-6 from the undershifted-6 alignment, with everyone converging on the inside defensive guard.   The left end ignores the wingback and comes in at a 45-degree angle.   (See Figure 136.)

Fig. 136. Goal line defense vs. single wing.

The *left tackle* converges at a 45-degree angle.

The *left guard* converges over the outside shoulder of the outside offensive guard.

The *right guard* penetrates through the inside offensive guard. He must be low.

The *right tackle* moves just inside the offensive end to give

him a better position to converge over the outside shoulder of
the left offensive tackle.

The *right end* converges at a 45-degree angle.

The *fullback* and *center* have similar responsibilities. They
are lined up just outside their defensive tackle and a yard and
a half off the line of scrimmage. From this position they are
responsible for the outside on running plays and the flat on
passes. On this defense everyone converging must be responsible for his inside and if they meet pressure from the inside
they must fight down the line of scrimmage and must never
release to the "back" side of the offensive pressure. Defensive
backs still have zone responsibility but should be in position
to come up quick outside. They should not be as worried
about a deep pass from this defense as there will certainly be
a lot of pressure put on the passer.

DEFENSING THE SPLIT "T"

Since the advent of the split "T" there has been a gradual
change from the common defensive alignments, namely, the
6-2-2-1, 5-3-2-1 and the 7-diamond. It is generally conceded
that you cannot consistently stop the split "T" without a 5-4-2
set-up. If the opposition is as good or better than you are it
will take some variation of this set-up to stop them. There will
be a place for normal "T" defenses on certain down and distance. The recognized coaches of the split "T" generally concede the 5-4-2 alignment commonly associated with Oklahoma
is the best (this is the inside 5-4-2).

This defense may be played quite differently by adjusting
your personnel. The major problem in converting to a "box
defense" is the necessity of revolving with flankers. As soon as
the offense realizes you are playing box defense they force you
out of it by setting flankers or putting a man in motion. In
rotating it is necessary to have a linebacker or end playing

defensive halfback. This is a radical change of their normal responsibilities and immediately creates a defensive weakness. To solve this situation let the fullback go to either side as the outside linebacker. He will go toward a flanker or if there is no flanker he can go to the width of the field or to the strength of the offense. In doing this you will always leave the two deep men—composed of either of the halfbacks and the safety man.

Fullback left and fullback right

The fullback should delay his position by lining up in the middle opposite the offensive center. He then waits until the offense lines up and goes to his position. The halfbacks and safety will semi-revolve away from the fullback. The pass defense becomes a quick problem: Are you going to play a man to man defense or stick with your basic zone pass defense? Sometimes it seems difficult enough to stop a passing attack with three deep men. And now you have the problem of trying to stop it with two. It has been proven that you get better results by staying with the basic zone pass defense. This can be done with this line up even though the safety man and semi-revolved halfback are in a little awkward position. You can still keep from having the touchdown pass thrown on you. To help protect the halfback away from the fullback he is allowed to play five to six yards off the line of scrimmage. It puts him in better position to still get back and play his third of the field on pass defense which is usually the short side of the field or away from offensive strength. (See Figures 136a and b.)

For pass defense with the fullback left or right, the two deep men should always be at least ten yards deep. (See Figures 137a and b.)

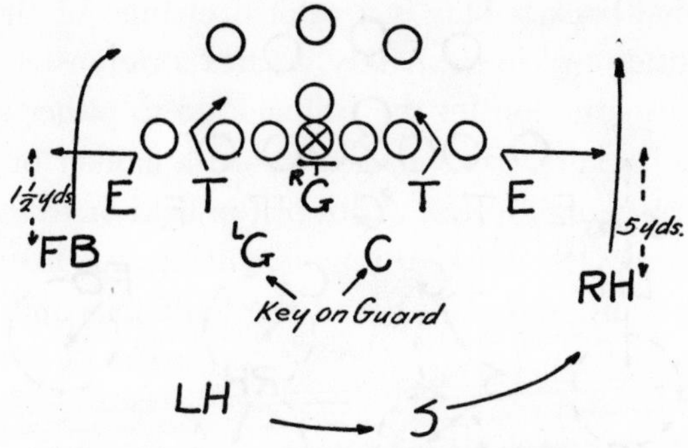

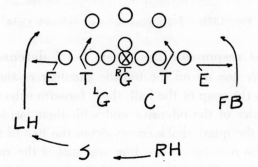

Fig. 136a. 5-4-2, fullback left.

Fig. 136b. 5-4-2, fullback right.

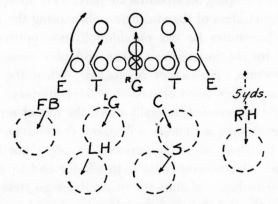

Fig. 137a. 5-4-2 pass defense, fullback left. (Ends use a hard delayed rusher.)

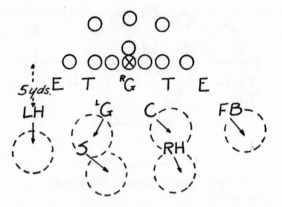

Fig. 137b. 5-4-2 pass defense, fullback right.

Individual responsibilities, basic 5-4-2 defense

The *ends* line up on the outside shoulder of the offensive ends. On the snap of the ball, they "forearm shiver" the outside shoulder of the offensive end with their inside foot forward. If the quarterback comes down the line of scrimmage his way, he remains on the line and makes the quarterback come to him. This gives the end the responsibility for the quarterback keeping on an off-tackle play. The most common error is penetration of the end *before* diagnosing the play. If the end penetrates he has put himself in a position to be optioned by the quarterback. The end play must be slow and deliberate. He cannot be fooled. When the quarterback laterals there is no chance of a "keep it" play; then the end's angle of pursuit is laterally down the line of scrimmage.

Playing in such a manner will allow the end to figure in the sweep, where, if he penetrated, he might not figure in either one. A coaching point is to tell the end to make the play come to him. Should the quarterback go straight back for a pass, the end then rushes, delayed and hard outside, and is responsible for keeping the passer in the pocket. If the play develops away from him he slowly revolves away from the play and becomes a second safety man.

The *tackles* line up on the outside shoulder of the offensive tackle. On his initial charge he steps with his outside foot into the gap between the offensive tackle and end. At the same time he "forearm shivers" the outside shoulder of the offensive tackle. He must not be hooked by the tackle and should get penetration. He will get pressure from either the end or tackle. If the end should block *in* on him, he fights for every foot of penetration to force the play deeper into the backfield. If he can get a yard and a half of penetration he is doing a good job. If he is flanked by the end he is never asked to be responsible for tackling the runner on the play. It will help the tackle to let him know this; otherwise, he may get the mistaken idea that he is doing a poor job. If the tackle gives him pressure from the inside he tries to hold his ground with an outside position and tries to work back to the inside. This is his responsibility against the running game. If a pass shows, the tackle rushes hard either inside or outside of his block. Should a play develop away from him he is then responsible for following the ball from behind.

The *right guard* lines up on the offensive center's nose one-half yard off the line of scrimmage. On the snap he does not penetrate on his initial charge but "forearm shivers" the center. He forces the offense to use at least two men on him in the event they should run a trap over his position. In playing loose he is also in good position to pursue in either direction. Should a pass show he rushes hard on either side of his block.

The *left guard* and *center* have identical responsibilities. They line up a yard and a half off the line on the outside shoulder of the offensive guards. They each will key on the

guard on his side.   If the guard pulls their way they go with
him.   If he comes straight ahead they meet him in the neutral
zone.   If he sets, as on pass protection, they drop back and
cover the spot on their side.   If the guard should pull in back
of the center to the opposite side, he fills in to protect a trap
up the middle.

The *fullback* lines up three and one-half yards outside his
defensive end, and about one-half yard off the line of scrimmage.   He has the option of going to either side depending
on offensive strength or width of the field.   He has outside
responsibility on running plays and covers the flat zone on
passes.

The *left halfback, with fullback left,* has normal zone responsibility.   He can line up a little deeper at ten to twelve
yards.   With the *fullback right,* he moves up to five or six
yards off the line of scrimmage, three yards outside his defensive end.   He has outside responsibility on running play.
On passes he goes back to his original zone pass defense.   He
is handicapped by position but he can still keep the deep pass
from being completed.

The *safety man, with the fullback left,* semi-revolves away
from him to about head-on to the left offensive halfback.   This
will vary depending on the width of the field.   If the fullback
is left and the ball is on the right hash mark, he would keep
his normal position about over the ball.   With the fullback
right he semi-revolves in the opposite direction to the left with
similar responsibilities.   He should always remember that
depth is a big advantage in playing his position.

The *right halfback* has the same responsibility as the left
halfback but in reverse, depending on which way the fullback
goes.   Should the fullback go left he is up five to six yards
from the line, and three yards outside the defensive end.   He
has outside responsibility on the running game and is respon-

sible for his zone on pass defense. If fullback goes right he
assumes his normal position with at least ten to twelve yards
depth.

Tight stunt

The fullback can call this stunt on his side any time he
desires. It is a good charge off and will make the basic defense much better. Penetration by the end and tackle will
usually force a quick show of the quarterback and put quick
pressure on the passer. The end and tackle from their original
position converge sharp at a 45-degree angle. The left guard
or center on which side the tight stunt is called can loosen up
to about two yards and play the play, ignoring the guard.
(Figure 138a.)

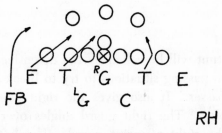

Fig. 138a.   5-4-2 stunts: tight stunt (only toward fullback).

Inside linebacker-tackle stunt

This stunt will be called by the defensive quarterback (who
is usually the center). This stunt is very good if the offensive
ends are consistently blocking in on the tackles and the offensive tackle blocking in on the inside linebacker. (See Figure
138b.)

The tackles converge hard over the face of the offensive
tackles and must not be cut off. If they receive inside pressure they must come down the line of scrimmage. The inside

linebackers key on the offensive end. If they block in on the tackles they fire over the offensive end's original position. If the end releases they remain in their position and diagnose the

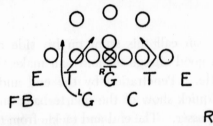

Fig. 138b.   5-4-2 stunts: tackle inside linebacker stunt.

play which will usually be a pass or a running play in the opposite direction. If a pass develops they cover the spot on their side. If a run develops they take their angle of pursuit.

Guards' stunt

A guards' stunt will be called by the defensive quarterback and is good on passing situations to try to break guards clean to rush the passer. It also gives the right guard a chance to vary his play. The right guard angles over the outside shoulder of the right offensive guard. The left guard fires directly over the left offensive guard. The center loosens up to a depth of two or three yards and plays the play. (Figure 138c.)

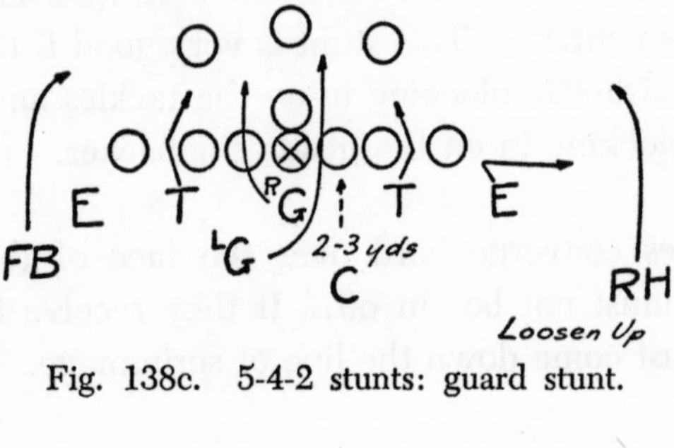

Fig. 138c.   5-4-2 stunts: guard stunt.

Gap stunt

Penetration hurts any offense, particularly the split "T" because the quarterback must maneuver close to the line of scrimmage. This stunt can be called on either or both sides by the defensive quarterback. The tackles, on the snap, drive hard into the gap between the offensive end and tackle. The inside linebackers, on the snap, drive hard into the gap between the offensive tackle and guard. The right guard, on the snap, should take one step back to position himself for a play up the middle and to eliminate any possibility of being trapped. (See Figure 138d.)

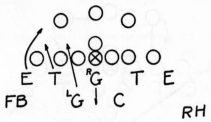

Fig. 138d.   5-4-2 stunts: gap stunt.

The *end and tackle away from the fullback* should have a stunt that will allow the end to cover the flat occasionally on

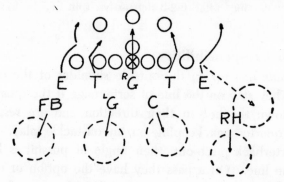

Fig. 139.   End and tackle stunt away from fullback (4-man rush).

pass defense. This is the weakness of the defense, but if the end will occasionally cover the flat on pass defense and make the tackle responsible for keeping the passer in the pocket, it will add strength to the defense. The end merely tells the tackle by a signal that he will be off if a pass develops. (See Figure 139.)

6-2-3 DEFENSE AGAINST THE SPLIT "T"

This defense has proven satisfactory against a true split "T" offense and will have its place if you are able to put it in. (See Figure 140.)

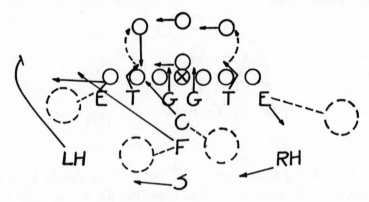

Fig. 140.   6-2-3 defense vs. split "T."

Individual responsibilities

The *ends* line up on the outside shoulder of the offensive ends. They stay on the line of scrimmage if the quarterback comes down the line in their direction and are responsible for the quarterback keeping on an off-tackle play. Should the quarterback pitch-out, their angle of pursuit is laterally along the line. On a pass they have the option of covering the flat zone or rushing the passer. In either case they must, by a signal, tell the tackle on their side.

The *tackles* line up on the outside shoulder of the tackles and, on the snap, they step with the outside foot and drive for at least a yard penetration. If a pass develops they will co-ordinate their play with the end, either keeping the passer in the pocket, or, if the end is off or rushing, either side of the offensive blocker if the end is rushing.

The *guards* line up on the inside shoulder of the offensive guards and are responsible for any play up the middle. They can vary their position from on the line of scrimmage to a half a yard off and still protect their responsibility.

The *center* keys on the quarterback and is responsible for the "quickie" play the way the quarterback goes. If a pass shows he covers the right spot.

The *fullback* lines up about three and one-half yards deep and goes with the quarterback and is responsible for the outside pitch-off. He can easily protect this responsibility if he will go with the quarterback and not run an arc. He can tackle for no gain if he will correctly play this responsibility. If a pass develops he covers the left spot.

DEFENSING SPREAD FORMATIONS

There is no need to try and go into detail in covering the various spread formations now commonly employed. If you have a good scout report and a team is using a spread formation as an element of surprise, the important thing is to have one sound defense and not to make defensive mistakes or have defensive personnel out of position. Most spread formations are basically passing formations, so pass defense should take priority.

Basically you should try to defend all passes from spread formations and never rush over four men. In doing this you can cover the width of the field with four men protecting both flat zones and both spots, still leaving three deep men to play their third of the field.

10

The Kicking Game

THE KICKING GAME plays a large part in football—from a field goal to a well-executed and planned punt return. I don't think anyone can put too much emphasis on this phase of the game. In practically every close game, it will be the kicking game that will decide the issue, either directly or indirectly.

In close games the punt will be used more than any other one offensive play. But too often the kicking game is pushed back into a less important role as if it was just something you "have to have" to play the game.

How many coaches include every phase of the kicking game in their practice schedule from the first week of training?

It is easy to overlook the kicking game because so much of the yardage on kicks is concealed. A part of the vital statistics kept for every game should include yardage of kicks, punts returned, and kickoffs returned—both offensively and defensively, in addition to the net distance of the actual kick. This will sometimes tell you why a team won or lost. Keep these statistics for your team. In this way you can discover what you are doing with the kicking game.

Always be alert and on the lookout for a good punter or place kicker. When you find one, exploit him to the fullest extent. Joel Hunt has a good explanation of the difference between a kicker and a punter in his two little verses:

KICKER   PUNTER

I can kick the balls *When I kick, I control the ball,*
 High into the air; *Right or left out of bounds they go;*
Where the pigskin falls, *Quick-kick over safeties you know.*
 I know not where. *I don't kick—I punt the ball.*

There have been many great kickers but few great punters.

The kicking game can be broken down into the following parts:

THE PUNT: (1) Mechanics, (2) Protection, (3) Fielding and returning the punt, and (4) Blocking the punt.

THE PLACE KICK: (1) Mechanics, and (2) Protecting the place kick.

THE FIELD GOAL.

THE KICKOFF: (1) Line up and coverage, and (2) Returning the kick off.

Almost any well co-ordinated athlete can learn to punt a football well enough to come within four or five yards of his target. Such a punter comprises an offense in himself. His punts may be planned to gain ground, to penetrate the enemy territory, or to put pressure on opponents when the ball must be surrendered to them. This is "concealed yardage," which will always figure prominently in any close ball game.

Many great coaches have built their offense around the kicking game.   General Bob Neyland, my old coach, and Wallace Wade probably exploited the kicking game more than any other coaches.   During the 1930's Coach Wade always had a great punter.   The punter would keep backing the opponents up with the kicking game till all Wade's team needed to score was a break.   When the opposition made a mistake it was often in the danger zone, which usually resulted in a score.

PUNT MECHANICS

Two natural drawbacks face the beginning punter.   First, the football is not round and is different from any other ball. It is an elongated speroid and must be handled and punted differently than a rounded object.   Second, the punter does all his work on one leg so that he must develop an unusual sort of balance different from that required in any other sport.

On the other hand, when inflated to its official size the ball will remain constant and the punter can develop a high degree of efficiency and consistency if he works on certain elementary fundamentals.   Some boys are naturals and require little or no coaching.   When you find a boy that is unorthodox in style but still gets distance and accuracy, do not make the mistake of trying to change him.   You can't improve on results, and performance is all you are striving for.

Dropping the ball

If the ball is held and dropped differently by the kicker each time it will react differently each time.   If it is dropped and handled with a uniform release it will tend to react similarly each time.   So it follows the kicker must adopt a standard manner of holding the ball.

The best way to hold the ball is to place it in the right hand with the middle finger resting along the line of the bottom seam. Make sure the hand is forward enough to have control of the ball—if this isn't done the ball will fall forward and down resulting in punting the ball in a different manner each time. The laces will be up usually, but this isn't too important as long as the hand has the correct position.   In this way you can control the drop of the ball to punt a high, medium, or low ball.

The left hand merely serves to balance the ball and should be placed very lightly against the front left side of the ball. Make sure the left hand doesn't exert any pressure since this will cause the ball to fall out of the line of release.

Be alert for beginners tossing or jerking the ball on the drop. This is the main reason for variations in punting and it can be corrected.

When dropping the ball the arms should *not* be extended full length.   If they are, it will cause the punter to put too much weight forward and tend to expose more of a target to enemy charges.

Have the punter work on *dropping* the ball many times before he even tries to punt the ball.   Make the punter watch the ball all the way to the ground—usually a perfectly dropped ball will bounce backward after hitting the ground.

Body balance

Body balance is *the* prerequisite for a good punter. He must be relaxed and balanced.

You will usually find that a boy has a definite "drift" when he punts the ball. Usually a right-footed kicker will "drift" to the right and a left-footed kicker to the left. This "drift" can be cut to a minimum by a slight correction in stance.

The punter must be made to realize how important the eyes and the left foot are in punting. The left foot serves to give direction—the ball will tend to go in a line with the foot on which he is balanced.

Never let a punter kick without thinking: Is he in the middle punting for distance? Is he kicking from either hash mark or kicking for the "coffin corner"?

Every time a punter kicks it is under different circumstances and he must be conscious of this difference at all times or he will not be able to punt with intelligence before a crowd.

In the act of kicking, the toe should be pointed in the direction the player wants the ball to go. The kicking foot will seek a parallel with the balanced foot at the completion of the kick.

Never let a boy get the idea that he can punt better by leaving the ground with his balanced foot. He *may* do this naturally and do a good job. If so, certainly don't change him— but it is contrary to standard punting form.

No one can control a ball if he is in the air. For perfect control the foot on which the kicker balances should be kept solidly on the ground.

Stance

The punter should have a set stance. The stance should be close to a heel and toe alignment with the *kicking* foot forward. The knees should be slightly flexed and the arms should be well-extended. This gives the center a good target to snap the ball about waist high, and it gives the punter a good position to go after a bad snap.

Always work on punters handling a bad snap from the center. They should always be ready for a bad snap; if they get a good snap, the bad snap idea leaves in a flash. If they get a bad snap on any down other than the fourth they should be prepared to pick the ball up and run rather than try a delayed kick from an awkward position. If it is fourth down they should be prepared to get the ball off no matter where the ball is centered.

Steps

After receiving the ball the punter should take a short step with his front foot and then follow with a full step on the balanced foot. The kicking foot then comes forward and up for contact with the ball. This is the common step-and-a-half form. Some coaches refer to it as the "hop, step, kick" style, which is a slight variation from the step and a half but a little quicker and covering a little less ground.

Acceleration and contact

After the second full step the kicking leg starts gaining momentum. The leg swing should use power without exertion. Contact with the ball should be made with the toe pointing downward to get a spiral; then the leg is slightly bent, locks, and swings into the ball. This is the real power in the leg snap. The timing obtains distance and results.

Contact should be made about knee high.

Follow through

The follow through is important in every phase of athletics and has a definite place in punting. Follow through insures that the ball will reach its objective and retains rhythm. The drawback of the arms to the hip will add to the effectiveness of the follow through.

Summary

1. *Brain*—use it on every punt.
2. *Eyes*—estimate angles and distances on the ball while in possession.
3. *Body*—almost relaxed.
4. *Hands*—positional control for the drop and placement.
5. *Leg*—swing power without exertion.

6. *Leg snap*—the real power.

7. *Foot*—toe down, fitting the ball for spiral or end-over-end.

8. *Follow through*—insures objective and obtains rhythm.

PROTECTING AND COVERING THE PUNT

Punt protection is a vital part of a team's practice. It must be put in your practice schedule and worked on—both dummy and at full speed. Too many coaches work on trick plays and naked reverses before they ever work on this important phase of the game.

Punt protection is easy to overlook because you cannot *win* a ball game directly through punt protection. But rest assured there is no quicker way to *lose* a game than to have a punt blocked or partially blocked.

There are two basic types of punt protection. It behooves every coach to include both in their coaching because they each have their place. The two basic types of protection are *spread protection* and *tight protection*.

Spread protection

The "spread" has one great advantage over the "tight" in covering the punt. However, there is one important thing you must consider before using spread protection. *You must have a center who can snap the ball at least thirteen yards with some degree of accuracy.* If you can't find a boy who can do this, spread protection will be eliminated automatically.

Alignment of personnel

Start by switching the guards and tackles in the offensive line up. This will give you more speed and coverage where it is needed, and it gives you more protection where it is needed. (See Figure 141.)

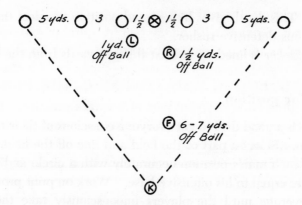

Fig. 141.   Spread punt protection lineup.

Spread punt protection line up

The *center* will take his position first; he will be in his normal position.

The *tackles* should take a yard and a half split from the center.   It is very important that the tackles line up correctly or no one will have their correct position.

The *guards* line up with a three-yard split from the tackle. (Be sure that every boy knows how far three yards is.   You will find a great variation in their idea of three yards.   The usual mistake is they will tend to cut down on this split.)

The *ends* line up with a five-yard split from the guard.   This is the minimum but there may be more if they desire, particularly if they should have the width of the field on their side.

Close backs.   The left close back is one yard off the line of scrimmage.   The right close back is one and a half yards off the line.   This will enable them to carry out their responsibilities without interference.

The *fullback* lines up six to seven yards deep with his left foot keyed on the center's right foot—just room for the ball to clear.   This depth gives him a good position to select the most dangerous defensive rusher.

The *kicker* is lined up at least thirteen yards from the ball.

Drill for position

Here is a good drill to get everyone conscious of their relative position.   Select a part of the field and line off the field, marking off each man's position accurately with a circle and with a diameter equal to his offensive base.   Work on punt protection and coverage until the players unconsciously take their accurate position.   It is most important that they keep the base of the triangle—don't let them cut down their splits.   The base should be not less than 22 yards.

Blocking rules for spread punt

The *center* blocks the man over him.   If there is no one over him he leaves on the snap to cover the punt.

The *tackles* take the first man to their outside.   They do this regardless of how many men are inside, then they consistently take the first man to their outside.   They take a passive step back and to the outside.   They should not be aggressive.   If no one shows up in this zone after the initial snap, they release and cover.

The *guards* take the man directly over them or the first man to the outside (if they can reach him with one lateral step), then cover.   Note the exception—a guard blocks this way unless there are two men on the line of scrimmage between him and the tackle; if this situation exists he takes the first man to the *inside*.   (Do not count men unless they are on the line of scrimmage.)

The *ends* go on the snap of the ball and protect the outside for a punt return, unless there are two men between them and the guard. Then the end "bumps" the first man to the inside and covers.

Close backs. The left close back steps up into the line on the snap and across laterally and takes the first man to show. With an aggressive block from an inside angle he should be able to knock the man into other defensive rushers and eliminate over-loading his zone by blocking the first man into others. The right close back steps up and to his left, "sleeving" the left back, and he takes the first man to show in the same manner. Using this form of cross blocking these two men can block three or four men. This will not give the defense a chance to fake them and go either way—a possibility that exists when they block straight ahead.

The *fullback* is the "safety valve." He takes the first most dangerous man. He should look to his right first to defend the kicking zone. If no one looks dangerous in this zone, he should look back quickly and decide who he considers the most dangerous rusher. This is an important assignment. A mistake here can lead to a blocked kick. (Be sure that you have a drill in which two or three men are allowed to get as far as possible so that the fullback can have some experience in deciding who is the most dangerous man.)

Punter. With a good snap he should punt in 2.1 seconds. (If you ever get a punter who can punt in two seconds flat, you will never have a punt blocked even if you don't slow anyone up on the line of scrimmage.) Don't let the timing get over 2.2 seconds. This is the danger time.

Covering spread punt protection

See Figure 142.

The *ends* leave on the snap and cover fast to the outside in the first wave.

The *guards* protect their responsibility and cover from this position. They may be in the first or second wave.

The *tackles* protect their responsibility and cover in the second wave.

The *center* protects his responsibility and goes for the ball. He may be in the first or second wave.

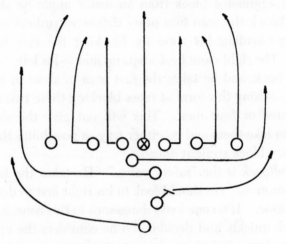

Fig. 142.   Covering from spread punt protection.

The *close backs* protect their responsibility.

The *left back* covers right, and *right back* covers left, with outside responsibility.

The *fullback* protects his responsibility and covers right.

The *punter* covers left.

Tight punt protection

"Tight" punt protection is necessary and should be a part of your offense. It is needed when kicking from the goal line and the punter cannot get his required depth of thirteen yards for the spread protection. There will also be days when weather factors will make it very hazardous for the center to snap the ball thirteen yards. When you need tight protection, you need it badly.

Tight protection line up

A "cup protection" formed by eight men with everyone responsible. Form is outside foot to the outside foot of the inside man. (See Figure 143.)

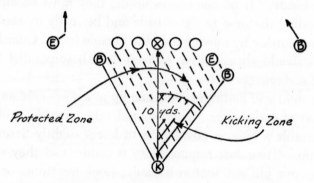

Fig. 143. Tight punt protection line up. The punter is responsible for kicking over the protection.

Individual protection responsibility

The *center's* first responsibility is to get a good snap of the ball to the punter; then he is responsible for his own base. He must not leave too soon and create a gap for delayed rushers trying to block the kick. *A safe rule is for all linemen to delay two seconds before leaving on this protection.* (To have them estimate two seconds accurately, have them repeat, after the snap, "one, one thousand, two, one thousand," then release.)

The *guards* and *tackles* take a normal base with about a twelve-inch split. Don't allow them to close the gap between them and the inside man. If the guard and tackles cut down on their base and split they automatically cut down the protected kicking zone. On the snap of the ball the guards and tackles broaden their base and at the same time shift their inside foot forward with a quick stagger of both feet. This position should be a low crouch because they are waiting passively to absorb the charge of the defense. They must not be *aggressive*—that is the way gaps are created. They should never move more than one foot at a time after taking position until *after* the two second interval. Their responsibility is first to the inside. If no one comes inside, they must be alert for overloading the zone to the outside and be ready to, secondly, help out outside by moving only the outside foot. Guards and tackles should always strive to keep their base parallel to the line of scrimmage.

The *right end* and *right back* line up at a 45-degree angle to the line of scrimmage. They should take as wide, still, and comfortable a base as possible, with knees slightly flexed and head up. Their first responsibility is inside, and they should never move but one foot at a time. Look for stunts or overloading in this zone. Ends must be ready to help out if the loaded zone is between them and the right back. They can help out by a step with the outside foot and by snapping the elbow up level with the shoulder to give more blocking base, again never moving the inside foot. These two men have the most important part in this protection because they are directly in front of and protecting the kicking zone.

The *left back* lines up at a 45-degree angle to the line of scrimmage in a position where he can touch the left offensive tackle's hip. His responsibility is similar to the right end, but he does not have to help outside. He maintains his base and forces anyone to rush the kicker from the outside so that to get to the kicking zone they must run an arc. They musn't reach the kicker's foot going in a straight line.

The *left end* goes on the snap on anything other than fourth down punting. On fourth down punting, he should move in and bump the defensive end as he releases for coverage.

The *wingback* lines up eight to twelve yards from the offensive tackle and leaves on the snap.

The *kicker* should punt in two seconds flat. Be sure that the punter is aware of the protected zone; if he wants to kick to his left he must move over to the right to compensate for the kicking zone. *Everyone on the team should realize the zone they are protecting.* The punters must always kick *over* their protection. There have been many punts blocked because the punter did not kick over his protection.

Covering the tight protection

From tackle to tackle the line protects for two seconds, then fans out to protect the width of the field.

The *right end* covers outside in second wave.

The *left end* covers outside in first wave.

The *right back* covers quick to the outside in second wave.

The *left back* covers outside in second wave.

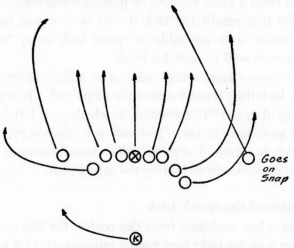

Fig. 144. Covering from tight punt protection. The line protects two seconds before covering.

The *wing back* goes for the ball without any outside responsibility in the first wave.

The *punter* covers to his left.

Summary of punt protection

There cannot be any mistakes in punt protection. If the opponent blocks a kick on an offensive mistake you are doing a poor coaching job. Work on punting from *all* positions on the field. The greater part of this work should be done off or behind your own goal line; this is where you get more pressure on the punting game and where you can stand the least. A mistake here is usually a touchdown mistake.

A final reminder—you can never over-rate the offensive kicking game.

THE QUICK KICK

The quick kick can be a very helpful offensive weapon under certain conditions. The quick kick is a surprise punt usually executed from a basic running or passing formation.

For the best results the kick should be low and end-over-end. Usually it is advisable to quick kick *away* from the safety man as well as over his head.

I have always been a firm believer in a little different type of quick kick than is most commonly employed. It is particularly helpful in the "T" formation in which your left halfback is often your best kicker. You will get consistency, a good roll, and it has more deception—which usually assures you an excellent opportunity of fooling the safety man.

Mechanics of the quick kick

Taking a low lead-pass from the center, the kicker takes a short step with his right foot, then a full step with his left foot, and drives off his balanced foot. He is facing the sideline. Swinging his kicking foot in an arc and turning his body, he strikes the ball about three quarters away from the end. The ball should be held very lightly with the left and right hand at each end.

With a kick of this type you get maximum impetus on one end, resulting in maximum roll. It will usually catch the safety man going to his left and the kick can be very easily and naturally kicked to his right. This kick is very easy to coach and will get the needed results.

The other type of quick kick that can be employed with a fullback in the "T" formation, or a tailback in single wing, is the "rocker step." The kicker assumes his normal backfield stance and receives the ball from the center at the knee of his kicking leg. Taking a short step back with his left foot and a full step forward with the same foot he kicks the ball end-over-end by dropping the ball evenly on the top of his foot.

Protecting the quick kick

There are a number of methods of protecting the quick kick, but generally they should all be aggressive blocks on the line of scrimmage. These blocks will keep the defense low and therefore protect the low flight of the ball over the line. Quick coverage must be stressed to take full advantage of the kick. (See Figure 145.)

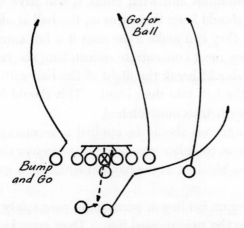

Fig. 145. "T" formation quick kick protection and coverage. Line blocks should be low and aggressive.

Covering the quick kick

On a quick kick as well as on a normal punt, stress the importance of covering as fast as possible.   When a team has to start in the danger zone after receiving a quick kick, many times subsequent breaks will set up a score for you.   Go back and find out who made the tackle on the kick and give him "credit" for making the touchdown possible.   In this way you build up a sense of the relative importance of covering the kick with as much speed as possible.

FIELDING AND RETURNING THE PUNT

Fielding.   You must find out by practice who are your best men in handling punts.   There is no set form for fielding and returning punts, but there are certain fundamentals that will help to guide you in coaching this:

1. *Fielding men must study the punter in each game.*   Get all the information you can on his kicking habits.   This will help the safety man to line up correctly.

2. Fielding men should always be conscious of the wind and weather conditions and what effect it will have on the punt.

3. They should keep their eyes on the ball at all times.   By split vision they can make a decision if a fair catch is a possibility.   They must concentrate on catching the ball first.

4. They should break the flight of the ball with their hands and bring the ball into their chest.   This should be their control speed with arms outstretched.

The same factors should be applied to receiving a bouncing kick.   Once in complete possession, the receiver should change the ball from his chest to the hand in which he is going to carry the ball.

In working on fielding of punts make your safety man handle punts inside the twenty-yard line.   They must know when to let the ball go and when they are justified in fielding the ball in this zone. A good general rule to apply is, "*A punt should never be fielded inside the 10-yard line.*" This would be true if the punt has normal coverage. There would be exceptions only in the case of a quick kick or a punt over the safety man's head on which the punter has out-kicked his coverage.

The only way to be sure of no mistakes in the twenty-yard area is to spend most of your time fielding punts in this area. There are just as many chances for bad breaks in other areas of the field, but they are never recognized because they are not as costly.

You can work your punters and safety men as a group, letting the punters kick high for the ten-yard line or angle for the "coffin corner." In this drill you will be working both offensively and defensively.

Punt returns

When it is executed well, the prettiest play in football is a sideline punt return that goes all the way. It is relatively simple to put in your practice schedule and is well worth the time and effort.

You must first sell your boys on the idea that they are going to return the punt all the way—that once the safetyman hits the sideline he should go all the way. The blockers must all be conscious of timing their blocks according to the length, height, and direction of the punt. Usually, the first man down in the wall will be the key blocker because everyone will be timing their blocks on him. His responsibility should be to allow the runner to hit the sideline.

Individual responsibilities

The following responsibilities are for a 6-3-2 alignment with the return up the right sideline. Assignments are simply reversed for a left sideline return.

The *right end* lines up nose-on to the left offensive end.   He legally delays the end from covering the kick as long as possible, then sprints for the sideline.   When he is about ten yards from the sideline, he turns at a right angle and goes straight down the field.   If he is sure the runner can get to the sideline without making him move over into the center of the field, he makes his block at about ten yards from the sideline. If the ball should be kicked on the opposite side of the field, he may have to come over to pick up the runner.   He then positions himself and takes the first man to the inside in this zone.

The *right tackle* lines up head-on to the left offensive tackle. His play is the same as the right end, except that he will space himself approximately seven to eight yards from the end and that he will block the first man to the inside in this zone.

The *right guard* and the *left guard* line up on the offensive guards respectively and carry out the same responsibility.   If any of the men in the wall find no one in their zone to block they should look to the inside to see if anyone has filtered through the wall, and, if they have, they should block them out.

The *left end* and *left tackle* line up on the outside shoulder of the right end and right tackle respectively.   They rush the kick hard and try to force the kick down the middle.   The left tackle goes on into the sideline and becomes part of the wall. The left end comes over and remains on the line of scrimmage and is the "safety valve"—he takes the last man, who will usually be the kicker.

The *right halfback* gets an outside position on the left offensive end and "dogs" him from the outside to keep him away from the exchange or fake of the ball.   He then blocks him, making sure to make his block at the right time.

The *center* sprints to position himself on the left offensive

end from the inside. After the right halfback has blocked the
end, the center should clean up and put him on the ground
again. This is the key block and should enable the runner to
get inside the wall. The fullback comes over quickly in front
of the ball and takes the first man to come in this zone. His
responsibility is to protect the exchange or fake of the ball.

Exchange and fake of the ball

The twin safeties have a primary responsibility in the execution of an exchange. They must be "actors"—the way they
carry out their fakes will largely determine the success of the
return. They must always keep distance between them.
They cannot fool the men covering the punt if they are too close
together, and they will make the fake or exchange too soon,
which will allow the men covering to adjust. If the ball is
kicked between them, the one who fields the punt should give
ground, if necessary, to keep this distance. The one who fields
the punt always goes in front. This shields the keep or exchange better. The ball carrier should retreat if necessary to
hit the wall.

Double safety sideline return

The correct maneuver for the double safety sideline return
is shown in Figure 146.

Drill for sideline punt return

The sideline return needs a lot of dummy work to practice
timing position and blocks with the keep or exchange. This
drill can be used for a running drill to end practice.

Put two dummies about ten yards from each sideline on the
line of scrimmage. With this set up, work the exchange both
left and right, making the men in the wall go around these

dummies. It is very important in the return that the men in
the wall do not cut the corner.

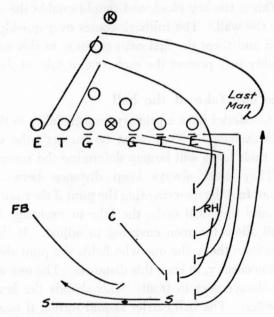

Fig. 146.   Double safety sideline return, right.

Double safety middle return

The middle return helps the sideline return in that it will
keep the covering team "honest" in playing the sideline return.
(See Figure 147.)

Individual responsibilities

The *guards* line up on the offensive guards, legally delay
them as long as possible, then sprint across to a position in front
of the exchange or keep of the ball. They try to form a lane
about ten yards wide down the middle of the field. The guards
will be the first men in the wall and should take the first man to
the outside in their zone.

The *tackles* line up head-on to the offensive tackle, legally delay the tackles as long as possible, then swing to the inside and position themselves about eight to ten yards from the guard and block the first man in their zone.

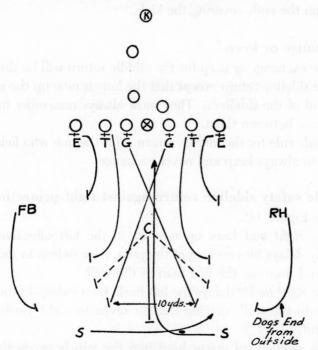

Fig. 147. Double safety middle return. The center has three options.

The *ends* have the same responsibility as the tackles. This gives three men on each side of the lane, and if no one comes into their zone the ends should then look into the lane and take anyone in the middle.

The *fullback* positions himself outside the right offensive end and "dogs" him from the outside to help protect the keep or exchange. The *right halfback* has the same responsibility on the left offensive end.

The *center* is allowed to vary his responsibility, particularly if the team covering is trying to use him as a key to determine quickly the direction of the sideline return. The center may drop straight back and protect the exchange or block to either side on the ends covering the kick.

Exchange or keep

The exchange or keep for the middle return will be the same as the sideline return except that the lane is now up the middle instead of the sideline. They must always remember to keep distance between them.

A safe rule for the middle return is for the one who fields the punt to always keep and never exchange.

Single safety sideline return against tight protection

See Figure 148.

The *right end* lines up nose-on to the left offensive end, legally delays his covering of the punt, then swings to the sideline and becomes the first man in the wall.

The *right tackle* delays the left back, then swings to the sideline into the wall, spacing himself seven to eight yards from the end.

The *right guard* drives hard into the gap between the left offensive tackle and the left offensive guard. If he drives for quick penetration he should be able to force both men to block him and thereby delay the coverage.

The *left guard* drives similarly into the gap between the center and the right offensive guard, then swings over and becomes part of the wall.

The *left end* and *left tackle* rush hard on the inside to try to force the kick down the middle. The tackle then goes into the wall and the end remains on the line of scrimmage to pick off the last man.

The *fullback* crosses quickly to the other side of the field to help the right halfback double-team the left offensive end.

The *center* drops back and takes the first man down on his side. He should time his block so as to allow the safety man to come back up the middle before he swings over to the sideline to pick up the wall.

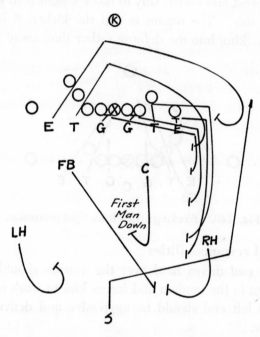

Fig. 148. Single safety sideline return against tight protection.

The *right halfback* gets an outside position on the left offensive end quickly and "dogs" him from the outside. Keeping the ends attention will give the fullback a good blocking angle to take the end out.

The *left halfback* blocks the right end out.

The *safety man* should bring the ball up the middle and hit the sideline between the fullback and center's blocks.

BLOCKING THE PUNT

Blocking the kick from tight protection

Blocking a punt from a tight punt protection is shown in Figure 149.

The quickest and easiest way to block a punt is to go in from the *strong side*. The reason is that the kicker, if he is right footed, is kicking into the defense rather than away from it.

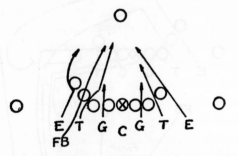

Fig. 149.   Blocking a kick from tight protection.

Individual responsibilities

The *left end* drives hard over the outside shoulder of the outside man in the tandem and forces him to work to the outside. The left end should be aggressive and deliver a good initial blow.

The *left tackle* drives hard into the gap between the No. 2 back and the offensive tackle, forcing the back to help the offensive tackle. This drive by the tackle is the key to this maneuver.

The *left guard* lines up in the gap between the tackle and the end and penetrates quickly into the kicking lane. This will usually force the tackle to help block him to the inside.

The *right guard* lines up in the gap between the weak tackle and guard and penetrates.

The *right tackle* charges the gap between the No. 3 back and the weak tackle.

The *right end* charges head over the outside shoulder of the No. 3 back and goes for the kicking zone. The fullback tries to conceal this position by lining up just outside the left defensive end. From this position he masks his charge just long enough to let the left end, left tackle, and left guard draw pressure. They should open up a hole between the No. 1 and No. 2 backs through which he can go directly into the kicking zone.

The *center* lines up about five yards deep and is ready for a run or a pass in case of a bad snap. The maneuver is set up for the fullback to block the kick but you will find that anyone may be the man who will have the opportunity to block it, depending on the reaction of the protection. I have seen four different men block a kick from this maneuver. *Sell everyone on the idea that they are going to block the kick or they will not carry out their responsibilities.* Every defensive man who is in any position at all to see the kicker should, as he kicks, raise their arms and drive for as much height as possible and cross about two yards in front of the kicker's foot. With a slice or a hook you never know who may block or partially block a kick.

Blocking the kick from spread protection

It is much more difficult to block a kick from a spread protection because it has been proved that with a good fast snap from center and a quick punter you can get the ball off without delaying anyone on the defensive line.

However, we do try to put pressure on the punter from the spread protection because, when he is kicking from thirteen or fourteen yards deep, about one out of three times the snap from center will be a little off and will give the defense an opportunity to block the kick. (See Figure 150.)

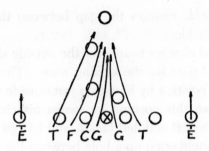

Fig. 150.   Blocking a kick from spread protection.

Individual responsibilities

The *left end* and the *right end* play slow and are ready for a run in case of a bad snap, or a pass.

The *left tackle* drives hard over the outside shoulder of the right offensive tackle for the No. 1 back's outside shoulder.

The *fullback* drives from the outside shoulder of the right offensive guard for the inside shoulder of the No. 1 back.

The *center* lines up head-on to the right guard, and works to the middle.

The *left guard* and the *right guard* line up on the outside shoulder of the center, drive hard to the inside, and make the No. 2 and No. 3 backs take them.

The *right tackle* drives hard over the left offensive guard for the kicking zone.

This play will always put pressure on the kicker, and it gives the left tackle, fullback, or center a good chance to break clean.

The most important factor involved in blocking a kick of any kind is to find the boy who has a particular knack and desire for "finding" the ball.   He may be a third stringer, but if he has this ability we put him in in this situation and exploit his talent.   Always look for a boy who has this important natural ability.

THE PLACE KICK

Mechanics

There is no better word than *mechanics* to start this phase of the game—place kicking *must* be mechanical.

Selection of kicker

In selecting a place kicker the coach must first look for a big boy who has good "snap" in his leg, but *any* boy who has snap in his leg may be a fine place kicker.   He should have patience and be willing to pay the price of hard practice to be a good place kicker.   It takes practice, *practice,* and *more* practice—until it becomes mechanical.

Make a "T"

The first thing to do is to instruct your place kickers to always kick from a "T"—either real or drawn on the ground. Any sort of "T" is satisfactory so long as it eliminates the goal posts as a factor in the kick.   (See Figure 151.)

The "T" can help the place kicker in the following ways:

1. It lines up the kick.

2. It helps to develop kicking "straight through."

3. It allows the kicker to check his non-kicking foot position at the time of the kick.   This foot must always step in the same place.

4. The place kicker can never develop accuracy unless he keeps his steps and foot position the same each time he kicks.

Form

Form for the place kicker is as follows:

1. Step with the kicking foot.

2. Step with the left foot about two and a half inches away from both lines of the "T."

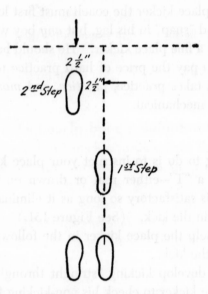

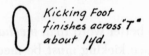

Kicking Foot
finishes across "T"
about 1yd.

2½"

2ⁿᵈ Step   2½"

1ˢᵗ Step

Fig. 151. Place kick "T."

3. Start the swing of the kicking foot. Be sure the swing does not start too far from the ball. Kick *through* the ball and finish through in front of the "T" with the third step. If the swing of the kicking foot is too far back you will not get accuracy on a straight-through kick.

4. *Finish the swing and the kick,* keeping your head down, your body slightly bent, and make sure you watch the foot go into the ball. Eyes should remain on the "T" until the kicking

foot hits the ground; then you look up. *The kicker should see the ball go over the goal post.* (A good beginning drill is to make the kicker walk five steps after kicking the ball. This will help to accentuate the follow through.)

The kick

It was necessary to leave the actual kick out of the form and to take it up in a separate discussion. *The kicker must lock his knee to get the snap and create the pendulum from the hip.*

If the kicker is slicing the ball the coach can show him where he is hitting the ball by putting some chalk on the toe of his shoe. After the kick the coach can examine the ball and show the kicker exactly where he is hitting the ball.

Some aids in developing a good place kicker

1. *Eliminate all preliminary movements before the kick.*
2. *Place kicker must always have the same movements and develop rhythm.*
3. *Never kick when the leg is tired.*
4. *Start to kick when the ball hits the holder's hands.*
5. *Kick a spot on the "T" and not the ball.*

The holder

The ball holder is important but not as important as is commonly insisted—if you have a good place kicker. With proper form the place kicker can kick any ball from the "T" through the goal post, regardless of who holds the ball.

The holder should line up seven yards from the line of scrimmage with both knees on the ground at about a 30-degree angle to the line of scrimmage. His hands should be outstretched in front of his chest to give the center a target. Do not let the holder give the target over the "T." This is an awkward and dangerous position to handle a snap that is not directly into his hands. The holder determines when the ball should be snapped. He should ask the kicker first if he is ready, then give a set signal for the offensive line.

Protection of the place kick

Protection for the place kick is passive blocking, for everyone on the line of scrimmage, including the two backs. Everyone is responsible for the area from his outside foot to the outside foot of the first man to his inside. This is commonly referred to as "cup protection," and any rush must come from the outside. (See Figure 152.)

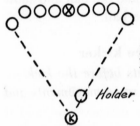

Fig. 152. Protection of the place kick. Everyone is responsible to the inside.

From end to end this protection can be best carried out by shifting the inside foot to a forward position and at the same time by broadening the base with the outside foot. A low crouch to make a low block will tend to lower the defensive charge. The offensive line should not know when the ball is going to be snapped. This will help keep them from being aggressive on their initial charge.

Protecting the extra point or field goal will be relatively a simple matter if no one is aggressive or leaves his initial zone. If someone does it will create a gap for the defensive men to penetrate. If the two outside backs will retain their base and force any rush *outside* of their position, the kick will be gotten off.

THE FIELD GOAL

The field goal, of course, is similar to the extra point. It is a valuable weapon and very often it is as good as a touchdown. If you have a good place kicker on the team, determine his range on field goals and keep this weapon in mind. Let the team know you are going to use it when the occasion presents itself.

Protection for the field goal is the same as for the extra point. The only difference is that the holder may have to vary his position slightly on bad kicking angles to insure kicking inside the protection. The kicker will adjust the angle of the "T" to the goal post.

THE KICK OFF

The kick off can easily be made into an offensive or defensive break. On most kick offs, try to return the ball to the 35-yard line. This will put you out of the danger zone, and if you don't make a first down you can surrender the ball to your opponents with a slight advantage in position.

The kick off is a long place kick with basically the same form. The kicker should back up five to ten yards to muster extra power and momentum. He can adjust his steps so as to run through the ball without slowing up.

Covering the kick off

Individual responsibilities

Put your fastest, best-tackling men at the ends of the line. (These will usually be backfield men.) Send them for the ball without any outside responsiblities.

Next in position should be your ends; they flare to the outside and are responsible for any sideline return. They usually have this type of responsibility on defense so you will tend to get better execution from this lineup.

The covering alignment of the rest of the personnel is not too important, but try to keep some sort of balance. Don't have all of your slow men on one side or your best tacklers on one side. Try to space them alternately.

The kicker covers, and the safety man remains on the 35-yard line and is exactly what the name implies. He should be the man who is your regular safety in your defensive set up.

Once you line up a set from end to end, keep it constant and be sure that any substitutes in the middle know their correct position. If you are sure an opponent is returning kick offs by numbering the kick off team you can occasionally let the third and fourth men cross and switch assignments. This may help to confuse blocking assignments.

Everyone except the kicker should line up on the 35-yard line and be turned facing the inside with the inside foot back. Wait for the kicker to reach the 35-yard line; when he is "under control" move ahead one step behind him. Watch him kick the ball, then cover.

No one should ever be off-side on the kick off, either covering or receiving. This is an unpardonable sin.

Kick off returns

Line up five men in the restraining zone at least two yards past the 40-yard line. Don't let them take a step back until the ball has been kicked to insure a legal formation. Switch the tackles and guards to give you a little more speed where it is needed on certain returns. The ends should normally be lined up around the 25-yard line about fifteen yards in from the sideline.

The *fullback* should be lined up in the middle of the field on about the 20-yard line.

The *halfbacks* should be lined up about fifteen yards from the sideline at about the 5-yard line.

The *safety man* should be lined up on the goal line. This gives you good position to field any bouncing ball or short kick. If a kicker is a consistently short kicker everyone should make adjustment by moving up accordingly. (See Figure 153.)

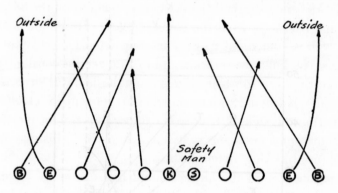

Fig. 153. Covering the kick off.

Side line return

A power sideline return with double blocks on the key men executed against a team of equal ability should carry to at least the 35-yard line. The return is not designed to go all the way.

Individual responsibility

The right sideline return is executed as follows (Figure 154). (A left sideline return would mean a reverse of the assignments.)

Number the kick off team by counting in from the right sideline.

The *left guard* and *left end* double-team a No. 4 man from the sideline.

The *left tackle* and *fullback* double-team the No. 3 man.

The *center* and *right tackle* double-team the No. 2 man and try to take him out.

The *right end* and *right guard* take the No. 1 man and block him out.

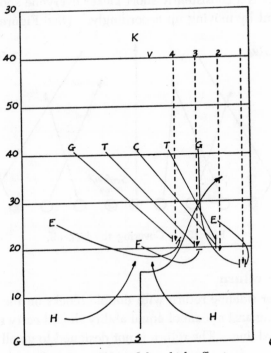

Fig. 154.   Right sideline kick off return.

The *left halfback* sprints to get ahead of the safety man and take the first man to show.

The *right halfback* swings inside and to the middle and is personal interference for the safety man.

The *safety man* should start up the middle first depending on the length of the kick then swing to the sideline between the No. 2 and No. 3 men on the kick off team.

In any return on any kick, timing of blocks is by far the most important thing. A well-timed poor block is better than a good block poorly timed.

Always make your team conscious of the distance and height in a kick.

Middle kick off return

First number three men from the kicker on each side, starting from the inside but ignoring the kicker. (See Figure 155.)

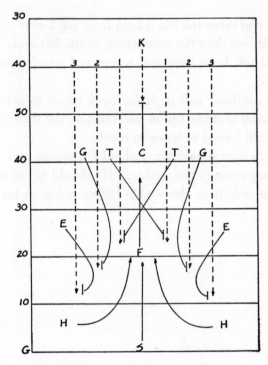

Fig. 155. Middle kick off return.

Individual responsibilities

The *left guard* takes the No. 2 man from the kicker on his side.

The *left tackle* takes the No. 1 man from the kicker on the opposite side.

The *center* takes the kicker. Give him the option either to go up quickly to take the kicker or to drop back and time his block with the rest of the team.

The *right tackle* takes the No. 1 man on the opposite side of the kicker.

The *right guard* takes the No. 2 man from the kicker on his side.

The *left end* takes the No. 3 man from the kicker on his side.

The *right end* does the same thing as the left end.

The *fullback* drops back and is personal interference for the safety man.

The *left halfback* and *right halfback* sprint to get ahead of the ball carrier and line up on the fullback; the three men form a wedge until forced to leave to block.

The *safety man* should stay behind the wedge and make the kick off team come to the wedge. He should get as much distance as possible from the wedge before going on his own.

11

Preparation and Game Organization

THE SUBJECT OF preparation and game organization is almost inexhaustible. It is well-recognized in the coaching profession that coaching is a year round job. Preparation is as necessary to successful coaching as weather is to the weatherman—i.e., there must be some of it every day.

As to organization: We believe we have reached a state in coaching in which there is little to choose between systems and coaching "philosophies." The big difference between teams is found in organization and preparation.

We sincerely believe that a coach must have good material *plus* good preparation and organization to win. We believe that a coach can have great material and poor preparation and organization and lose.

Selecting the staff

The success of any head coach depends to a large extent on his ability to select a good staff. It is good fortune indeed when the one responsible for the football program is given a free rein in the selection of his aides.

A good staff is not necessarily made up of individuals who are alike in every respect. We believe it is well to have men who are different in temperament, who are different somewhat in background, who are different in age. There is, perhaps, a place for the eternal optimist, balanced by one on the pessimistic side. There is a place for youth with new ideas and enthusiasm, to be counterbalanced with age, maturity, and experience.

A staff of "yes-men" is not desirable. New ideas, occasional differences of opinion, and constructive criticism should be encouraged. Certainly all this should take place in the staff meeting, for once decisions are made everybody should "come out of the huddle with the same signal."

One of the earmarks of a good head coach is his ability to take suggestions from his staff, and his ability to "bring, bind, and blend" them together into a workable program.

Loyalty, of course, is fundamental to the success of any coaching organization. The staff should win together and lose together. There should never be any "second guessing," either publicly or privately.

As for the qualifications of the individual member of the staff, we think there are two general qualities he must have: (1) We think he should have a genuine love for working with boys, and (2) He must have a genuine love for football. In addition to these qualities, each coach should be well-versed in the phase of the game he is coaching—and, in addition, he should be a good teacher. There are many great football players who do not do well coaching because they cannot teach. There are many average football players who make successful coaches because they have made the teaching adaptation.

Preparation for the season

Perhaps one of the most vital things a football coach (especially in high school) should do in preparing for the season is to visit the home of each boy who is to be on the squad. He should accomplish the following things by his visit: (1) Let the parents know of his interest in the boy not only athletically but in every respect, (2) Explain to the parent the necessity of their cooperation, in order to accomplish the most for the boy and the team, (3) Talk frankly with the parent regarding their son's ability (don't let them expect too much), (4) Talk with the parent regarding training rules, (5) Explain to the parent the necessity of each boy complying with regular squad rules of procedure, such as the importance of the squad traveling together on out of town trips (discussed later in this chapter), and (6) Observe the economic conditions of the home (there are a good many high school boys who fail to develop because they simply do not have enough to eat).

These visits will not only pay dividends in the won-and-lost column, but they will give the coach a backbone of support that will carry him through some lean seasons when his "fair weather" friends desert him.

A second important part of any preparation is to be sure that each boy has a medical examination. This is not only protection for the boy but also for the coach.

A good managerial system is a fine part of any football organization. Managers should be selected from the different grades in school, so that you always have one coming "on." They should be given team letters and coaches should respect them and have their boys respect them.

Spring training

The foundation of a successful football team is usually laid during spring training.

A coach should take full advantage of spring training for any experimentation he has in mind. It is a time for introduction of new defenses, new pass patterns, new formations, plus any new ideas of individual technique.

Changing personnel from one position to another should, if at all possible, be done during this period rather than during the regular season.

Spring training should be the time when the fundamentals are stressed to the "*n*th" degree. Blocking and tackling, which are the essence of a great football team, should have priority during spring training.

Phases of the game that require a great deal of individual instruction, and also have a certain injury risk that cannot be taken during the regular season, should be stressed during this period: place kicking, protecting the kicker, returning punts, returning kick offs, pass protection, and so on.

We feel that because of the objectives of spring training, it is necessarily a period of *contact*; thus, by its very nature it affords the coach an opportunity to see "who wants to play."

Blueprinting the season

The last days of August are usually "days of decision" for the "high command." It is necessary that allover season planning be "wrapped up" at this time. All movies, charts, and statistics of the previous season, and especially those compiled during spring training, should be studied. After careful deliberation, decisions should be rendered as to personnel.

After all the material has been evaluated, the staff should decide their basic offensive and defensive plans. All available material on the opposition should be gone over with a fine-tooth comb. It is a very good idea to assign individual staff members to make a "pictorial analysis" of the teams that are to be met during the season.

Arrangements should be made for "skull sessions" two or three times weekly during the season. (Some high schools arrange for these sessions to take place during the P.T. periods, home-room periods, etc.)

Finally, over-all practice plans for the season should be set up. Of course, this practice schedule should be flexible and should be set up with certain objectives for the season in mind, rather than immediate objectives. In other words, we think of this schedule as a "servant," not as a "master."

Early fall practice

We believe football teams are "made" during spring practice and early fall practice. We find that actually 50 per cent of our working time is gone after these two training periods have been concluded.

Early fall practice is given over primarily to conditioning, with some individual instruction included. After the fall work has been completed, about all the time remaining is needed for team work and polishing.

We usually have three weeks of work preceding our first game, and we work twice daily during the first ten days of the fall session. The morning work consumes about one and a half hours. The afternoon program lasts for about an hour and forty-five minutes.

We try to have two scrimmages weekly, on Wednesday and Saturday. The scrimmage on Saturday is under game conditions. After our fall training is concluded, we hold contact work to a minimum.

We like to do a great deal of our work in groups, and we feel if there are a sufficient number of coaches and adequate man-power that most can be accomplished if group work is done the first hour, and teamwork for the remaining time.

Because situations will vary so much it is impossible to present a schedule to fit every situation. We offer the following suggestions as to what should be covered in early season practice:

1. *Calisthenics.* Every boy should be sufficiently warmed-up before he goes into practice, and calisthenics should also be used for conditioning. We also believe in lots of running during this part of the training period, however, we feel that hard running should be done at the end of practice rather than the beginning, thereby getting better play execution before your men tire.

2. *Getting off on the ball.* This is fundamental to the success of any football team.

3. *Line blocking.* All phases: guards pulling, cross blocking, one-on-one drills, releasing, downfield, etc.

4. *Defensive play.* Against two-on-one, three-on-one, charging, looping, angling, rushing the passer, rushing the kicker, tackling.

5. *Offensive backfield play.* Taking the ball, watching the hole, faking, blocking for passes, backfield timing, open field blocking.

6. *Defensive backs.* Coming up on sweeps, covering pass receivers (linebackers and ends should be included in this drill), forming interference on intercepted passes, open field tackling.

7. *Offensive team work.* Getting off on ball, new plays, dummy scrimmage, pass patterns, kick protection, pass protection, regular scrimmage.

8. *Defensive team work.* Co-ordinated defense, shifting defense, dummy defense, thin line scrimmage, regular scrimmage.

9. *The kicking game.* Place kicking (extra points, field goals), kickoffs, returning kicks, covering kicks.

10. *Lecture sessions.* At least forty-five minutes per day should be given over to lecture sessions. Insist on each boy keeping a good notebook.

A typical week during the season
Sunday afternoon (a time convenient to coaches)

1. Review your game of the past weekend, discuss weakness, personnel changes. This should be done after movies, charts, and statistics are reviewed. In this connection, I think it is well to have your own team scouted once or twice early in the season. If movies are available, every player should be graded.

2. Review the file on the team coming up for the next game. If movies are available, they should be reviewed. (Note: It is well to take hometown newspapers of each team on the schedule.)

3. Have a scout go over his report on the opponent coming up. If he has scouted them several times he should have a complete "pictorial analysis" drawn up.

4. New defensive and offensive maneuvers should be decided upon.

5. Practice plans for week should be set up. Plans should be set up only in broad outline. It is important that each day's practice be reviewed *immediately* after the session ends so that the next day's practice schedule can be set up. We feel that it is advantageous to set up the schedule while the staff has "well in mind" the deficiencies noted during that day's practice.

Conditions vary so much we feel it impractical to set up a rigid schedule for every day of the week, but we feel that the items listed below should be stressed in addition to the regular routine practice.

Monday. If the game is played on Saturday, Monday should be a "light" day. Each player should be given a report on his past Saturday's performance. Overall plans for the contest coming up should be discussed with the squad. The scout should give the group a comprehensive report on the opponent of the week. If at all possible, each player should receive a mimeographed copy of the scout's report.

Tuesday. All new offensive and defensive techniques for the coming contest should be given to the squad. A lot of "dummy" scrimmage is probably in keeping at this time.

Wednesday. If any contact work is in order it probably should be done on Wednesday. All new offensive and defensive plays should be thoroughly checked.

Thursday. Polishing should be the order of the day. All details should be checked thoroughly. All men should be given written tests on their offensive and defensive assignments.

Friday. Short workout. Review new plays, go over the kicking game, go through kick off procedure, let place kicker practice a few kicks with entire team taking part. (All this work, of course, in "dummy.")

We might mention that every day we expect certain of our specialists (punters, place kickers, kick off men, passers, pass receivers) to report early.

The day of the game

If the game is to be played at home, we think it is important that the boys attend class. After leaving class we insist they stay off their feet.

We feel it is very important that they have their pre-game meal together. This is a very good time to give them their last minute instructions as to taping, etc.

We do not like our team to dress too early, since we feel the tension tends to wear them out. However, it is bad for a team to have to rush in order to complete their dressing in time.

1. Pre-game warm-up:

We like to be on the field for about a twenty-minute warm-up period. We think it is very important that the squad be well informed as to what should take place during this period. Unless it is well-organized, this particular period is a likely time for the players to suffer injuries from collision, etc.

We feel that it is very important that the specialist get well "warmed up." All players should go through the warm-up in full game equipment. After about twenty minutes on the field we return to the dressing room for final instructions, to check equipment, and to make last-minute decisions on kicking, receiving, etc.

2. *Aides during game:*

We feel that during the game the coaches should be at their best. Every decision is vital, and the smallest detail can have an effect on the final result.

We try to be so organized that we can give our boys every aid possible.

First, we like to have a "phone man" to give us instructions from the press box. He should be completely familiar with the offensive and defensive plans for the day. In the press box with him we like to have a chart man who keeps a chart on the offensive and defensive play of our team. These charts, samples of which are shown in Figures 156–159, are especially valuable for half-time use. They are good for a review of the game with the quarterbacks (defensive and offensive), and, of course, should become a part of the permanent file, to be referred to in preparing for the same opponent the following year.

Another type of chart which we feel is a good one to keep as the game progresses is shown in Figure 160. This chart can be kept by any individual who is familiar with the offense being used and who can check defenses.

We feel this chart is especially valuable in teaching quarterback strategy and also valuable in keeping up with the game as it progresses.

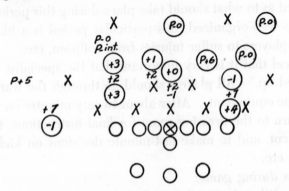

Fig. 156. Game chart, 5-4-2 defense. Explanation of symbols: −1 = run for one-yard loss; +2 = run for two-yard gain; P+5 = pass for five-yard gain; P-int. = pass intercepted; P-O = pass incomplete. A symbol in a circle indicates the play was run the first half.

3. Seating arrangement:

We like our men who are not in the game to be seated by positions. This, we feel, is very important for two reasons:

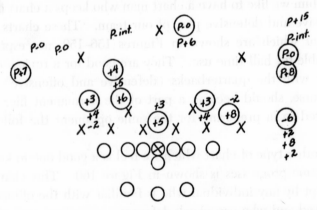

Fig. 157. Game chart, offense against 6-2-2-1 (loose 6) defense. (See Fig. 156 for explanation of symbols.)

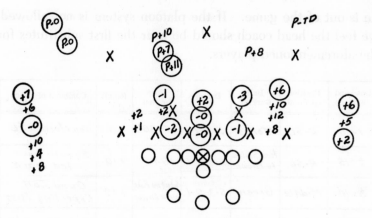

Fig. 158. Game chart, offense against 6-2-2-1 (loose 6). (See Fig. 156 for explanation of symbols.)

(1) It is much easier to find substitutes if they are seated in position groups, and (2) Men who are going in and out of the game can pass on information to their teammates. We usually like the head coach to sit near the offensive quarterback, when he is out of the game, and near the defensive quarterback, when

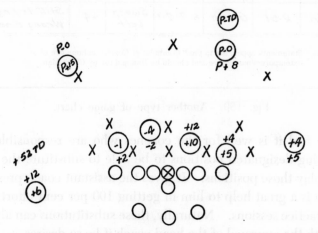

Fig. 159. Game chart, offense against 5-3-2-1. (See Fig. 156 for explanation of symbols.)

he is out of the game.   If the platoon system is not allowed, we feel the head coach should be near the first substitutes for the aforementioned players.

Down and Distance	Position on Field	Ball Carrier	Defense	Pass or Run	Result	Comment of Coach
1-10	R-SL	Jones	5-3-2-1	R-38	-5	Too close to SL
2-15	R-SL	Pass Smith to Brown	5-3-2-1	36 YS	+10	Should have led more
3-10	Middle	Green	5-3-2-1	Statue Fake with Draw	+12	Good Call Expecting Pass
1-10	Middle	Jones	5-4-2	28S	+6	OK
2-4	L-SL	Green	6-2-2-1	Sweep Left	-2	Poor Call Run inside End
3-6	L-SL	Green kicks	5-4-2	Quick-kick	55yds.	Good Call
1-10	Middle	Smith	6-2-2-1	QB Sneak	+7	Good Call Surprise Play
2-3	Middle	Pass Smith to Jones	5-3-2-1	P38	+5	Good Call Poor Run by Receiver
1-10	R-SL	Green	6-2-2-1	Sweep Left	-4	Still trying Wrong End

Note: Statements appearing in the "Comment of Coach" column are of an extemporaneous nature and should be listened for by Chart Man.

Fig. 160.   Another type of game chart.

We feel it is well for the coaches who are responsible for coaching designated positions to be able to substitute the men who play those positions.   It gives the assistant coach prestige, which is a great help to him in getting 100 per cent effort during practice sessions.   Naturally, these substitutions can always be with the approval of the head coach if he so desires.

4. Half-time:

These are twelve precious minutes. Of course, how they are used depends on the progress of the game. First, though, the boys should go directly to the dressing room. People not connected with the game should be kept out. Extreme exuberance or extreme pessimism should not be exhibited by the coach or players.

Players should be made comfortable (have their faces wiped by the managers), and comparative quiet should prevail during the first few minutes, during which the coaches may in a quiet manner seek information from key players and also study the charts. If the team is playing poorly the coach should bring that up in a firm manner during the first part of his talk. Then, strategy, blocking assignments, and overall planning for the second half should be gone over.

During the last two or three minutes, the squad should be encouraged, or, if the game has been easy, warned about overconfidence.

5. After the game:

The coach should talk with the boys after the game. The type of talk depends on how the team played, not necessarily on how the game came out.

The coach should check for injuries. If at all possible the team should eat or have refreshments together.

If the game is played out of town, the boys should ride home together. This is a *MUST*, we believe, for these reasons: (1) It is dangerous to have boys riding in a dozen automobiles after a game, (2) It keeps down "cliques," (3) It prevents boys from staying out late and perhaps breaking training, and (4) It builds team spirit.

Saturday

If the game takes place on Friday or Friday night, the coaches should hold a critique on Saturday at which weakness and strength should be noted. A complete game analysis should be made for next year's scout and for the permanent file. And then the game should be wrapped up, put away and forgotten (if the wolves will let you).

Now it is Sunday and the cycle starts again. Yet, some people wonder what coaches do!

12

The Coach and Public Relations

A FOOTBALL coach can master every technical trick of the trade. He can have outstanding material. He can have every modern physical facility. But he must also understand and practice good public relations principles if he wants to become a success in his chosen profession.

He must always be aware that he has off-the-field responsibilities—to his assistant coaches, to his players, to school officials and alumni, to boosters groups, to press, radio and television, and to the general public.

A successful coach must remember that he is an important citizen in his community, and he must be ready to live up to the responsibilities involved.

Relations with press, radio, television

A coach can do what he may think is a wonderful job (and the job may really be commendable from a technical standpoint), but he is still not a success until he becomes one in the eyes of the public. The best method of reaching the public is through newspapers, radio, and television. Here, then, is a good starting point for the coach's public relations program.

First of all a coach must devise some means of keeping his news sources supplied with information. They often do not have the staff to attend all his practices, to "dig up" information about his coming games, or perhaps even to attend all the contests.

A college coach should make room in his budget for a sports publicity man to handle press relations—on a full time basis if possible, or at least a part-time worker. The high school coach with no possibility of securing a publicity man for his team should find a capable and interested follower to take care of these duties. Usually this volunteer publicist will be repaid at least in part by the sources he furnishes with the news, like an urban correspondent for a metropolitan newspaper. If this does not work out the coach should keep the news sources posted himself.

The coach should always be friendly—sincerely friendly—when discussing his team with newsmen. He should put his cards on the table, good and bad, and not try to deceive newsmen into writing "poor-mouth" stories about his ball club in the hopes it will make him look better if he wins on Saturday. If the coach deals frankly and fairly with newsmen he will find they will be just as frank and fair with him.

The coach should always be available for interviews—but he must be careful not to say anything rash in defeat. He should never criticize assistants or players through news sources.

The coach must learn early in the game to take criticism in print or on the air from newsmen. If he feels he has been wronged in such criticism he should talk to the newsman calmly and quietly about it, explaining his position on the matter under discussion. He will find that when he takes this approach newsmen will listen and be fair. The coach should never try to "fight" newsmen in public because they can reach too many more people with very little effort.

Pictures should be taken of players and made available to newsmen, or they should be cooperated with when they desire to take pictures. In order not to interfere with practice sessions, it is usually good to set a time before practice to take such pictures.

Remember that when a newsman is covering ball games he is working, and wherever he is seated for the game is his "office" of the moment.

Here are some other things a coach can do at games to help his public relations with newsmen:

1. Provide newsmen with a place to sit down where they can get an unobstructed view of the game at all times, and where they can place their typewriters or microphones.

2. Provide them with "spotters" who will keep them informed on the players during the game. If there is a public address system for the press box, which can keep all informed, so much the better.

3. If there is not a publicity man to do so, arrange for some capable person to keep statistics on the game and furnish these to newsmen at halftime and at the end of the contest.

4. For the benefit of the fans, as well as the press, be sure the player jersey numbers listed in programs are in numerical

order and are correct.   Have these checked just before game time and notify both public and press of any changes.

5. Provide refreshments for newsmen at halftime whenever possible.

6. Keep everyone out of the press box, radio and television booths, except bonafide workers.

The newsman working in sports is usually doing so because he loves it just as the coach does.   Give him cooperation and he will repay in kind.

Relations with the public

Football is one of the greatest spectator sports in the United States today, and the coach can make it the greatest in his community by good public relations with the public.

Of course, it always helps to have a winning football team, but everyone cannot win all the time.   The coach can assure continued support of his team by looking out for the comforts of fans, and by dealing fairly with them in every way.

The coach should make it a rule never to show favortism to any one outside group.   He should put tickets on sale on a first-come-first-served basis, after the alumni have been taken care of (the alumni are considered "in the family" and not an outside group).

There should be efficient policing of the stands at all games. There should be ushers to show fans to their seats.   There should be clean and adequate toilet facilities.   There should be well-located concession stands dispensing food, soft drinks, coffee, pennants, cushions, and other such things the fans might find need of after arriving at the game.   There should be accurate programs for sale at a moderate price.   A public address system should be installed and properly manned with a well-trained person who is careful to announce only the bare essentials necessary to keep the fans informed on the progress of the game. There should be enough entrance gates manned with ticket sellers and takers to keep the traffic flowing before the game, and plenty of exits to clear out the stands afterwards.

Relations with school officials and faculty

The coach should realize from the beginning that his work is with just one segment of the complete school program. Football is recognized more and more as an important factor in the well-rounded education of a young man, but the basic purpose of the school's existence is still the classroom. Keeping this in mind at all times, the coach should do everything within reason to be cooperative at all times with school officials and with the faculty of his school.

The coach will soon find that his thinking and his expressed beliefs will have great influence over the boys he is working with—often a greater influence than the boy's own parents. Use of this influence to encourage the boys to attend classes regularly, to study their lessons and cooperate with their teachers, is sure to put the faculty in the right frame of mind to act with sympathy when the coach's problems are put before them.

Every coach is in the "limelight" in his own town at least, and therefore usually has more opportunities than anyone connected with his school to meet the public. The coach should take advantage of such opportunities to "sell" the complete program of his school and thus cooperate with school authorities in advancement of school projects.

Actually the coach, the school officials, and the faculty are all working toward the same goal—advancement of the school in every way possible. Each have separate but related duties to perform toward that goal. Mutual recognition and respect of the problems involved, and assistance to each other whenever possible, is sure to benefit all concerned.

Relations with the players

Of course every coach realizes the necessity of good "public relations" with his own players. He must learn early in the profession to find that delicately balanced position with the boys in which they feel personally close to him without familiarity, and that enables them to look up to him with loyalty and respect.

The coach should be extremely careful not to let personal likes or dislikes sway his judgment of an individual as a player.

The coach should be careful of promises made to his players, because it is essential that all such promises be fulfilled. The players must never be allowed to feel that the coach has in any way let them down.

The coach must be sure not to have any obvious favorites on the squad; it is always detrimental to allow individuals or groups special privileges. Each player must feel the coach is unbiased and is just as interested in his development as the next fellow's.

Probably the most important public relations principle to be followed in dealing with boys is one that holds true in every walk of life. With exceptions for special cases, the coach should not criticize a player before his teammates. Whenever possible, the place to administer criticism is in the coach's office with the door closed.

The coach should encourage his players to consult him in any problems they might have, he should make himself easy to reach for such consultations, he should listen with interest and respect to even the most seemingly trivial of complaints, and he should strive always to be helpful and understanding.

The coach who genuinely loves boys and loves working with boys will usually be loved by them in return. The coach who does not love working with boys should not be coaching.

Relations with alumni and "booster" groups

The coach will find that alumni associations and other "booster" groups are usually the school's most loyal followers —but because of their high feelings they can also be the severest critics. He must find ways to channel the enthusiasms and loyalties of such groups to the proper paths where they will be most beneficial. The groups should be made aware of the line between helpfulness and interference.

The coach will find that most of the demands on him by such groups are those that he can and should readily fill. They will want him to attend meetings now and then, and to speak before them. The coach can help keep their enthusiasm bubbling by loaning them game movies. They will ask the coach for needs of the squad that they may tackle as club projects. Cooperation by the coach is the key here, as it is in most phases of public relations with groups or individuals.

Relations with the staff

A coach should strive to gain the respect and confidence of members of his own staff.

First of all, he should *encourage* suggestions from staff members. Each suggestion then received should be treated with respect, its merits carefully weighed, and, if it is rejected, the originator of the idea told why it will not fit in with the plans.

Although the head coach must be the boss while in his working clothes, he should be just "one of the boys" at all other times. The basis of his relations with his assistants on or off the field should be mutual respect and confidence.

Relations with other coaches

It is important to a coach's advancement in his profession for him to be cooperative with coaches of the other sports at his school. He must never forget that their objective is the same as his own—to succeed for themselves and the school. During off-season the football coach will be able to find many ways in which he can be helpful to the other school coaches, and he will find it will pay off in loyalties thus gained.

The successful coach also does everything within reason to insure good public relations with coaches of other schools. Pleasantness in dealing with coaches of other schools will always reflect to advantage when such problems as schedule changes come up. The older and more experienced coaches should always make it a practice to be helpful to the young men in the profession.

13

Scouting

SCOUTING is the act of accumulating advance
information on your opponents. The job of scouting is just
as important a part of coaching as the work done on the field
during the week. It is absolutely essential that the report of
the scout be correct through-and-through.

The calibre of your scouting will be reflected on the score-
board during the ball game. The scout report provides the
ground work for both offensive and defensive strategy of the
game.

The purpose of scouting is summarized in these words by
Lynn Waldorf:

> *How can we win?*
> *Where can we gain?*
> *What must we stop?*

Qualifications

A scout should possess a sound and thorough knowledge of football fundamentals and formations.   He must be a keen student of the game.   He must be able to discern the slightest variances in both offensive and defensive standards.   He must evaluate quickly the opposition—as individuals *and* as a team. He is cognizant of all formations, maneuvers, and stratagems. He is at all times an enthusiastic worker.   He records all information.   He trusts nothing to memory.

Pre-game preparation

It is a good idea to complete your scouting schedule during the summer months.   Then your coaches will know well in advance the teams they are to scout.   If feasible, arrange the scouting schedule to have two members of the coaching staff at every game scouted.   They should work as a team.

Try to schedule two scoutings of the opposition before you are to play them.   It is best to cover them in the two games immediately preceding your game.   The only deviation from this rule would come about if your opponent scheduled a "breather" (against a weak team) in one of those two games. The overall thought here is to scout your opponents twice, see them in two tough ball games, and to be as current as possible in your scout report.

Before leaving town the scouts will review all available information on the team they are to see.   This will include movies, scout reports, and newspaper accounts.

The scouts should arrive at the stadium at least an hour before game time.   They should have already memorized the names, numbers, and positions of the first twenty-two men and specialists.   (In platoon football this would be offensive and defensive elevens plus specialists.)   They are well supplied

with notebooks, mimeographed forms, and pencils to use before and during the game.

Warm-up

The scouts go to work when the teams come on the field for
their warm-up.

They check and record names and numbers of all types of
kickers: punters, kickoff men, extra point, and field goal kickers.
Particular attention is given to the punters: their distance from
the center, steps taken in kicking, the time in getting the kick
off, and the distance and height of their kick. Special attention is given to any quick kick warm-up.

Notes are taken on the passers. Their speed in getting set
and their types of throws are recorded. We classify as *specialists* all backs who throw beside the regular passers. (We consider quarterbacks and tailbacks as "regular" passers.)

From the sidelines one of the scouts picks up their snap
count and most popular count. Timing of the quarterback in
approaching the center and beginning his snap count is especially noted. This, along with the snap count, is important if
you shift your defenses.

The game

The two scouts work as a team during the game. One observes the offense while the other does the writing. Then on
defense the procedure is reversed: the scout that was writing
observes and his partner takes over the writing chores. Of
course, either scout, when writing, is employed as an observer
as much as his time permits.

We chart every offensive play that the team runs. We use
a mimeographed form. Holes are punched in the margin to
enable us to carry the forms in a loose leaf notebook. At the
top of the page we have blanks to indicate the quarter and di-

rection of the goal for that quarter.   Immediately under these two blanks is a horizontal line calibrated in five yard units. We use a perpendicular line through the calibrated line to indicate the position of the ball as to yard lines on the field.   A blank is provided for the downs and one for the distance to go for a first down.

To the right, spaces are provided for substitutions made between plays.   If the play that the team runs is exactly like one we have in our attack, we merely record the number of the play at the bottom of the page.   Also recorded is the gain or loss on the play, which we indicate by a plus or minus sign.

If the play run is different from any in our attack, we draw in the backfield fake and line blocking.   In case a pass is thrown, we utilize the halfbacks and safety man in our diagram to draw in the pass routes correctly.   The backfield fake is also recorded on the pass plays.   The number of the ball carrier on a running play and the numbers of the passer and receiver are recorded on a pass play.   A vertical line on the right or left margin indicates the play was run from a hash mark. No vertical lines on either side indicate the play was run from the middle of the field.   We devote one page to each offensive play.   (See Figure 161.)

We also use a mimeographed form to chart their defensive alignment on every play of the ball game.   On this form we record only the number of linemen on the line of scrimmage and the number of linebackers.   In a separate notebook we diagram their team defenses, stressing linemen's charge and team adjustments to flankers and spread ends.   We also fill in their pass coverage for each defense.   (See Figure 162.)

We have six headings on our defensive form.   We record defenses under the heading that the down and distance indicate.   The headings are:

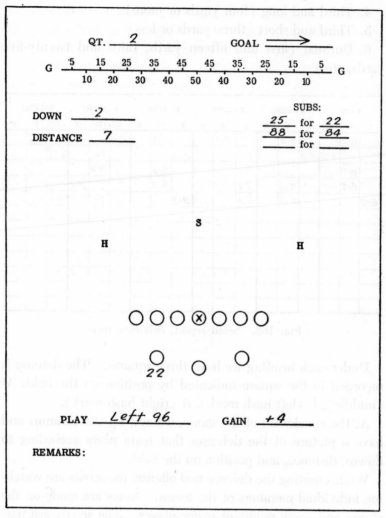

Fig. 161. Scout report, offensive game.

1. First and ten
2. Second and long (six yards or more)
3. Second and short (five yards or less)

4. Third and long (four yards or more)

5. Third and short (three yards or less)

6. Unusual (first and fifteen yards, third and twenty-five yards, etc.)

1 - 10			2 - LONG			2 - SHORT			3 - LONG			3 - SHORT			UNUSUAL		
L	M	R	L	M	R	L	M	R	L	M	R	L	M	R	L	M	R
	6-2			5-3			7-1			5-3		7-1				1-15 5-3	
		6-2	5-3				7-1		5-3				7-1			3-25 5-3	
	6-2				5-3	7-1				5-3			7-1			1-5 7-1	
	6-2			5-3		7-1				5-3				7-1			
6-2				5-3		7-1				5-3			7-1				

Fig. 162.   Scout report, defensive form.

Under each heading we have three squares. The defense is recorded in the square indicated by position on the field: *M* (middle), *L* (left hash mark), *R* (right hash mark).

At the conclusion of the game, we add up the columns and have a picture of the defenses that team plays according to downs, distance, and position on the field.

While charting the defense and offense, the scouts are watching individual members of the teams. Notes are made on the strong and weak points of every player. The scouts are particularly watchful for any tip-offs on plays.

During the game, diagrams or notes are kept on punt and kickoff returns, punt and kickoff coverage, pass defense, and miscellaneous topics.

Post-game organization

As soon as possible after the game the scouts organize their forms and notes.   If they are to see the same team again they will consolidate their information as quickly as possible after that game.

The scouts should meet with the coaching staff as early as possible to go over the strategy for the coming game.   The scouts make their recommendations for the game and answer questions about the opposition.

The scouts make up a report for the players.   In this report they include lineups, notes on personnel, random notes, favorite running plays, favorite pass routes and a breakdown of the opponents' offense.   This offensive breakdown shows favorite plays from all different formations.

On white cardboard squares the scouts draw up running and pass plays of the opponents, which either a "B" team or freshman team can run against the varsity.

If possible, the scouts should attend the ball game to aid the head coach.   They both will be of greater assistance if they station themselves up top on the telephone instead of sitting on the bench.   In the press box or high in the reserved section, the scouts will be viewing the opponents from the same angle they had scouted them.   From their vantage point they can offer helpful suggestions.   After the game, the scouts should check themselves for reliability in their scout report.

The scout report, play cards, and all other data should be filed away for future reference.

Scout report

The following scout report is for the coaches' use only.   If given in part to the players, it is done on the field orally.

SCOUT REPORT

(1) SNAP COUNT
    Popular Count
    Pre-Shift
(2) SPECIALISTS
    Punter
    Extra Points
    Kickoff Man
    Punt Returners
    Kickoff Returners
    Favorite Receiver
    Best Runner
(3) PUNT RETURN: KICKOFF RETURN
(4) PASS DEFENSE
    Man-for-man or Zone
    Revolve with flanker—Counter flanker—End spread
    Personnel
(5) ALIGNMENT OF BACKS: LINE SPLITS
(6) SCORING PLAYS INSIDE 10-YD. LINE
(7) PLAYS INSIDE OWN 20-YD. LINE
(8) TIPS
    Personnel
    Position

Personnel

The first two teams and specialists are listed according to position, number, name, height, and weight. Each individual's characteristics are summed up as concisely as possible, preferably in one or two sentences.

Pass routes

Mimeographed pass routes of your opponent are indicated. Favorites are pointed out. Ends' routes and backfield maneuvers are shown for each route.

Running plays

Mimeographed running plays of your opponent are included. Only the running plays that differ from those of your attack are drawn up. Plays that are the same as yours need not be drawn up.

Offensive breakdown

The offensive breakdown is a composite of all running plays from all formations used by your opponent. This information is obtained from your charts of his offense. If your opponent runs a number of formations such as the single wing, box, and "T," we will show all the plays run from each formation. If your opponent runs only the "T," we will show all plays run from the "T" as well as flanker formations of the "T."

The plays are drawn up in a vertical line or series over the offensive hole in which they are run. Use your own numbering system for these plays. (For plays not in your attack, consult the sheet of running plays for line blocking and backfield faking under the number that you have given the play on the breakdown.) Under each formation we list the favorite plays.

For example, Figure 163 shows plays lined up according to the hole in which they are run.

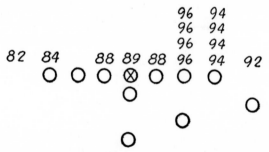

Fig. 163. Scout report. Plays lined up according to the hole in which they are run.

Random notes

In general notes on your opponent, include any information not previously written into your scout report. Use this heading if you wish to inject a note of the psychology you think might be used against your opponent.

Actuating the scout report

With the distribution of all paper work to the coaches and squad, the scout report is "put into action." Now the purpose of all this work becomes apparent.

The coaches study the overall picture of the opponent's offense and defense. They attempt to counter his strong points and exploit his weak points.

All players who figure in the pass defense study the mimeographed pass routes noting the backfield fakes.

All players in the rushing defense study the mimeographed running plays as well as the offensive breakdown. This enables them to know not only the plays from different formations that will be run at them but the blocking as well.

The "B" team or freshman team will run the opponent's passes and running plays against the varsity during the week. They use the play cards drawn up by the scouts.

14

Training

E VERY school participating in athletics should have some arrangement for having injuries cared for. The desirable situation is to have a competant, full-time trainer with the team at all times, and a physician who is available in case he is needed. Most colleges have trainers and doctors, but it is understood that often for many reasons high schools have to have a student or a coach do the training duties.

This chapter, therefore, is directed primarily to the schools below the college level that do most of their training without a full-time, experienced trainer. Some individual must care for the athletic injuries and be responsible for the care and treatment of injuries. This person should be an assistant coach or a student manager with some sort of basic training. This chapter will present, for the unexperienced trainer, the basic things he should know in order to run a training room for any institution.

Duties of the trainer

1. Supervise room or area set aside for treatment of injuries, seeing that the room and equipment is kept clean and that the supplies are adequate.

2. Prevention of injuries by equipping players properly and by use of necessary strapping, padding, and bandaging.

3. First aid and administering of medicine under the supervision of a doctor.

4. Operation of therapeutic devices.

5. Act as contact between players and coaches.

Team physician

No coach or trainer should have people participating under him in any sport without provision for quick medical care and medical advice on all athletic injuries not receiving emergency treatment.

The doctor you employ should have an adequate knowledge of athletic injuries. It is also very desirable that he has played football during his college career in order to be more familiar with the game and the types of injuries occurring.

The trainer should report to the team physician on all injuries and have a decision made by the physician as to the procedure to be taken. If the injury requires the services of a medical specialist, the team physician will know who the proper doctor is that should be consulted.

Your team physician should be interested in your sports program and be willing to come to your aid at a moment's notice. He should attend every game, and practice sessions if possible. If he is not able to be in attendance at all times, it is desired that his offices be close enough so that he can help when needed.

The coach or trainer is accepting too much responsibility

when he does not have a doctor on hand at all times. The coach's problems are numerous enough without having the dread of injuries occurring without prompt, proper medical attention.

Training room

Type of training room desired

1. Your training room should be close to your dressing area and shower room.

2. The room should be large enough for the necessary equipment and large enough to take care of the size squad you anticipate.

3. The lighting should be good. The ideal situation is natural light during the daylight hours.

4. Good ventilation and temperature control are necessary.

5. The room should be so constructed as to facilitate cleaning. Numerous floor drains in a concrete floor make it easy to mop and disinfect frequently.

6. There should be an area walled off in which to locate your tubs, baths, ice boxes, and hydrotherapy machines. This keeps the water from flowing or being tracked over your work area.

7. All equipment and room walls should be of a color (usually white) that dirt can be easily detected upon. When dirt is detected it should be cleaned off immediately.

Training room equipment

1. *Hot water.* A centrally located sink with hot and cold connections should be in such a position that work can be done on the training tables without too much walking. Hot water connections should be available for what hydrotherapy machines you may have. Hot and cold water connections must be available for foot and ankle tubs or hand basins. If

possible, have a seven-foot bathtub with hot and cold water connections.

2. *Towels.* Towels are necessary to apply hot applications and treatment.

3. *Tables.* Tables are used for taping purposes and treatment of all injuries. Have as many tables as space will permit. The dimensions of these tables should be 6 feet 6 inches long, 26 inches wide, and 30 inches high. Tables should be constructed of heavy material to support weight firmly and should be covered with a plaster or leatherette material to facilitate cleaning.

4. *Cabinets.* Lockable storage cabinets for your medicines and medical supplies should have a large storage space for bulk items; there should be at the bottom a work shelf 36 inches from the floor, the upper part containing medicines and instruments for treatment.

5. *Electrical devices.* Schools on high school level are unable to invest large portions of their budget in electrical equipment for the training room, but the following are recommended: Infra-red heat lamps, Medcolator, and Diatherapy.

6. *Hydrotherapy machines.* Whirlpools are expensive items and high schools usually cannot afford them, but there are several practical whirlpools that you can afford costing less than $500.00. If the money is available, these are the quickest, most practical of the mechanical treatment devices in the average training room.

7. *Ice box.* There should be an ice box or refrigerator for storage of ice for treatment purposes; it should be lockable if possible.

8. *Foot bench.* We require all of our athletes to paint their feet with a skin toughener before each practice for the first ten days of practice. Provide a bench with a powder box and containers with paint brushes to do the painting. This foot paint bench will save you many hours of work on blisters.

9. *Stools and benches.* Benches should be placed in the Training Room for waiting athletes. Stools are needed in conjunction with some treatments.

The above equipment constitutes the bare essentials in a training room. Other devices that may aid you in the treatment and care of injuries should be added as your budget permits.

Training room supplies and their use

1. *Methialate or Nitrotan*—for painting and cleaning abrasions, scratches and insides of blisters and superficial cuts.

2. *Benzoin or "Tufskin" (Cramer)*—for painting feet for the prevention of blisters.

3. *Talcum and corn starch*—a half-and-half mixture to use on feet after painting with Tufskin or Benzoin.

4. *Boric acid solution*—one teaspoon to a pint of water; for an eye wash used with eye cup.

5. *Surgical soap, Phisodern, alcohol, peroxide, S-T 37.* These are used in training room for cleaning out wounds. The type of wound and the ability of the boy to stand the pain of burning will help to guide you in which to use.

6. *Furacin soluble dressing*—to be used on boils, abrasions, and open wounds that have had an unusual amount of dirt in them, to prevent infection.

7. *Athlete ointment and sulfa thiozaint*—used on abrasions and open wounds where pressure of the bandage might cause the bandage to stick to the wound.

8. *Burn ointment*—used on sunburned necks and legs and other parts of the body that have been exposed to heat.

9. *Athlete's foot ointment and liquids*—for treatment of fungus infection. Many standard brands are satisfactory.

10. *Rub-down liniment.* We use a patent medicine in conjunction with a baby oil.

11. *Liquid soap*—used to give athletes rub downs the morn-

ing after a ball game. The athletes first soap in tubs of hot water for five minutes before rub downs.

12. *Salt tablets.* During hot weather athletes should take two tablets after each practice.

13. *Aspirin*—the only medicine we have in our training room for headaches. Given after concussions.

14. *Dextrose*—given to boys any time they desire in one or two tablet doses; made available at halftime to all who like to take them.

15. *Laxative tablets*—to be dispensed on the advice of the physician.

16. *Antihistamine and cold tablets.* Antihistamine tablets will help prevent certain colds or reduce the severity of the infection. Cold tablets will help relieve the discomfort of the cold to a certain extent but there is no cure for a cold at the present time.

17. *Sodium bicarbonate*—bought in tablet form and given in doses of one or two tablets for acid stomach.

18. *Sulfa diazine tablets*—given on the prescription of a physician.

19. *Emetics and anti-acids*—medicines for food poisoning and upset stomach, to be prescribed by the physician.

20. *Nose and throat spray*—dispensed with atomizer to boys who have congestion of throat and nose.

Bandages and instruments

1. *Adhesive tape.* We buy tape cut in one-inch, one and a half inch width and two-inch widths. Ninety-five per cent of all of our tape is the one and a half inch cut.

2. *Sterile gauze bandage*—in pads of two-by-two and three-by-three inches. For dressing open wounds, abrasions and cuts, boils, etc.

3. *Non-sterile gauze bandage*—two-inches wide, ten-yards

long; used as covering for ankles, hands, etc. before tape is applied.

4. *Sterile cotton*—for application of antiseptics to wounds.

5. *Lee cotton*—non-sterile cotton used for applying analgesic packs.

6. *Cotton tips*—for applying liquid antiseptics.

7. *Tongue depresser*—for applying ointments and creams to bandages and affected areas.

8. *Scissors.* Bandage scissors, five and one-half inch; four and a half inch small curved surgical scissors; four-inch straight surgical scissors.

9. *Eye droppers.*

10. *Nail clippers.*

11. *Tweezers.*

12. *Adjustable knife handle and blades.*

13. *Ankle wraps.* Ankle wraps are used to help prevent ankle injuries. All boys are required to wear ankle wraps if their ankles are not being taped. The ankle wrap is put on over the socks in a figure eight or heel-lock style wrap.

14. *"Band Aids" and plastic band aids, flesh colored.*

15. *Sterile gauze bandage*—two inches wide for bandaging areas not covered by pads.

16. *Elastic bandages*—bought in two, three, four, six and eight-inch widths for applying pressure to injured areas or for application of hot packs.

17. *Elastic adhesive bandage*—two and three inches wide for taping of knees, wrists, and other areas where applicable.

Training room rules and procedures

Players should know the following rules and procedures:

1. No dressing or undressing in the training room.

2. Players stay out of training room unless they have specific business there.

3. No "roughhouse" or "horseplay" can be tolerated. Serious injuries have resulted from such activity.

4. Shower before coming into training room for treatment of minor cuts and skinned places.

5. No profanity is allowed.

6. No player is to operate training room equipment.

7. No player is allowed to have ice or ice water from the training room after a workout.

8. Help keep dressing room and training room clean. Place all trash in containers.

9. Do not ever try to treat any type of injury yourself.

10. You will be treated in the order that you appear. Await turn on benches provided.

11. Report every injury or blister, no matter how trivial it may seem to you.

15

Treatment of Common Athletic Injuries

IN DISCUSSING the most common injuries occurring in football we will start by defining types of injuries and their causes.

The *contusion* is probably the most frequent injury of all in contact sports since some tissue is susceptible to bruise on the slightest contact. The definition of contusion is *the bruising of a muscle, joint, or viscera by an external force.* The contusion is more commonly known as the "charley horse."

The *sprain* is also very common in contact sports, due to the tremendous twisting forces that the joints must endure. We define a sprain as *a partial or complete tear or stretching of one or more ligaments about a joint.* This also is accompanied by tearing of other tissue in the joint.

323

The *muscle strain* in athletes is produced by muscular contraction and is a result of inco-ordinate reaction and unbalance of protagonist and antagonist muscle groups. These are commonly called "pulled muscles" and can occur at the attachment of the muscle to the tendon or in the belly of the muscle. The degree of tear can vary from a few fibers to a complete severance.

In the three types of injuries explained above the pathology may be described in four stages. The first stage is *the actual occurrence of the injury,* with a hemorrhage being emitted internally. The second stage is *the formation of the hematoma.* The next stage is *the absorption of the hematoma.* The fourth stage is *the healing of the injury by fibroblastic proliferation.*

In addition to the above injuries, we also have frequent fractures and dislocations. The coach should be able to recognize these immediately and have the team physician reduce and prescribe treatment. This type of injury should never be tampered with by the trainer or coach and only first aid should be administered in order to transport the athlete to where the doctor may administer treatment.

We will now discuss the areas of the body that are frequently injured and list in chronological order the exact steps that are taken from the time the injury occurs until the player is able to participate once more.

Knee

Sprain or contused

1. Immediately after the knee has been examined by you and your team physician and the type of injury has been diagnosed, the affected area is strapped with an elastic bandage snugly, and crushed ice is packed around the knee and left on

for a period of thirty to forty-five minutes. This ice is placed in a towel and completely encircles the injured knee.

2. After the icing, a dry elastic bandage is placed on the knee, the athlete is issued crutches, if necessary, and the knee is X-rayed for the possibility of bone fracture.

3. The elastic support is left on the knee (to minimize the amount of swelling) for a period of twenty-four to thirty-six hours. The time will vary as to when additional treatment is started with the amount of swelling occurring during this period.

4. Heat treatments are started as the next step in the treatment process. This heat can be applied with hot towels or by the use of a hot water whirlpool. After each hot water treatment we apply analgesic balm packs. Massage is not used on the knee area for about four days; however, massage may be used on the other parts of the limb to stimulate circulation and to aid healing during this time.

5. Twenty-four hours after the injury occurs, the player should start exercises designed to maintain the tone of the muscles in the quardracep group. This can be done without bending the knee.

6. When the boy has recuperated to the point he can perform some of his duties, the knee is strapped as shown in Illustration III. He is tested as to what he can actually do by the trainer before he is allowed to take part in any activity on the practice field. The recuperation period for a slightly sprained knee in our experience has been from two to four weeks. The recuperation period for a badly sprained knee, involving serious damage to ligaments and cartilage tissue, usually requires from four to six weeks and then the athlete may not be able to compete without surgical repair.

Ankle

Sprains

1. Elastic bandage is placed on the ankle immediately and the affected area is encircled with crushed ice in a towel or is immersed in an ice bath for twenty to thirty minutes.

2. The player is then issued crutches to be used in case there is a fracture of the bone, and he is X-rayed immediately. If there is no fracture we would rather he walk on the ankle if the pain is not such that it prevents him from doing so.

3. For twenty-four to thirty-six hours an elastic bandage is kept on the affected area to minimize additional swelling. We also ice the ankle again during this time, if the amount of swelling indicates more cold applications advisable.

4. Heat treatments, consisting of the use of hot towels or a hot whirlpool bath, are begun after the twenty-four to thirty-six hour period. Massage is started after three days.

5. The athlete should have his ankle strapped as shown in Illustration II as soon as he is able to report back to practice field. He should be very diligent in keeping himself in good condition although he is unable to do much running.

Shoulders

Separation of acro-clavicular joint

1. Ice the area with crushed ice for thirty to forty-five minutes immediately after the injury occurs.

2. Strap the shoulder as shown in Illustration IV and X-ray the part for possible bone fracture and also to determine the extent of the separation. To show the extent of the separation X-rays must be taken of both shoulders.

3. Strapping is very important in this injury during the con-

valescent period. The clavical must be held in its normal position in relation to the acriom so that in healing the joint will not have excessive space between these two bones. The shoulder is strapped for a period of seven to fourteen days depending on the severity of the injury and progress of healing.

4. Heat with hot towels, diathermy, heat lamps, or any other method you have at your disposal may be started after twenty-four hours. Replace the strapping after each treatment. Massage of the arm and shoulder muscles may be started with the initial heat treatment.

Dislocations

1. Reduction of dislocations is a very much discussed item among trainers and we are of the opinion that unless reduction can be accomplished by simple manipulation the trainer should not attempt to place the joint back in place. A doctor should be consulted immediately.

2. Steps of treatment and rehabilitation in this injury are the same as those discussed in the explanation of the acro-clavicular joint.

Head injuries

1. Procedure on the field when the injury occurs is very important because the trainer or coach at this time has to decide how badly the boy has been injured. A simple rule to follow in the case of a concussion of any type is to *never move the boy without the aid of a physician until he has regained consciousness to the point where he can walk from the field without aid or support. Never hurry.* An athlete's life may be at stake and you must be *certain* that the boy is not injured seriously enough to cause permanent or fatal injury if he is moved.

2. When the player is on the side line, even though he seems to be conscious and coherent, the team physician should make

as thorough an examination as he can on the field at this time.

3. We recommend overnight hospitalization for observation for any boy who has been shaken up by a blow on his head enough to cause him to be out, even if he is unconscious only for a short time.

4. *Never let a player return to the game or compete in subsequent practices until he has completely recovered from a blow on the head.* This can be ascertained by examination by your team physician in most cases; however, the athlete in his eagerness to compete will sometimes neglect to tell you of the effects he is having from the injury; therefore, you must impress upon him the great importance of his telling you the truth about how he feels. A second blow to the head during the period of recuperation may cause very serious damage ending his athletic career. Be sure he is well before he competes.

"Charley horse"

Contusion to fleshy part of quardracep muscles of thigh is common. All contused muscles are treated in the manner discussed below. The quardracep group receives a large number of injuries of this type; therefore, it can be discussed as an example of the typical "charley horse."

1. The contusion muscle is immediately bound firmly with an elastic bandage to control hemorrhage, and the player is asked to take a full knee bend position in order to tighten the muscle fibers in the thigh and also to prevent hemorrhage. He holds this full knee bend position for several minutes then he is sent to the training quarters and crushed ice is packed around the leg and left for thirty to forty-five minutes.

2. An elastic bandage is placed on the injured part firmly and is worn for a twenty-four to thirty-six hour period according to the severity of the blow.

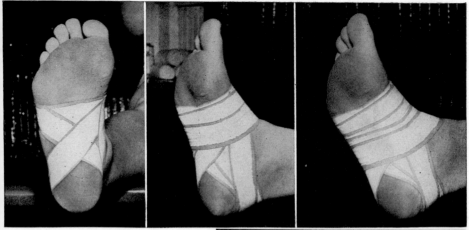

ILLUSTRATION I. Taping to support muscles and ligaments of the great arch of the foot. Two types are shown, the injury determining which type should be used. Injured man should sit on a table, foot extended over edge and at right angle to lower leg. (Top left) Place anchor just posterior to ball of foot, using 1½″ tape. Begin taping on outside of sole; pass diagonally across inner side of main arch, around heel, and tie onto anchor on outside of foot. (Center) Second piece starts on the inside of the arch, passes diagonally across the first strip, around heel, and ties onto anchor on inside of foot. (Top right) Additional support is added by three or four strips of tape around arch, beginning at anchor and overlapping ¾″ to the rear. (Lower right) Taping of an arch for which more pressure is needed to provide comfort. Tape is started on inside of lower leg, passed across front of ankle and pulled up snugly on inner arch, then tied to outside of lower leg. This is repeated four or five times, each successive piece overlapping ¾″.

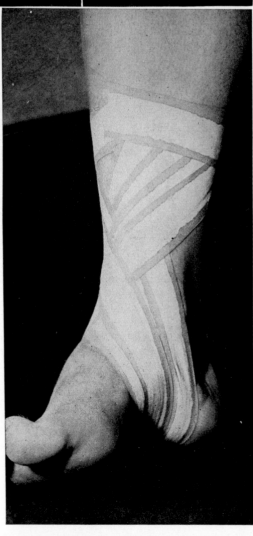

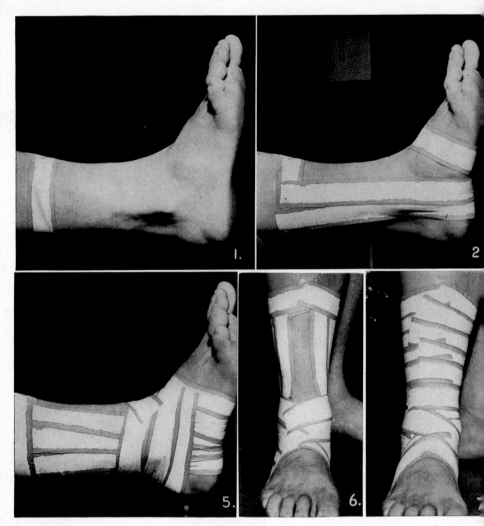

ILLUSTRATION II. Ankle strapping: general support for strained ligaments. Injured man should sit on a table, with foot extended over edge in
natural position, as if standing straight on floor. Use 1½" tape. (1) Place anchor
strip as high above ankle as possible without affecting contraction of gastrocnemius.
(2) Strip also around arch of foot. Starting at anchor on inside of ankle, run
stirrup piece under heel and outside ankle behind the malleolus. Start second
strip anterior to first strip on inside anchor. Tape under heel and across malleolus
anterior to first piece. (3) If the man has a large leg, use another stirrup piece
for additional support. (4) Put a figure eight horizontally across the malleolus.
(5, 6, 7) Starting on the inside of the arch anchor, about 1" from the sole of the
foot, place horizontal strips, overlapping ¾", until the support is closed to the
top anchor strip. (8) Put another figure eight strip around the malleolus.

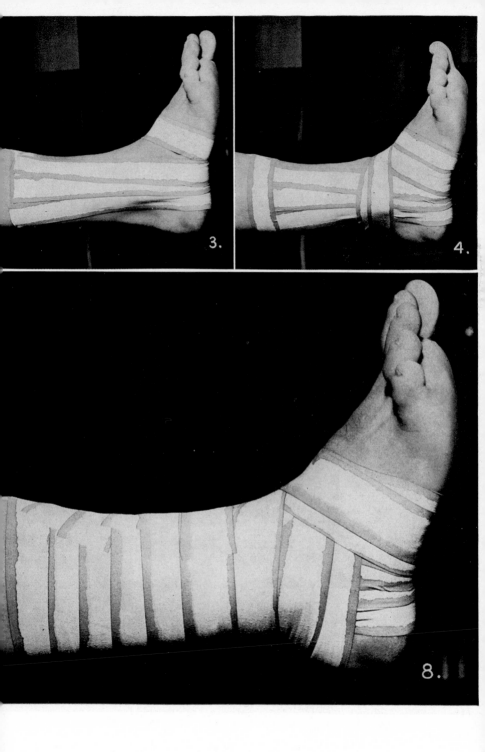

3.

4.

8.

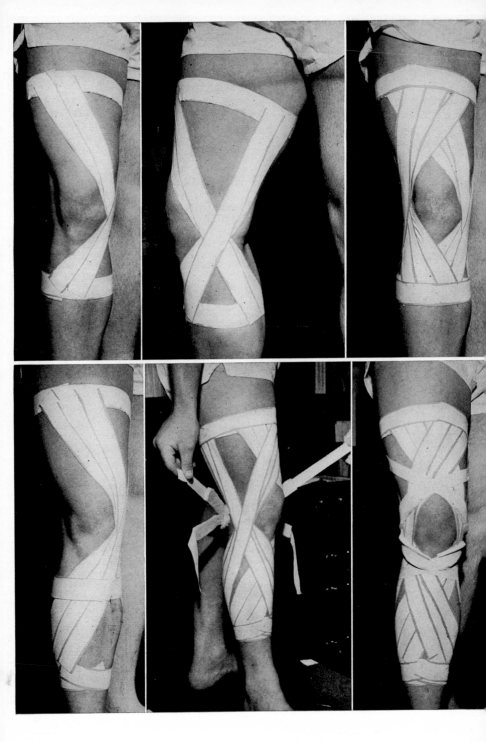

ILLUSTRATION III. Knee strapping: support for internal and external lateral ligament weakness and cruciform ligament slippage. The amount of support needed is determined by the stability of the knee and the length of time since the injury. The injured man should stand on a table, knee slightly bent with some weight on it, toes straight forward. Use 1½" tape. (Top left) For light support place anchors two-thirds up the thigh and midway the calf. (Center) Starting at lower anchor on mid-posterior calf, pass diagonally across joint on inside anchor on middle thigh. Second piece starts on mid-foreleg at lower anchor, passes diagonally up across first piece, and anchors on mid-posterior thigh. These diagonal pieces are continued four or five times, overlapping ½". If support is needed on lateral side of knee, repeat this process on outside. (Right) The diagonal pieces are anchored by horizontal strips on the thigh and calf, closing in as close to the knee as possible without causing chafing at the joint. (Lower left) For injuries requiring more support the same process is followed except that the lower anchor is placed just below the gastrocnemius. The diagonal strips take the same pattern, extending to the lower third of the leg. (Center) A felt cradle is added for stability. The back of the knee is padded with cotton before the cradle is placed. (Right) The horizontal anchors are applied: below the knee, above and below the calf; above the knee, from the knee to the thigh anchor. Dimensions and mounting of the felt are shown on the right page.

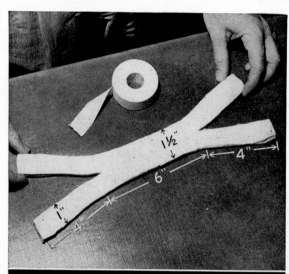

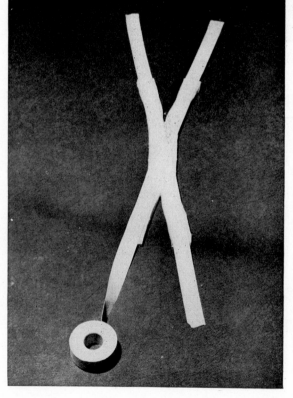

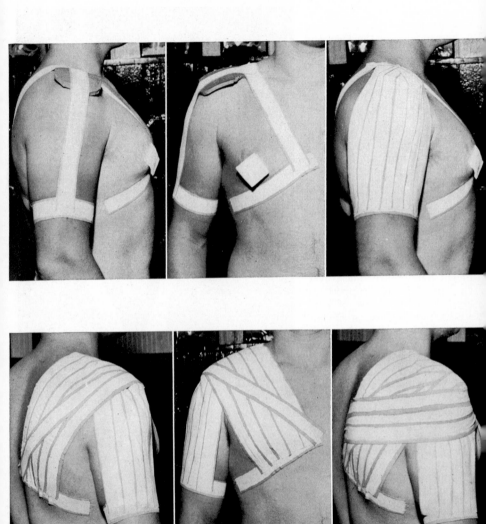

ILLUSTRATION IV. Shoulder strapping: for contusion and slight acro-clavicular joint sprain. Injured man should sit straight on table, injured shoulder raised 1" higher than other shoulder. Use 1½" tape. (Left page) Place rubber pad (4" x 4" x ½") over acro-clavicular joint. Place anchors below pectoral muscle, on upper arm two-thirds down from shoulder, and on back of scapula. Starting at center of upper arm, work alternately, overlapping ½", to the outside of the arm over the rubber shoulder cap. Pressure is put across cap, starting at the back and overlapping ½" onto the front. To hold arm down strips are placed as shown in lower right photo. (Right page) The strapping is then anchored down and an elastic bandage put over the tape to hold it firm.

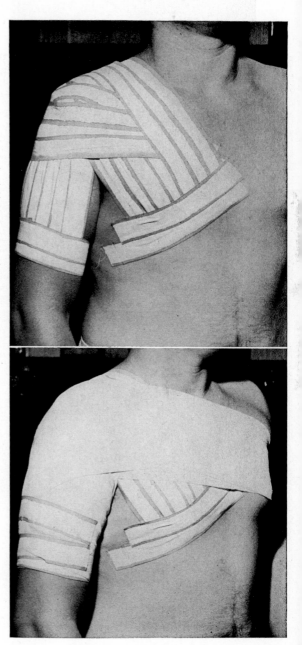

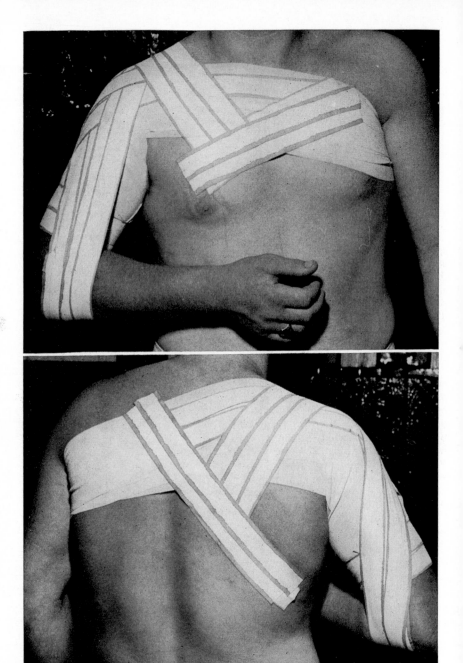

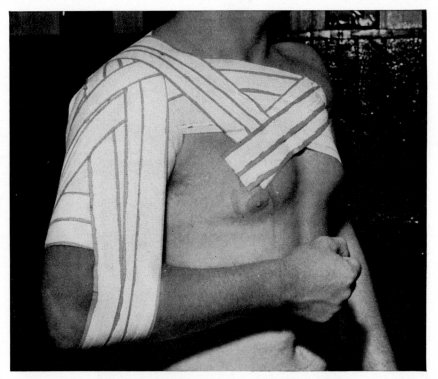

ILLUSTRATION V. Shoulder strapping: to support shoulder after reduction of dislocation and severe acro-clavicular joint sprain. Injured
shoulder should be pulled up 1″ higher than other shoulder, arm bent
and held across front of body. (Top left) A 4″ elastic bandage is put
on in figure eight fashion, running under the opposite arm. Anchors
are placed on the chest and back. (Lower left) Tape strips are started
on the front anchor and go across head of clavicle to the anchor on the
back. (Right) This procedure is followed four or five times, overlapping
¾″, pulling up on the elbow and putting pressure at the acro-clavicular
joint.

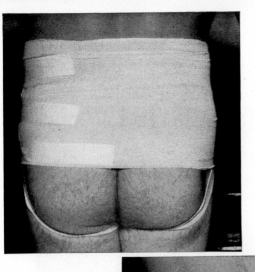

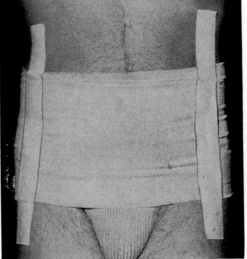

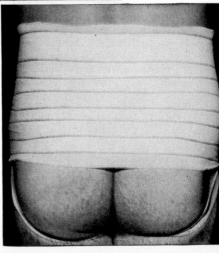

ILLUSTRATION VI. Strapping of lower back: for muscle strain or ligament sprain in lumbar and sacroiliac region. Injured man should stand on floor or low table with feet together. (Left page, top) A wide elastic bandage is wrapped around the body firmly at the level of the injury. (Center) Using 2″ tape, anchors are placed on the front. (Lower left) Staring ½″ from lower edge of the elastic bandage and tying onto front anchors, the tape is put on firmly, each layer overlapping ½″. (Top right) Diagonal strips are added for support. (Lower right) The back tape is anchored as shown.

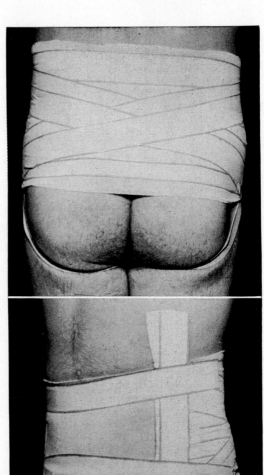

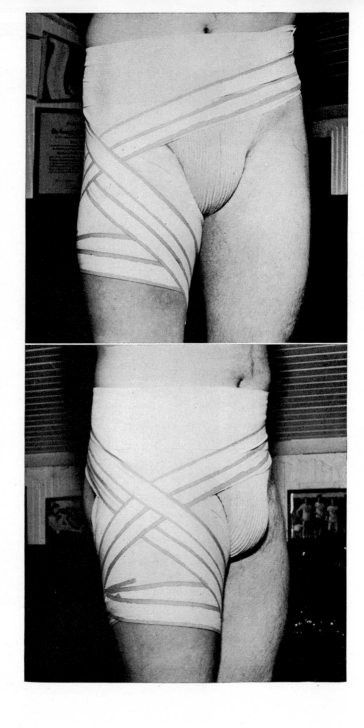

ILLUSTRATION VII. Groin strapping: for pulled muscles and tendons. Injured man should stand on table, legs spread sufficiently to facilitate strapping, heel on 2½" block. (Left page) 4" elastic bandages are wrapped around affected area and upper thigh, circling the body for added support. The elastic bandage is anchored on the thigh. Using 1½" tape, work from the inside of the thigh diagonally across the affected area to the lower back. (Right page) Start the next strip on the back of the leg and pass across the first strip. Continue, alternating these strips, overlapping ¾", until pressure is applied to the uppermost point of the groin. Anchor all ends down.

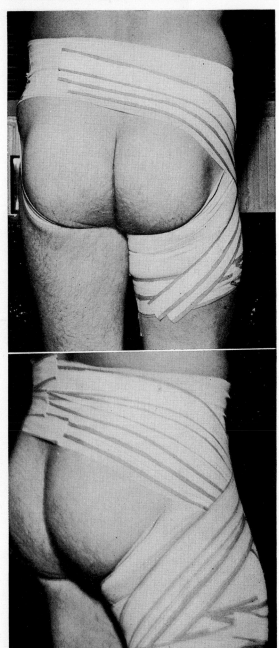

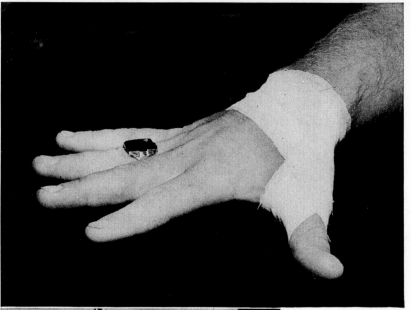

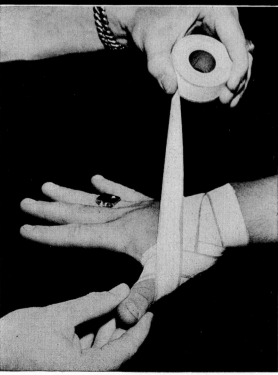

ILLUSTRATION VIII. Thumb strapping: for support of sprained first metacarpal. Hand is spread, wrist straight. (Top left) Using 1″ gauze wrap thumb. (Lower left and top right) Using 1″ tape, follow same pattern as gauze, taping from the roll in one continuous piece. (Lower right) In order to prevent the thumb from being overextended, a strap is put between the thumb and forefinger.

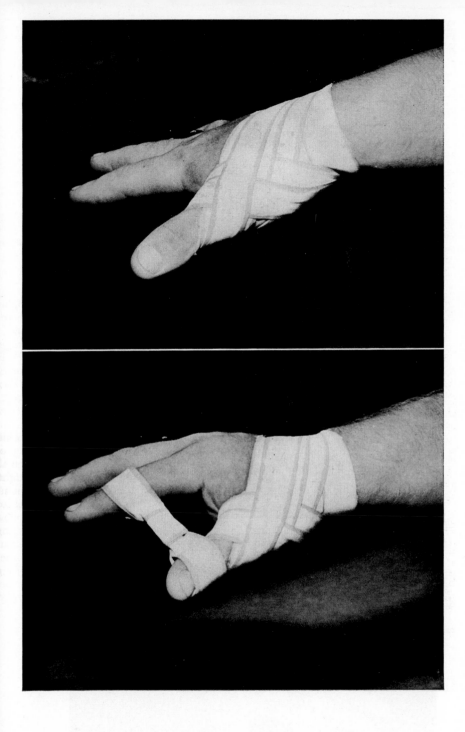

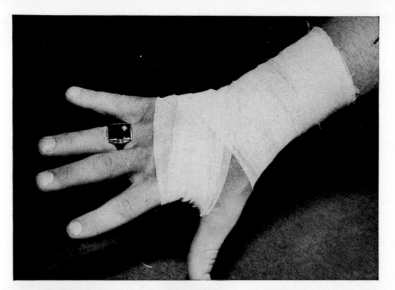

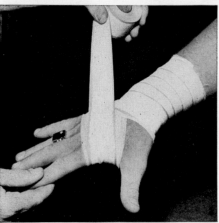

ILLUSTRATION IX. Wrist strapping to support sprained wrist or prevent sprain while hands are being used in competition. Wrist is straight, fingers extended fully. The fingers must be extended throughout taping process or circulation will be impaired. (Top) Wrist is wrapped with 2″ non-sterile gauze bandage going around the hand. (Center) 1½″ tape is placed over same area, starting on the forearm and working from the roll. Care must be taken going around the hand not to get the tape too tight. (Lower) We recommend taping through the hand so the tape will not slide back with movement and thus lose its effectiveness.

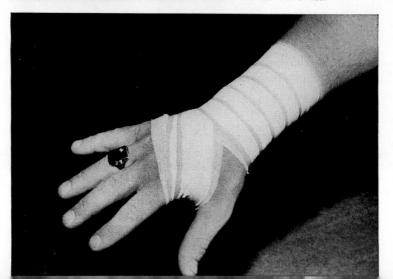

3. Heat treatments are begun after the twenty-four to thirty-six hour period by means of a hot whirlpool or hot towel applications. *No massage is used on the area for a week or ten days.* There is a danger of creating myositis ossificans if there has been any damage to the periostium. *When massage is started it should be of a very mild and gentle nature.*

4. Exercise is recommended during the convalescent period of a "charley horse." At all times during the exercise period the leg should have an elastic bandage on it and after each heat treatment the analgesic balm pack is applied.

5. Severe "charley horses" should be protected even after the player seems to have complete function of the muscle because a blow in the same area would eliminate him from work for quite some time. We protect the quardracep muscle contusion by building up the thigh pads so that they cantilever over the injured area. Plastic thigh guards with convex surfaces can be purchased that are very helpful in protecting this injury. The convalescent period is not as long as we have with sprain joints because function returns more rapidly and usually the muscles can be protected satisfactorily.

"Pulled" muscles

Strains of the ham-strain group of the thigh are the most typical type of pulled muscle occurring in athletics. The treatment discussed here applies to all pulled muscles.

1. Restrictive bandaging is applied immediately upon injury and the area is iced with crushed ice from thirty to forty-five minutes.

2. The elastic bandage is placed on the leg firmly and is worn for a twenty-four to thirty-six hour period.

3. The whirlpool bath or hot towel applications are started after the twenty-four to thirty-six hour period and after each

treatment a hot pack is applied firmly to aid support and continue the treatment.   No massage is used for a period of seven to ten days.

4. Strenuous use of the muscle is usually the cause of its being strained; therefore, *the athlete should do nothing in the way of exercising the limb.*   Exercise may re-tear the fibers that are trying to heal.   In other words, *no running.*   When the limb has healed sufficiently an elastic bandage should be snugly wrapped on the leg each time the athlete works out.   From this time on, the boy should keep in mind that the limb that has been injured has to be thoroughly warmed up when he is to compete or practice; otherwise, it is very easy to tear the muscle in the same area.

Equipment

Purchase

Standardize your protective equipment and clothing.   Check the leading manufacturers and obtain samples of what you intend to buy.   Buy your pads, shoes, and helmets with protection of the player in mind.   Do not buy inadequate, poorly constructed gear because it will only cost you more in the long run.   It will also subject your players to more serious and frequent injuries.   Good, protective equipment can be reconditioned several times at a fraction of the original cost.

Select the types of hip and shoulder pads you think will give the best protection and service and stick with them until something better is produced.

All gear should be fitted on the player in the coach's presence so that he can see the fit and give instructions on how the gear should be worn.   Many injuries are caused by poorly fitted equipment and by the player's not knowing how his equipment should be worn.

Clothing such as jerseys, pants, and sweat clothes should be purchased with the idea of having only to add to the sets in future years. Use colors that can be matched by any manufacturer and that can be laundered easily. Fancy, high-priced game equipment that is worn only once a week can soon be the biggest item on your budget. Avoid extra striping, panels, bordered numbers, and so on.

Much consideration should be given to practice gear. Well-fitting, properly constructed practice uniforms will cut down on injuries and add to the effectiveness of your practice sessions. No boy can do his best when his gear does not fit well. Most colleges now are trying to equip their players in the same style, weight, and texture materials for practice periods and games. High schools can do the same type of purchasing since the development of nylon synthetics has made durable well-fitting garments available at reasonable prices.

16

The Spectator

W E FEEL that football is the greatest of all spectator sports, and we believe that regardless of the class of football—from junior high to the best in college or professional football—there is nothing that can afford as many thrills and spine-tingling chills in one afternoon as the sharp block, the long run, the well-executed pass, the long punt return, the game-saving tackle, the long field goal, or even a blocked kick (especially if it is not against your team), plus all the other glamor, glitter, and "extra-curricular" activities that are to be had at a football game.

Don't be cheated

Even with all the things taking place in a game that the fan enjoys and understands, we feel that there are many other things that the average spectator misses. There are actually

332

only twelve or thirteen minutes of action (when the ball is in play) during a two-hour game.   Therefore, we feel that a fan who spends $3.00 or $4.00 for a ticket is being cheated if he doesn't avail himself of the opportunity to really "get in the game," and, as we say, "play the game," from whistle to whistle. Perhaps a few suggestions will help the spectator to get more out of the game.

Pre-game preparation

The fan who really enjoys the game is the one who actually "knows" the player, so we feel that to really become acquainted with "your" team, as well as the opponent's, you should follow the sports pages of the newspaper.   Television and radio, with their sportscasts and game broadcasts, are also fine media for learning something about Saturday's performers.

We know from personal experience that it is much more interesting to watch a contest when you are well acquainted with the personnel.   For example, although we see the Yankees only once or twice per season, we feel that we are well acquainted with Mickey Mantle, Phil Rizzuto, Gil McDougald and practically the whole gang—yet, we've never met them; we just became "acquainted" by following their progress throughout the season.

When you get to the stadium

A real football enthusiast likes to arrive at the stadium at least thirty minutes before game time, and his first act is to buy a program.   We believe that by knowing the numbering system in general use the fan can become well-acquainted with the players and their respective positions before the game.   A standard numbering system is used by practically all teams in all sections of the country at the present time.   The system follows this pattern:

ENDS	80–89
TACKLES	70–79
GUARDS	60–69
CENTERS	50–59
BACKS	10–49

The warm-up

The warm-up is interesting as well as "educational" and entertaining.   There are many indications of things to come that the spectator can foresee by watching the pre-game warm-up. First, it is interesting to watch the punters—check them with and against the wind and you will get a good idea of the part the wind will have in the game.   It is also well to check on whether the opponents should try to block or return the kicks (in other words, does the kicker kick fast or slow?), and will he out-kick his team?

The passers give the fans an opportunity to do some prognostication—always look for the left-hander; if he is a halfback, there is a good chance for some reverse passes.   (Of course, this also holds true when there is a good right-handed passer at halfback.

Field goal possibilities can be checked pretty well during the warm-up period.   And some teams put on a pretty good "floor-show" with their linemen during the pre-game warm-up.

Starting the game

The flip of the coin is a very interesting feature of the game if the spectator understands the mechanics involved.   It is well to know that the visiting captain calls the toss.   The "winner of the toss" is designated by the referee by placing his hand on the shoulder of the player.   The winner is given the choice of kicking or receiving, or the choice of goals to defend (this choice is in reality predicated on the wind). The respective choices of the captains are indicated by signals by the official, which are easily interpreted. If these proceedings are followed closely it gives the spectator a chance to start his mental processes working a little earlier.

During the game

A lot of coaches will say that blocking and tackling are the things to watch during the game—not the ball carrier. However, we find that when we take a "busman's holiday" and go to a football game, we follow the ball. Since, however, most of the game action takes place near the ball carrier, we would like to make a few suggestions about other things to watch for besides the ball carrier.

First, look for the blocking at the line of scrimmage—downfield blocking is a thing of beauty when well executed. Certainly, the defensive maneuvers that are employed are a great part of the game. It is very interesting to pick up the type of defense being used, and this can be done fairly well by observing two things: First, is there a man "on" the center's nose? If so, the formation is called an *odd defense,* and it is usually a five, seven, or nine man line. If there isn't a man on the center's nose it is an *even defense,* and usually is a four, six, or eight man line.

Secondly, there are two types of defense generally employed in the secondary. One is called a *box defense*—i.e., one without a safety—the other, of course, is one with a safety, and usually has what is called a "three-man-deep" type of pass defense.

Pass patterns also are very interesting to watch. On every pass there is a duel between the potential receiver and the defensive man. Watch the technique of the pass receiver—as he uses the head-fake, change of pace, and other tricks of the trade to get open. The development of the patterns themselves will afford thrills that the average spectator misses.

The time between plays should never be neglected—this is the time to really "quarterback" the game. Check the down and distance, keep the time, wind, and score in mind, then "call" your play. Watch for soft spots in the defensive setup.

Don't forget your kicking game; possibilities of a field goal always afford the spectator interesting moments of contemplation.

Remember, too, the *defensive* team must be "quarterbacked." It is interesting to maneuver your defensive team mentally into different alignments.

Do all this "quarterbacking," then check your thinking with the field general actually running the team. Always remember that he is operating under a lot more pressure than you are, and he doesn't get a "second" guess.

The officials

It would be impossible to have a football game without officials—and we should all realize their great value to the game. The spectator should realize that officials are men of the highest character and integrity. They have spent years in preparation for their job. Usually they are men who have made a success at a profession and they officiate because they are asked to and they feel they owe football something. In their work they are forced to make decisions that carry "severe" penalties (especially if they are against your team). Yet, this is a part of their job and if they didn't call these fouls the team against whom they were committed would be treated unfairly.

It should be recognized that 40,000 pair of eyes sometimes detect fouls that aren't detected by the four or five officials who are watching the twenty-two men involved. But remember, also, sometimes the official who is trained for the job sees infractions which you as a spectator don't see.

Be charitable in these things. Spectators can follow the game with a lot more interest if they will learn the officials' signals used for rule infractions. These signals are to be found in most programs, and it gives the spectator a lot of self-satisfaction if he is able to know immediately what infraction of the rules has taken place when it happens and the signal is given.

Sportsmanship

Football is one of our great American games. It is the duty and responsibility of each of us to see that it is kept in its proper perspective, and that it is *protected*. We should see that it is used to attain the objectives that mean so much to our way of life.

We feel that the spectator can be most influential and instrumental in helping to achieve these objectives, if he will develop the right attitudes. May we suggest a few?

First, and foremost among these attitudes that must be developed, is the realization that in football there *must be a winner and a loser* (excepting the occasional tie). The fan who recognizes this principle gets a great deal more enjoyment from the game than one who becomes irritated, aggravated, and rambunctious when "his" team loses. We would never minimize the importance of winning, but it is very unfair to the coach, the player, and the school when the fan forgets it is impossible to "repudiate the law of mathematics"—i.e., there must be a winner *and* a loser.

It is important that each of us develop the art of appreciating great plays made by the opposition. We should always give our opponents credit, rather than criticize our team when the opposition makes a great play. We believe perfection in the execution of a great play in football is to be admired and appreciated, just as we appreciate and admire the work of a great artist in any field.

The spectator should remember the football players are just human beings. They perform at times under great pressure, and they, as all other earthly inhabitants, are likely to make mistakes. It behooves all of us to remember, "To err is human, to forgive, divine."

Finally, we should always keep uppermost in mind that football with all its glamor, glitter, thrills, and chills, plus everything else that makes it great, has one thing more important than all of these combined—that is, the *BOY* who plays it.

Index

339